D1509802

JOURNEY DOWN A RAINBOW

By J. B. Priestley

Fiction

Bright Day
The Good Companions
They Walk in the City
Let the People Sing
Black-Out in Gretley
The Doomsday Men
Benighted
Festival at Farbridge
The Magicians

Angel Pavement
Daylight on Saturday
Faraway
Wonder Hero
Three Men in New Suits
Adam in Moonshine
Jenny Villiers
The Other Place
Low Notes on a High Level

Plays

Volume I
Dangerous Corner
Eden End
Time and the Conways
I Have Been Here Before

Johnson over Jordan
Music at Night
The Linden Tree

Volume II
Laburnum Grove
Bees on the Boat Deck
When We Are Married
Good Night Children

The Golden Fleece
How Are They at Home?
Ever Since Paradise

Volume III
Cornelius
People at Sea
They Came to a City
Desert Highway

An Inspector Calls
Home is Tomorrow
Summer Day's Dream

Essays and Autobiography

Delight
Midnight on the Desert
English Journey

Self-Selected Essays
Rain upon Godshill

Criticism and Miscellaneous

Meredith (E.M.L.)
Peacock (E.M.L.)
Brief Diversions

The English Comic Characters
English Humour (*Heritage Series*)
Postscripts

By Jacquetta Hawkes

Archaeology of Jersey
Prehistoric Britain
Early Britain
Symbols and Speculations
  (*Poetry*)
A Land

A Guide to the Prehistoric and
  Roman Monuments of Eng-
  land and Wales
Fables
Man on Earth

J. B. PRIESTLEY : JACQUETTA HAWKES

Journey Down
A Rainbow

LONDON: HEINEMANN-CRESSET 1955

917.9
p94j

First published in 1955 by
William Heinemann Ltd., 99, Great Russell Street, London, W.C.1
and The Cresset Press Ltd., 11, Fitzroy Square, London, W.1

Printed in Great Britain at the Windmill Press, Kingswood, Surrey

TO
CARL GUSTAV JUNG
The Wise Old Man

Someday—over the rainbow
(Popular song—Second World War Period)

*From the depths of the kiva emerges the ladder, its
two long poles pointing towards the sky; here is the
rainbow, sacred pathway of the gods . . .*
(Guide to New Mexico)

*Only gods succeed in walking on the rainbow bridge;
mortals fall to their death, for the rainbow is only a
beautiful semblance that stretches across the heavens,
and not a road for corporeal human beings: they must
go through underneath . . .*
(C. G. Jung: The Integration of the Personality)

FEB 27 '75

HUNT LIBRARY
CARNEGIE-MELLON UNIVERSITY

CONTENTS

CONTENTS

PREFACE

This is not another of those books about America. True, it begins like a travel book, and perhaps right to the end it never entirely loses its resemblance to one. Those readers who insist upon travel books are not going to be warned off. If what they want are glimpses of the American South-West, they will find them in many of these chapters: the peepshow is working. But we had no intention of adding one more volume to the pile, already too high, of books about America by visiting authors from Europe. The proper time for such books has gone. We are already in another age, when America mostly pays the piper and calls for most of the tunes. There is no longer any point in leaving Leicester Square and Coventry Street in order to describe Broadway, which merely has more electric light, newer Hollywood films, larger cafeterias. English readers have not to be conducted across the Atlantic now to observe the American style of urban life: it can be discovered in the nearest town. It is now the great invader.

Why choose America, then? The answer is that if you wish, as we did, to compare some of the earliest men with some of the latest, to make a contrast between two very different ways of life, the American South-West offers you an opportunity not to be found elsewhere. For there, neighbouring states, are New Mexico and Texas. In New Mexico some of the earliest inhabitants of America made their homes; and their successors, the prehistoric Basket Maker and Pueblo Indians, have left in their mesa-top villages and cliff-dwellings some of the most remarkable remains of any primitive people in the world. What is more, and very important for our purpose, the modern Pueblos, a peaceful sedentary people who have never moved from their ancestral lands, still preserve much of their ancient culture, far more (as we shall see) than is generally realised by European archæologists and prehistorians. They are still living more or less as they always did, and, in spite of all the assaults of Western civilisation, still offer us insights into prehistoric ways. So much for New Mexico.

But why Texas? Because there, just across the state line from New Mexico, warmed by the same hours of sunshine, may be found the latest men, living in what are for their size the richest and most rapidly expanding cities in our Western world. If our newest urban civilisation cannot be found here, then where can it be found? (One small example. We rarely pass through the main street of any town now without seeing the crimson-and-gilt façade of a Woolworth's store. The largest Woolworth's store in the world is in Houston, Texas.) Dallas and Houston represent the newest, the most prosperous, the most 'progressive' America, just as American life itself represents a pattern of society to which all our urban Western civilisation is beginning to conform. Here, you may say, is the social and cultural pattern of the mid-twentieth century. What may be as yet only dimly seen in many English and West European cities is here in these Texas cities, because they are new, wealthy, vigorous, all blazingly evident.

It may be objected, by the kind of reader who believes you cannot be in earnest unless you are deep in Blue Books, White Papers, official statistics, that the life of these Texas cities has here been sampled somewhat frivolously. Such a reader will declare that football games, night clubs, TV programmes, hotel festivities, can be ignored and certainly should not be high-lighted by the serious social critic. This view is itself more frivolous than anything in these chapters; it has already proved itself to be a disastrous attitude of mind, resulting in the world being changed, mostly for the worse, under so many uplifted noses. For it is not when people are toiling and trading—or are being sent to prison, certified as lunatics, operated upon, carted to the cemetery, or in any other fashion finding their way into statistics—that they best reveal themselves and the character of their society. It is when they are spending the money they have earned, when they are feeling easy and relaxed, when they are most impressionable, that the pattern blazes out. And what is tonight for them may be tomorrow night for the rest of us.

So that is why we went where we did, separating only at the last moment, as it were, one turning right for the desert of New Mexico, the other turning left to visit the Texas cities, so that the earliest men and the latest, ancient and primitive cultures and the newest triumphs of civilisation, could be examined as close together as possible, almost brought into one focus. We were not writing another book about America. Perhaps we were not writing a book about anything, but only assembling some essays and notes, not all of them in deadly earnest, that would enable a reader to take a quick look at one kind of life, then an equally quick look at another, very different. We did not set out to prove a theory; the territories were new to us; we did not know what we should find, nor what we should think and feel about what we found. But what happened, outside our heads or inside them, has been honestly reported, with no inventing, no cheating. What we enjoyed, what we disliked, it is all here. We may not be in entire agreement about everything; but our broad conclusions bring us to the same point. That point need not be made here because it will be found, differently stated, over and over again in the chapters that follow.

Another point, however, we must make in this place. It cannot be too strongly emphasised. From the high Mesa Verde in Colorado down to Houston on the Gulf of Mexico, nearly a thousand miles, we met with nothing but immediate helpfulness, kindness, generosity, to a degree that would astonish anybody not familiar with the hospitable tradition of the American South-West. If we rarely mention names, it is not that we do not remember them, gratefully too, but because not all the persons concerned might welcome being associated prominently with ideas and opinions they do not share. We can only hope that nothing printed here will make any of them regret their kindness. We can assure them that for all that is enduring, true, belonging in essence to their great sunlight region, we too have a deepening affection. It is a good part of an earth that deserves something better from all of us.　　　　J. B. P.

J. H.

J. H. Goes to Albuquerque I lay back comfortably in my seat in the long coach; they are excellent these train seats, tipping nearer to the horizontal than any I have encountered in aeroplanes, even the most luxurious. I was in that state of railway drowsiness when one isn't asleep, yet cannot control one's thoughts. I kept trying to force mine into a useful channel, directing them towards the questions of what Indian sites I ought to see, what it was I really hoped to get out of seeing them, what general ideas I had about primitive life that could be tested against the remains of these ancient Americans. Like a rider pressing a reluctant horse to a jump, I strove to rein my thoughts towards these important matters, but always they shied away and were soon straying off, playing with odd and irrelevant memories.

My will had one success, however, and that was in a mental exercise I have often practised before. First, I imagined the interior view, four long lines of passengers supported semi-prostrate in this steel tube with its dim, deep-sea light, each one aware of himself as an individual going on his own particular journey. Then, leaping in imagination to some near-by eminence, I saw the gigantic train, nearly half a mile of it, like a thick snake or a blind-worm moving through the night and the vast fields of the Middle West. Squeezing my imagination for greater accuracy, I decided that there would be no red glow or streaming fountain of sparks such as one sees in our coal-burning engines coming from the four diesel monsters drawing us; nor, perhaps, would the serpentine shape show darkly like an English train, for surely the bright steel coaches with their fluted sides would have a peculiar pallor, or might even be gleaming in the moonlight. So I pictured a ghostly train rushing steadily south-west across the map of America, a blind-worm driven by human insistence to hurry over prairies and through mountains until it reached the Pacific.

Rather after one o'clock at night I roused myself, for we were nearing Kansas City where Jack was to leave me and catch a train for Dallas. We climbed down on to the platform (and it really is a climb from these towering American coaches) and said good-bye. I remember the heavy smell of oil and steel which seemed to make separation on the dark platform all the more forlorn. I was back in my seat and trying to settle down again, when I became reluctantly convinced that the insistent male voice which was repeating 'we have the inside seat' must be directed at me. I looked up to where the wide, curled brim of a man's felt hat was just visible in the gloom, and protested that this was impossible, I had come from Chicago and was going on to Albuquerque. I made no attempt to move.

'Let my daughter have her seat. The inside seat is hers.' The voice was flat, unpersuasive—and indeed to my ears insulting. I appealed to the attendant. The man was quite correct, the seat I was sitting in had been booked to his daughter and I would have to move into Jack's vacant place. It was quite reasonable, and I should suffer very little discomfort, yet my protests went on—it was disgraceful I should be disturbed in the middle of a long journey, it was a piece of abominable mismanagement, and so forth. I made an ass of myself.

I am usually far too inclined to surrender anything for a quiet life, and, like any other treacherous woman, smile placatingly at the waiter when Jack occasionally complains of abominable food or service on our travels. Yet there I was at Kansas City making a useless and unwarranted fuss, helping to confirm half a coach-load's worst prejudices against the English. It was very stupid, and I can only think I was giving way to an alien's nervous aggressiveness, an emotion I hold in contempt. It was a warning; after that scene I held my peace, even when a New York taxi-man persisted in his belief that he knew where I wanted to go better than I did. It cost me time and money, yet I smiled and said good-night to him.

The train reached Albuquerque in the middle of the afternoon, and I stepped gladly out of the dead, over-heated air of the coach into brilliant, but not dazzling, sunshine and that delicious air which is sun-warmed, yet has an underlying coolness that will come into its own at sunset. The weather was to stay like this, save for a single day of snow, for the whole of my time in New Mexico. In spite of this dependability and the land's great need for rain, every morning I would be

3

greeted with 'lovely morning' or 'beautiful day' by all kinds of people who seemed daily to experience a fresh delight in their climate. I am certain this couldn't happen in England, where after a week of such sunshine we should be complaining of drought, heat-fatigue and monotony.

I had reserved a room in the Alvarado, one of the Fred Harvey chain of hotels. This concern dominates public catering in the South-West, managing most of the large hotels here and all the restaurant cars on the Santa Fé railroad. It is unassailably mediocre; its hotels, its food, range from tolerable to good but are never excellent. I had received a flowery telegram from the Alvarado telling me that my train would be met; it wasn't, but as the hotel proved to adjoin the station, a porter and I were soon advancing on it through exaggeratedly Spanish precincts. On the way I peered through the windows of the Hispano-Indian Museum (the only museum in Albuquerque) which is run by the hotel and contains some first-rate material. It is arranged in a haphazard, bazaar-like abundance which it is still possible to prefer to the rational, hygienic order of an up-to-date museum.

Here, within a few minutes of arrival, I was being introduced to the two points of attraction in the cultural life of New Mexico—the Indian and the Spanish. The main tides of modern life there are moved by oil, ranching, and now by uranium and atomic fission, yet as days went by I was only to become more and more impressed by the tremendous effect the creative force of these ancient peoples had upon their American conquerors. Because theirs were cultures which had grown

4

slowly from the land and the imagination, they created patterns, shapes, combinations of colour, which can be distinguished as belonging to them and them alone in all time and space. The Americans, who in spite of their marvellous feats of engineering and engineered architecture, have never so far as I know produced so much as a formal moulding peculiarly their own, are most strongly attracted towards the arts and traditions of these poor and materially powerless peoples.

There was no doubt about the Spanish influence on Fred Harvey. In the Alvarado I entered a world where painted beams, Moorish tiles, and lanterns, firedogs and other wrought-iron curlicues of every sort, almost concealed the bars, reception desk, and ordinary electrical fittings. The manager apologised for failing to meet the train, declaring that he had been at the station but could not identify me in the crowd, a statement which was such an evident yet gracious untruth that I concluded the Spanish atmosphere in which he lived, sham though it was, had permeated his soul.

When the porter shut the door upon me in a hotel-modern and quite un-Spanish bedroom, the confined space and cessation of motion seemed suddenly to confront me with the truth of my position. I was committed to an expedition, yet my ideas about its objectives, and the best means of attaining them, were equally half-baked. I stood there in a kind of desperation and with a feeling of imprisonment; I can still remember how the sparrows chirped in the dusty *patio* outside one window while the noises of the Santa Fé railroad penetrated through the other.

There are advantages in setting out with little pre-

paration—advantages of freshness, flexibility and freedom from prejudice, yet it must always bring moments
like this one, when I was faced with a shameful and
terrifying knowledge of my inadequacy. I took the
modern man's easy way out, seizing a telephone to put
myself in the hands of another. I rang the owner of a
bookshop, who had been warned to expect me. He
sounded friendly, jovial, but passed me on to a lady who
he said was the wife of an official and 'interested in
books'. Although on the telephone this lady welcomed me as though I were a returning sister and
promised soon to take me for drinks at her house, I felt
discouraged. An official's wife and interested in books?
Even if this second qualification might have a more than
usually definite meaning for the owner of a bookshop,
the chances didn't look good. I expected a woman
either conventionally smart and full of deadly, kill-
silence chatter or one of those whose face and character
alike seem to have been eroded away by exposure to
years of cultural luncheons and miscellaneous lectures.
  The person waiting for me among the beams and
wrought iron of the foyer was unlike either of these
imagined horrors. I saw a large, untidy woman,
pleasantly ample in hip and breast, with humorous,
rolling eyes set in those full lids which often go with the
most naturally feminine kind of sexual attractiveness.
Her car was ample and untidy like herself; her house
filled me with delighted astonishment. That such a
place could exist on the fringes of raw, fast-growing,
commercial Albuquerque, and that it could belong to
the City Manager, was a telling lesson against making
easy assumptions. It was a genuine old hacienda, the

6

Hacienda del Lago, built about two centuries ago in the Indian adobe style now so often imitated in New Mexico. Outside, in spite of the rare possession of a lake, it looked shabby and even rather depressing at this dry time of year when garden and fields were withered and dusty. Probably it seemed more dreary to me then, on my first day, than it would have done later when I had become accustomed to the soft mud-brown and irregular forms of adobe, and to the bizarre effect of the *vegas*—the ends of the cross-beams supporting the flat roofs which are allowed to project a foot or more through the outside walls.

Inside it was very different. True it was unkempt, with dust making delicate curtains of cobwebs visible in some of the less used corners, but wonderfully rich, warm and careless. The long living-room was furnished with old Spanish and Indian things, painted pottery, rugs, carved images or *santos*, looking glasses and embroidery, and there were also modern American and European paintings and sculpture. Yet as we sat in front of a fire of four-foot logs drinking Old Fashioneds no room could have seemed more harmonious, unaffected and habitable. Women of character usually express something of their essential quality in their homes, and this house perfectly expressed my hostess's. Here were a lot of things she had liked, brought together, enjoyed and neglected; they looked just right. The whole house was as far removed as possible from the daintiness or false elegance of the 'gracious living' ideal of the women's magazines. Indeed, I am sure the lady editresses would have dealt most severely with her boudoir, which was overflowing with cats, cosmetics

7

and underclothes. But for me, though I myself lack the confidence to be half so untidy, the *Hacienda del Lago* was a delight and a happy reversal of all my earlier expectations.

Our drinks were mixed for us by the official. He, even more than his wife, was a warning against taking too much for granted in America. She was all of a piece, he looked very much like an official, yet, so far as I could judge, was contented and at ease in a home so very unlike the home appropriate to a regular fellow. Except for his habit of driving at very high speed with one finger on the wheel and all the others occupied with beer and sandwiches, I was to find him a most likeable companion, tactful and modest with the Indians we were to meet together, and free from the slow speech and defensive pomposity which, I had better admit, irritate me in so many nice American males.

My host mixed more Old Fashioneds, the living-room became even more warm and attractive in the glow of whisky and firelight, and my travel weariness swam away. After quite a long time we went to dine at a Mexican restaurant in the old Plaza of Albuquerque. This square has recently been restored to something like its ancient appearance, with the pleasant wooden colonnades, or portals, which New Mexico has inherited from its Spaniards. The authorities have wisely forbidden hoardings and neon signs in the Plaza, so that at night its shadowy covered ways, lit only by shop and restaurant windows, are restfully unlike the glaring main street, where thousands of red green blue and red neon tubes flash and gesticulate.

If I were responsible for the plazas in this and other

8

Spanish-American towns I should go further still and forbid all motor traffic, turning them into urban cloisters where one could stroll along the portals sheltered from sun and rain, looking into shops, comparing menus, forgetting the noise, stink and glare of the streets. I remember how as a girl I was entranced by Sunday evenings in Perugia when the main thoroughfare was closed with chains and the citizens promenaded at leisure. In a city street it is wonderful to hear only the chattering of men and women.

The restaurant was pleasant, but the cooking very bad. Even at its best, I'm not particularly fond of Mexican cooking, and this was no more than a poor imitation. My plate was covered with skinny tortillas stuffed with sludge, and reddish slops which contained enough paprika to prick the tongue, but not nearly enough to turn the whole dish into a reckless gastronomic conflagration. Still, I was happy in the occasion, and went back to the Alvarado afterwards quite ready to sleep through the steely roars of passing trains.

Although I could hardly realise it until later, it was extraordinary how full an introduction to New Mexico these first few hours had given me. Already I had not only encountered the Indian and Spanish influences and the lingering traces of Mexico itself, but had also been prepared for the discovery (I repeat, I had arrived in a state of almost total ignorance) that the South-West is full of American refugees from the American Way of Life. Men and women who are nonconformists in their sexual loves, in the strength of their love for history and the arts, or in their desire to be able to drive an old car in peace, are glad to live there in the sun.

9

I had also on this first day encountered the hospitable friendliness which everywhere astounds European visitors to the United States, but which is probably at its best, most easy and spontaneous here in the South-West. It is sheer silliness to say 'Ah, but it soon wears off!' for how would it be humanly possible for it to go on? Once the stranger has been welcomed, plied with food, drink and company, of course he must shift for himself. I can only say that during the coming weeks I was often ashamed to receive so much more kindness than I had ever given to any stranger at home.

What I did not see until the following days was the desert scenery of the country. Its landscapes have been created by a climate of extreme dryness and occasional torrential rains, by crustal folding and volcanoes; its beauty depends upon the light that comes with spacious and brilliant skies and sunshine reflected from the countless hard facets of the desert. It is a clear light, allowing one to recognise a mountain fifty miles away, yet it is not hard, since at all times except the early morning, it carries a slight, mollifying shimmer.

The most characteristic landscape is one of level or rolling desert broken by the sheer cliffs of flat-topped mesas and dominated by jagged mountain ranges. The surface of the desert, brittle with angular stones, is sometimes bare, but more often covered with sweet-scented sage or other, more thorny, scrubs, and boldly spotted with the compact, dark shapes of pinyon and juniper. Watercourses are common, usually dry beds of gravel, smoothed rock and sandpits enclosed between vertical walls. In the Rio Grande and a few of the larger rivers there is always water, though for most of the year it fills only a tiny part of the bed; the smaller watercourses, or arroyos, fill only in the rainy summer season, or when storms burst in the mountains and send sudden walls of water hurtling down towards the desert.

Heavy rains striking upon dry and often loose volcanic soils have ornamented the landscapes with curious fluted effects. They are of every scale. The lower slopes of the great ranges are scored by channel after channel, each with a raised fan at its foot where flood water has spread its heavy burden of silt; below their level tops the mesa have the same flutings and fans, and so again have the sides of the arroyos; look closely at the smallest runnel by the roadside—there again you will see the same corrugations, the same channels, ribs and fans. This repetition of one motif at every scale gives these landscapes a most satisfying unity, an impressive natural architecture, and serves also to enhance the grandeur of the mountains whose jagged summits alone are above conformity.

The ranges dominating this part of New Mexico— the Sandias east of Albuquerque, the Sangre de Christo sheltering Santa Fé from the north, and the Jemez mountains lying to the west of the Rio Grande— belong to the southern end of the Rocky Mountains. In the heart of the lofty Jemez, the Via Grande, a basin rich and fertile in contrast with the crags and tumbled rocks all round, is said to be the largest volcanic crater in the world. But volcanoes have done much more than this in the building of the landscape. Rains of ash have formed tufa beds which wind and water erode into fantastic forms, into cones and arches hollow and riddled with holes, into stacks and domes sometimes suggesting Moorish architecture, sometimes rather the constructions of giant wasps or termites.

While these strange creations of the volcanic ash occur only here and there, the influence of vast floods of lava has been widespread. As the molten stuff gouted from the fissures it spread as a boiling sea over the countryside, hardening into immense flats, some of black basalt, some buff pink or red. These flats fissured and in great part were carried away, but islands large and small have remained, perhaps in places where the basalt cap was exceptionally thick or tough. Sometimes these flat-topped islands rising from the desert floor are small and conical, but occasionally they may be large enough to be riven by canyons. They were of great importance to the prehistoric Indians who built their towns and villages on their level summits, in their cliff walls or at their foot on the canyon floors.

The basalt is often compact of hexagonal columns, formed when the lava cooled. Where the edge of the flow is exposed at the mesa tops, these columns resemble masonry; with the smaller, conical mesas the likeness to a castle is so astonishing that one has the illusion of a desert Rhineland and imagines each one crowded with men-at-arms. The Black Mesa which stands in sombre isolation near the prehistoric ruins of Puye might well be the stronghold of the Devil himself; according to Indian legend a giant lived within it, dragging many victims inside its black basalt walls, before at last he was outwitted and slain.

Such are the structures of this desert scenery, but it lives in the light and colour which change with every

12

phase of the sun's course. In the morning the scene has a solidity and detail, the pinyon and juniper show their green against the buff of sagebrush or the pinkish yellow of bare desert; every rock and cliff has its firm outline, and the mountains look substantial, climbable —terrestrial outposts against the blue. After noon, colour fades and forms weaken, the whole world becomes an uninteresting tan, a dreary desert and nothing more. Then, slowly, life and significance return until with the evening hour the desert knows its full glory. Here in the South-West it is sunset and not dawn which is rosy-fingered. As its time approaches, the desert turns a soft pink, the little conifers blacken and send long shadows curving over the slopes; the arroyos are shadowy and everywhere the flutings and fans of the watercourses come into their own as lilac shadows lend them strength. The mountain ranges glow pink, soft blue, or lilac-grey, according to the quality of the evening; remote ethereal presences far beyond all human tracks. The whole evening realm in its tranquillity and loveliness appears wholly aloof, an existence which has not yet had time to notice the little flurry of mankind.

I have written of the New Mexican desert as though it were universal; in fact it is veined with cultivation. Along the banks of the Rio Grande and the other rivers which maintain at least a trickle of water at all seasons, there are Indian and Spanish villages with irrigated pastures and fields of maize, orchards of cherry, apricots and apples. Often, too, there are well-grown cotton-wood trees lining the edge of the rivers or spreading into groves. I myself have never seen this country

13

HURT LIBRARY
CARNEGIE-MELLON UNIVERSITY

during the season when the green of the irrigated lands shine out against their desert matrix, nor have I caught the best moment of the fall when on the mountain flanks the white-trunked, slender aspen display their intense yellow against pines and firs, while the cotton-woods repeat the colour, a few tones deeper, on the valley floors. When I first arrived at Albuquerque the leaves on most of the cottonwoods were already a cere brown, but everywhere, inexplicably, a few of the great trees were still aflame, adding much to the beauty of the countryside and doing something to redeem the ugliness of the town.

Unhappily, in New Mexico much of the handiwork of modern man is both ugly and squalid. All the places where he lives, whether considerable towns like Albuquerque or small settlements along the highway, are appallingly untidy, probably the untidiest places in the world. For this is not the humble, yielding squalor of poverty, but the squalor of a people possessing ample material wealth and an abundance of steel. Individuals lightheartedly fling discarded equipment outside their houses—gas-stoves, pots and pans, petrol tins or whatever it may be—while the community as a whole does just the same thing, making vast, steely middens round their towns formed of rubbish which will deteriorate horribly, but never rot away. Nor will any blade of grass grow to soften or screen it. We English hardly appreciate the kindness of our grass in mitigating urban ugliness and adding finish to our roads. It is the great tidier and softener. Here instead of grass there is only dust.

To my eyes there can be nothing more dismal than a

disused car dump in a setting of dust. The large, haphazard second-hand car marts surrounding many towns do nothing to add to the amenities, but the outer ring of dumps where the once-adored automobile finds its last ungrateful resting place is an abomination and disgrace. A dump may occupy several acres. Cars, vans and buses are chaotically tumbled, rusty, surrounded by broken glass, and with parts torn savagely off—wheels missing, bonnets left gaping after the plundering of some part of the engine—the victims of base mechanical violations. I believe in fact that these dumps are run as commercial investments and that the violaters actually pay for their loot. This makes it all the more surprising that in several small highway settlements (I cannot bring myself to call them villages) I saw cars which had simply been abandoned by the wayside, pushed on to a piece of waste ground or a vacant building plot and left to decay. I found myself trying to imagine in just what moment of boredom, irritation or sudden fortune a man might decide to leave his car by the road, much as in Europe a tramp will cast off an old boot.

It may give an idea of the confused and ragged appearance of the settlements if I add that these poor derelicts are not at all conspicuous, but merge readily into their surroundings. The medley of shacks, hoardings, filling-stations, private trading ventures in strangely run-up accommodation, new buildings in every stage of construction and shoddy old ones in every stage of decay, together with a tangle of overhead electric cables, make a few forsaken automobiles look quite at home.

Hoardings are the other outrage of man against

nature. There is something to be said in favour of the blare of neon signs in the towns; it is not very attractive, it is true, but then the buildings the signs conceal are even less so. Also they give at least an illusion of urban gaiety and warmth, making a brazen challenge to the dark wastes beyond. But the armies of enormous wooden hoardings carrying repulsive enticements to motorists seem to me quite inexcusable. They are seen at their worst along the fine highway leading westward into the desert from Albuquerque—the road I was to follow when going to the famous Shalako ceremony at Zuni. They stand for miles in close-set ranks, those on one side of the road facing away from the town for the benefit of incoming drivers, on the other facing towards it for those who are driving out. Among so many rivals one is not at all likely to notice the board which says WELCOME TO ALBUQUERQUE, nor if one sees it at all, to obey the one on the far side of the town —GOOD-BYE, COME AGAIN.

Even commercially these acres of advertisements must be worthless, for such arrays of hoardings, passing the eye one every second, cannot be apprehended. The motorist gets a hazy and nauseating impression of being cajoled, preached at, shamed or wisecracked into eating and drinking more, driving more powerful cars, and into taking the necessary antidotes to these courses (life insurance in the case of the motors), but no single advertisement can possibly win his attention.

When the town battalions come to an end then hoardings put up by roadside motels, cafés and trading posts begin; a single ambitious trading post sometimes destroys the beauty of scores of miles of highway. It is no sentimental prejudice to say they destroy beauty. The loveliness of desert scenery, depending as it does on subtle harmonies of colour and form, on stillness and space, is not merely damaged by this monstrous foreground, it is destroyed.

In Santa Fé I was to meet many Americans who felt just as strongly as I did. Parties had even gone out by night and sawn nearly through the supporting timbers to encourage the hoardings to fall in the next wind. Some impatient characters were contemplating arson, while others, more law-abiding but even less realistic, were busy taking photographs of some of the worst desecrations with the intention of sending them to the advertisers to convince them of their wickedness. It should be unnecessary, for here is a nuisance which really could be cured (like the hooting of tenor horns in New York) by simple legislation, without anyone suffering the slightest damage.

I hadn't expected to stay long in Albuquerque, for it was away from most of the prehistoric sites I hoped to see. However, as my new friends very kindly took me for long drives, I lingered a little, enjoying this opportunity to see something of the country. I also made an excursion that had always been one of the few fixed points in my programme, an excursion to a site (a cave-dwelling) which is associated with the earliest known inhabitants of America. It seemed the right place to visit first.

2

J. B. P. Goes to Dallas

From Chicago to Kansas City I had travelled with Jacquetta on the train that was taking her to New Mexico. At Kansas City, however, I had to catch the train heading south for Texas. Even though they were due to stop at Kansas City about the same time, there was no official connection between these two trains; if one were late the other would not wait for it. I might not have a moment to waste. So our midnight good-bye was hurried, a brief exchange outside the dim-lit hot steel coach. A few moments later I was walking the length of the gleaming snorting monster, following the red-capped porter towards the exit from the track. The Kansas City station is an old acquaintance of mine and I have written about it before. It is no ordinary station, not simply a place where tickets are bought and trains are boarded. It is an enormous dignified structure, a temple of transport in the heart of a continent. And after midnight it seems vaster still, with no end to it, like a station in some melancholy dream. In such dreams we find ourselves drifting down long mysterious corridors, up incredible stairways, into vast meaningless halls, with lights burning everywhere but no people about, as if we had arrived in some city of the dead; and when we wake up, before the dream memory fades, we marvel at our rich imagination, not knowing then that we are merely anticipating a late change of trains at Kansas City.

Even the red-cap porter might have been a dream figure. He was not the usual coloured man but a tall white youth, too young, too loud, too cheerful, to be carrying luggage at that hour. He made me feel he might be doing it for a bet, or to placate a stern father (perhaps a director of the railroad), or to write short stories, or to make reports to the F.B.I. But this may have been mere fancy, born of the hour and the excellent whisky I had recently swallowed in defiance of the laws, customs and outlook of the State of Kansas. It was probably just such fancifulness that had got whisky outlawed there. While I wondered about him, as I climbed up from the track, he vanished; but in the great hall, high above and far out of sight of the platforms, so that it might have been the cathedral of some stern sect, he reappeared from nowhere, without my luggage, to tell me my train to Texas was late and I would have at least an hour to wait. Promising to conduct me in good time down to the right track, he then returned to no-where, leaving me to wander about that immense hall like an insomniac in a midnight market-place.

Nobody arrived, nobody went; nothing happened. Some coloured folk, waiting for slow trains to unimaginable villages, slept on the benches. Nothing was lit up and open except a kiosk, brightly islanded midway down the hall. I felt I had to buy something there, so I asked a woman with tired eyes and an angry make-up for an orange juice I did not want, to discover that it had had all the flavour carefully iced out of it. The only other customers were three or four Air Force men, probably long-term regulars, for they were trim and hard, and had the manner, half-shy, half-contemptuous, of the professional soldier moving among civilians. Listening to them, I remembered how I had never set eyes on a uniform during my earlier visits to this country. Now, at every railroad or airport, whatever the hour, there were uniforms. It was another America, another world. But not, I reflected, altogether another America; and here was the rub. These service men at the kiosk embodied the new American dilemma, for they were conscious of their uniforms, their training and hard experience, their badges of rank and medal ribbons, all that set them apart from the civilian; at the same time they were young American males, who had grown up in a free-and-easy democracy and still wanted to be liked even by chance acquaintances. I took the line of thought away from the kiosk into the dusky outer spaces, where I strolled to stretch my legs. America's bewilderment, sometimes flashing into dangerous anger, was easily understood. How do you wield immense power and still remain a good easy mixer? How can you be the boss and yet still one of the boys? When we British were top-dogs we were represented by a ruling class that was arrogantly self-sufficient, not caring a damn whether they were liked or not. But the American grows up with a deep desire to be liked, and when he finds he is not liked, just because he is top-dog, then he is shocked, bewildered, saddened, and occasionally very angry.

20

It was well after two when I found my little steel bed-room, a cube of hot metal, and began undressing as the train went rumbling out. I have spent much time in American long-distance trains, and still enjoy them, even though the service and the food in them are not as good as they used to be. East of Chicago I prefer to fly, but in the larger and more promising spaces of the South-West I still like to rumble along, day and night, popping in and out of my metal hutch, thick with the sweet reek of Burleigh tobacco, lurching along the corridors in search of a martini and a magazine or chilled tomato juice and pork chops, pleasantly aware all the time that I am reading, eating, drinking, talking, shaving, brushing my teeth, that unwanted leagues of prairie are vanishing beneath the wheels; I am pre-paring myself for that moment in the early morning when the bar of the window blind, suddenly released and flying up, seems to work like an enchanter's wand—and we are rolling through a new landscape, far away from the land where the sun went down. A full night's journey on an express, particularly in the South-West, is always long enough to conjure this miraculous trans-formation. (The aeroplanes, for all their three hundred miles an hour, can never complete the trick, for they show you something like a relief map, and by the time you are down to earth you are in an airport, exactly like the one you left the night before.) This train to Texas, next morning, did not cheat me. My first peep through the window showed me autumn rolled out like a golden-brown carpet, a hundred miles of it ending in a faint blue smudge. I was rolling along, somewhere else.

My spirits rose with the sun that I hardly seemed to

have seen for months. Hastily and happily I washed and shaved—no small feat in a lavatory about five inches wider than I am, rocking and bouncing too—and then dressed in the light of a new earth. In the shape and colouring of my thought, in my conscious outlook, I tend to pessimism, but below that level there is an optimist still in me, a fellow who longs for and enjoys his breakfast, who still believes today will be different and so is ready to start all over again. (He is not hard to explain, this fellow. He grew up in the age of security, before 1914, and then discovered in 1918 that he had survived, with some horrible incidents along the way, bullets, bayonets, bombs, poison gas and shells of every calibre up to sixteen inches, in the most ingenious and systematic mass slaughter that history had known up to that time.) On my way to breakfast, I noted with pleasure the sober charm of the Oklahoma landscape, and thought what a pity it was that the old English water-colour painters, who loved wandering, had never wandered as far as this. Just after I reached the dining-car, we came to the outskirts of Oklahoma City, an improvised, shanty sort of place, with its edges buried under thousands of derelict cars and mounds of scrap metal, looking as if its civilisation, like a hurriedly knitted sweater, were now unravelling.

The voices I heard in the dining-car belonged to the South-West. The men's were deep, almost cavernous; the women's were higher than they are in the East, higher and more nasal, as if the summer dust compelled them to keep nose, throat, mouth, as little open as possible. The men, all middle-aged, were booming routine little jokes at one another, in a dutiful fashion, like hard-working character actors. While I waited for coffee and eggs there passed through the car, in the dark-blue uniform of the train staff, a solemn ebony giant, like some prince of the Niger. Now and again one sees a similar princely figure among the coloured dining-car waiters, as if some imperial family of the jungle had taken to serving orange juice and coffee; but these are infrequent. The majority always seems to me to divide itself into three strongly-marked types: oldish melancholy negroes, bent and furrowed with years of servility, later versions of poor Uncle Tom; then mischievous comedian types, who arrive and depart all one wide grin and can be overheard roaring with laughter just outside the car; and finally, certain paler, spectacled, younger men, efficient but almost haughtily withdrawn, who look as if they are taking your order for Navy Bean soup and pot roast only until they can complete their courses in sociology somewhere at the end of the line. And we diners might remember that between these sociologists, whose spectacles will coldly magnify our bad habits, and the comedians so apt at mimicry, and the diminishing glances of the giant black princes in disguise, not much of us will be left to bolster up our sense of superiority.

The sun climbed and blazed, the plain broadened illimitably; we were rolling through Texas now. At the end of a sleepy morning, the haze thickened into distant buildings, and, looking absurd in that plain as wide as a sea, skyscrapers came shooting up. The porters cried, 'Fort Worth—Fort Worth'. I was booked through to the neighbouring city of Dallas, but this railroad had no line there and so I had to complete my journey by bus.

The forty-mile highway between the two cities passes through several small towns ('Come Again to Arlington —The Centre of America's Future' cried one of them) and is lined all the way with trailer courts, motels, drive-in movie theatres, super-markets, gas stations, second-hand car dealers, and large facetious notices— 'If You Can't Stop—Wave!' and 'Fishworms with Fish Appeal'. Everything was new, belonging essentially to the automobile phase of our civilisation. At a first glance it was all as bright and attractive as a circus, but very soon a certain shoddy monotony began to be apparent. The high-speed traffic never thinned out; everybody who lived in one city seemed to be going at sixty miles an hour to the other city. An unfamiliar sun glared at the burnt brown plain beyond the roads. Feeling rather lost after the long journey, a crumpled and hungry man (I had had no lunch), not knowing where I would find a room and a bed that night, I stared through the bus window, wondering what—in the name of the foul fiend of restlessness—I thought I was doing there. This was probably one of my worst ideas, for I had come nearly five thousand miles, at horrible expense, for what? Dallas came towering up, then closed round me. One of its highest towers seemed to be made of dazzling tin. The bus reached its formidable terminus. As the brakes gave a final sigh of relief, I saw at once— for I am an intuitive type—that somebody had come to meet me.

The Local Enthusiast, who had had a letter about me from New York, explained that the hotel had no room that night because it was still housing a conference. (American hotels that refuse conferences, if any exist, should prominently advertise the fact. I do not know what these conferences do during the day, but at night their delegates, blazing with bourbon and Scotch, shouting over their poker games, breaking into close harmony, bidding one another manly farewells all down the corridor, murder my sleep.) So the Local Enthusiast proposed to take me to his house, which, he added with the quick generosity that is one of the most endearing American traits, was mine to command, if I preferred it, for the remainder of my stay in his city. I accepted gratefully for that night, but said that as I had booked a room in the hotel I had better occupy it next day, and stay there to take advantage of its central position in the town. He himself lived a mile or two away, in what I soon saw, as we went gliding and purring into it, was the best residential suburb, called Lakeside.

His car really did seem to glide and to purr, and appeared to find its own way about as he continued talking eagerly and pointed out various pleasant features of the district. His pride was by no means without justification. The place had charm. The long low houses, among winding drive-ways, with their careful lawns and trees all open to the view, were very well done, in varying styles but not idiotically eclectic like the houses of the rich in Southern California. If there was money to burn here, as obviously there was, taste and good sense had not been banished. Only the largest mansion he showed me—a Renaissance château about ten years old—was silly. The others were admirable of their kind. Here, in Lakeside, the city was out of sight and almost out of mind; the lawns, for ever watched and watered, were richly green; there was a glitter of water everywhere between the lower trees; most of the houses were tactfully placed and neither too showy nor too drab; some nice little problems had been nicely solved by the architects and landscape gardeners. No major problems of our new urban life had been solved, of course, for these involve an enormous number of people all with moderate incomes; here there were only a few hundred people to be housed, all of them well off and some as rich as emperors.

Still feeling rumpled and soiled after the train, still in want of a clean shirt, a sandwich, a drink, still wondering what I thought I was up to, I admitted—I hope not too grudgingly—that Lakeside was very well designed indeed, that there was much to be said in favour of the new American domestic architecture. I hope too that I was not already, in some dark corner of the mind, weighting a bias against people who lived behind those pleasant low façades, a cool white beyond the green; against the men who summoned architects across the continent and told them the houses must be up and ready for occupation within a few months; against the smart-looking women who passed us in cars even larger than my host's. We should remember, however much we protest, that there is envy mixed in our opinion of Americans. And Texans sincerely believe that all other Americans are envious of *them*. The afternoon lighting up our exploration was about the best I had seen since May; the car went gliding up one avenue after another like a gondola; my host, in his enthusiasm, never stopped talking, sometimes seeming to interrupt himself to get everything said; and sitting beside him, probably looking not unlike a figure symbolic of half-

26

ruined London, I did what I could to meet the situation.

In a pleasant interior, dim after so much brilliant sunlight, my hostess welcomed me with good-natured warmth; and in ten minutes, after hastily unpacking my large suitcase, in which a pound of tobacco had broken loose, I had made a fine trim bedroom look as if a platoon of infantry had passed through it. I descended to find the drink and the sandwich awaiting me, the first rill of what was soon to turn into a Niagara of hospitality. There was talk; there were high-fidelity records; there were visitors and much more talk. I was asked, and I agreed, to share the evening's social round my host and hostess had already planned for themselves. It began with a crowded party at a country club with cascades of champagne and steaming rosy hillocks of Lobster Newburgh, a hundred men with deep voices and nothing much to say, a hundred and fifty women, all smart as new whips, with everything to say. Introductions were formal and took precedence over all attempts at conversation; I must have heard, *May I present*——? a hundred times. They seemed agreeable people but I never had a chance to get to know anybody. After two hours of this, foaming with champagne, dubiously loaded down with Lobster Newburgh, and rapidly losing contact with reality, I was conjured away from the country club to the smoky candle-lit recesses of a restaurant, where we joined, belatedly, a large dinner party at a long table. We were just in time there to welcome a mammoth dessert, the largest I have ever seen—halves of giant pineapples came into it, I seem to remember—for I refused to tackle one. *May-I-present* began again, but this time, the hour being

27

later and many a bottle emptied, with rather less formality, with jokes booming out of the men and little
gurgles and screams of pretended delight coming from
the women. Later still, now in a hazy long dream, I was
up in somebody's apartment with a remnant of the
diners, staring at a screen on which were projected
coloured photographs of Florida, mostly of Miami,
which looked horrible. And even later still, deeper in
dreamland, I was having a Scotch-for-the-road—
though what road I would never know—with a man
originally from my part of the world, an old soldier too.
There we were, tough old campaigners, at ease together
high above the rabble, glowing in the warmth of a friendship that had lasted nearly two hours, wise and merry,
luminous with intuition, still shrewd in our judgment
yet ready to forgive the weak and foolish, filling and
emptying just another-for-the-road; there, I say, we
were, goggling across the broad spaces of his sitting-
room, roaring out those vast generalisations that seem
at the time so witty, so profound, and that so fortunately
drop out of memory.

On our way down to the hotel next morning I was
taken to what is claimed to be the largest book-store in
America. It is run by the Methodists. And certainly it
was a very fine store indeed, carrying an immense
stock, all neatly laid out. It had everything except an
intimate bookish atmosphere; it was a book-store, not
a bookshop. But opposite my hotel, quite small, only
one room, was a bookshop, the real thing. Now and
again one comes across these small bookshops in
America, usually run by women who have a genuine
interest in literature, and, like the one I found in Dallas,

they are generally places where people drop in for a gossip. There is much to be said in their favour. We could do with a few of them in England, where this kind of personal bookselling is now hard to discover, although we are so busy creating the cultural desert in which these shops are the oases. There is a world of difference between stores operated by sellers of merchandise and shops kept by shopkeepers. Books properly belong to the latter; they are not merchandise. I found some companionable souls in this little bookshop, and popped across all the more often because I took a strong dislike to my hotel. It offered me all manner of gadgets and arrangements I did not want, and refused me what I did want—peace, quiet, a little space. Up in my bedroom I could overhear at all hours the final words of business deals, marital quarrels and reconciliations, and an assortment of radio programmes. All day and well into the night, the main lobby was as busy as a city railway station. The restaurant was always crowded, even at breakfast-time, so I never patronised it. The staff were pleasant enough—I always found people in Texas cheerful, friendly, obliging—but that hotel to me was simply a bed, a bath, a telephone.

The companionable souls across the way would take me a little higher up the street, for more talk over a martini or two, to the University club, no monument of scholarship, it is true, but offering excellent hard liquor, equally excellent soft furnishings, and a large dim bar as a relief from the daylight glare and the night-time glitter outside. It was necessary to go to a club for a cocktail because the licensing laws had been designed by either a lunatic or an artful group of distillers. In this city you could buy at a public bar or in a restaurant only wine (not good) or beer, no spirits. On the other hand, you could buy as many bottles of hard liquor as you wanted at the many stores. So people dining out publicly or going to a dance-hall or a cabaret take their bottles of spirits with them. Where, in a sensible place, you would merely have a drink or two, here you would open, and sooner or later finish, a bottle. With the obvious result that people here tend to drink more, not less, than they do elsewhere. That is why I came to the conclusion that it was not the dry Baptists and Methodists that upheld these absurd regulations but the liquor trade itself. I have in fact never seen more hard drinking since the uproarious days of complete prohibition. All this comes of the good oppressing the wicked: Hell booms.

The parties, chiefly thrown my way by the Local Enthusiast, went on and on. I began to suspect that I recognised the staff of coloured people hired on these occasions to serve drinks and the baronial buffet suppers. Most of the hosts and guests were either 'in oil' or on the lucrative edge of it. In front of one house, large flambeaux were flaring, perhaps as a symbol. Everybody was hospitable and kind and very friendly, though we all kept off politics. I met only one person I thoroughly disliked, and this particular young man, I was told, was notorious; whereas, meeting the same number of people in London, New York, Paris, I would probably have run into dozens I thought detestable. On the other hand, I met very few people whose presence and talk made me feel eager to meet them again. The truth is, these parties had everything parties should have—genial men and handsome women in a good setting, first-class food and drink and service—except striking personalities and satisfying talk. I do not say the striking personalities did not exist; some of the older men, who had come up the hard way, were probably too shy or indifferent to reveal themselves. But the talk, though friendly enough, was poor, not to be compared with that of the companionable souls elsewhere in the city.

I have no tenderness for the epicene or all the sexual aberrations; but I am convinced that good talk cannot flourish where there is a wide gulf between the sexes, where the men are altogether too masculine, too hearty and bluff and booming, where the women are too feminine, at once both too arch and too anxious. Where men are leavened by a feminine element, where women are not without some tempering by the masculine spirit, there is a chance of good talk. And if there cannot be a balance of the two eternal principles, then let the feminine principle have the domination. But here was a society entirely dominated by the masculine principle. Why were so many of these women at once so arch and so anxious? There was nothing wrong with them as women. Superficially, everything seemed blazingly right with them. But even here in these circles, where millionaires apparently indulged and spoilt them, giving them without question or stint what women elsewhere were for ever wistfully hoping for, they were haunted by a feeling of inferiority, resented but never properly examined and challenged. They lived in a world so contemptuous and destructive of real feminine values that they had to be heavily bribed to remain in it. All

31

those shops, like the famous Neiman-Marcus store (a remarkable creation) here in Dallas, were part of the bribe. They were still girls in a mining camp. And to increase their bewilderment, perhaps their despair, they are told they are living in a matriarchy.

It is easy to see why modern America has been described as a matriarchy. There is all the fuss about Mother. Individual women wield far more economic power than they do anywhere else. Women's organisations have more influence than they have in Europe. Women run great enterprises. The adornment of woman is now the basis of a stupendous industry. A large proportion of American men are bullied by women—mothers, wives, daughters—all their lives. This is one country where Woman is the Boss. Here women are often so aggressive, demanding, dictatorial, that many men are only happy when they can get away from them. (A great deal of contemporary American fiction emphasises this fear of woman and the desire to escape from her.) So runs the argument, and it seems a strong one. But it misses the essential point. Life in America is dominated by the masculine and not the feminine principle. The values of this society are masculine and not feminine. It is ruled by Logos, not by Eros. If women become aggressive, demanding, dictatorial, it is because they find themselves struggling to find satisfaction in a world that is not theirs. If they use sex as a weapon, it is because they so badly need a weapon. They are like the inhabitants of an occupied country. They are compelled to accept values and standards that are alien to their deepest nature. Woman wishes to take root; this society is uprooted. She is deeply conservative; this society is nothing if not progressive. She wants slow but certain growth; this society is restless and for ever changing. She desires an erotic personal relationship, the life of Eros; what she gets is a muddle of hasty sex, social partnership, and a tangle of legalities, the creations of Logos. She wants a securely-rooted family tree; there are fewer and fewer of them in this society. She believes, in the ancient wisdom of her heart, that nothing matters except the quality of personal experience, what real men, women and children are feeling about life; but this society attends to everything except that, offering her in place of it technics, gadgets, graphs, statistics. She longs for prophets, seers, heroes, artists, magic males to adore; what she gets are pompous bank presidents, salesmen with ulcers, apologetic chartered accountants, advertising fakers, and lunatic designers of atomic bombs. Her essential nature cries out for a devoted lover, healthy children, a happy home filled with easy intimate talk, laughter, absurd or charming ceremonies, and nothing whatever out of cybernetics and science fiction, buildings two thousand feet high, travel at five hundred miles an hour, stainless steel robot attendants, and dinners arriving in capsules. She is the most traditional creature in the world, the most old-fashioned, imprisoned in a society that has said good-bye to every tradition, where everything is new-fashioned.

So she takes her revenge. If she has to be bribed, she demands the heaviest possible bribes. If sex must be her weapon, then she wields it day and night with ferocity. If she must compete on this alien ground, in the jungle of sharp enterprise and large profits, then she competes

aggressively and unscrupulously, bringing to the con-
flict her will power and hysterical energy. She will be
hard on men because it is they—or the principle they
represent—who are responsible for her feelings of deep
unease, frustration, insecurity. She projects on to them
her unconscious resentment of the triumphant masculine principle. Where it is super-triumphant, crowing
at its loudest, as it tends to be in these bursting Texan
cities, then, no matter what wealth is hers to scatter on
any whim, what deference she receives, she will remain
resentful at heart, often quite unfairly critical. So in
places of this kind women will exaggerate the faults of
the American male in general. He is too much concerned with business, sport, whisky and predatory
blondes. He is boring. He is bad-mannered—a palp-
able slander, this, for American men have better manners
with women than almost any others. He is not adult,
not mature, and so incapable of understanding and
pleasing a woman. So it goes on, when in truth they
have little or no real quarrel with their men as individuals. And the men, so often 'in the dog house', half
worshipping these magical beings (all the more magical
because they represent the defeated principle, the something that is lacking), half despising them for their wil-
fulness, their selfishness, their unfairness, are baffled
and miserable, telling one another that women have
always been like this, not knowing what they want, the
crazy creatures. But woman does know what she wants,
and has always been the saner partner. It is the society
these men have created, are still creating, that does not
know what it wants and is lunatic. It is the society of
the hydrogen bomb.

Handsome women and pretty girls were everywhere at these parties; but I hope I will not be accused of having exotic sexual tastes (and I haven't) if I declare that the one staggering beauty I saw was a young coloured waitress, who served our lunch at a newspaper office. She was not the familiar half-caste type, the 'high yaller' of amorous Deep South legend, but quite black, with negroid features exquisitely subdued and harmonised, a gentle smiling creature out of some lost world of feminine darkness. I found it hard not to stare at her, and must have neglected some of the talk round the table, talk that was lively and good. I am supposed to have had a long feud with American newspapermen, and I must confess that unwittingly they have done me a great deal of harm, prejudicing a host of American readers and playgoers against me. There has never been anything personal in all this. It is the result of a thoroughly bad tradition, which I thought was dead—and indeed I think it is in New York—but discovered, to my dismay, still showed some signs of life down in Texas. This is the tradition that the slightest adverse criticism of American life made by a visiting English writer is important news, to be played up, whereas anything pleasant he says can be ignored. And if necessary, for we all know these visiting English writers must be snooty fellows, some sharp nasty criticism can be invented for him. ('Says All Texas Men Are Bores' was the headline of an imaginary interview with me in a Houston paper, later. If I had believed this, I would never have had the hardihood to declare it on the spot; though I will put it on record here that several Houston women, after hearing my disclaimer, told me they were disappointed and that I ought to have said it.) There is no malice in all this; it is just part of the game; but to a man who depends for his living to some extent on public goodwill, it is not a game, and no joke at all, to be displayed to millions, who do not know him, as a conceited lout, a stupid boor, repaying hospitality and kindness with insults. But apart from these occasions when the bad tradition divides us, I always get along with American newspapermen and usually find them capital company, better in themselves than most of the papers that employ them.

Though often idiotic in their opinions, these Texas newspapers have one very sensible feature. They make use of their own local critics and columnists, many of them careful writers with a point of view of their own, instead of being content to buy the usual syndicated stuff. One or two of these local columnists, sardonic wits like Carl Victor Little in Houston, have a fine knack of puncturing the vast balloons of gas and gush floating up from the oil-fields and giant ranches. This is worth noting. American life may still be sillier than English, if only because there is so much more of it and it has so much more money to play with, but now it seems to me that American silliness is derided and denounced far more often, and far more effectively, than English silliness is. Any intelligent American knows mass nonsense to be mass nonsense; he may deceive others, he does not deceive himself. An equally intelligent Englishman now is not so sure, probably because his mass nonsense has been so cunningly intermixed with genuine traditional feeling. Thus, the post-war English, meeting the new huge silliness, the mass nonsense, with a kind of innocence without the hard sardonic streak there is in so many Americans and that finds expression even in the popular press, are in the more dangerous situation. Not, however, in politics. Alongside these satirical columns in the Texas newspapers were letters from readers that were terrifying in their complacent ignorance, their indignant lunacy. Their writers argued as if they were living on the back of the moon. To them China was not a huge ruin of an Empire where armies had been wandering for years, but some little thing that Alger Hiss or somebody had slipped to the Reds as a present. War was to be avoided by threatening with total destruction everybody who did not agree with the folks in Sweetwater, Eagle Pass or Brownsville. American forces were to keep order everywhere but no clean-living American boys sent to dirty places overseas. People not able to appreciate the free American way of life ought to be tracked down, arrested, locked up, chain-ganged, and generally knocked hell out of. I do not claim these are the views of the average Texan citizen; yet the editors trying to please him did not hesitate to print drivel of this sort—world politics out of this world.

The General, of course, was not so foolish. I was invited to meet the General and then listen to him giving an address to the Foreign Affairs Association of Dallas. I met him at a cocktail party at the Petroleum Club. This club is handsomer than its name, and has been designed for the leaders of the oil business. A man I went in with, speaking in a quiet reverent tone, said: 'More than a billion dollars are represented here.' He was not himself 'in oil' but he seemed to have an almost tender admiration for the richest and most powerful oil-men, seeing them as epic figures, misjudged by an envious world. He tried to convert me to this view of them, stressing the fact that their fortunes were 'clean', gained at nobody else's expense. The trouble with these tycoons, however, as my more radical acquaintances were quick to point out, is that they are not content merely to fly around in their private planes and smoke the longest cigars; out of gains handsomely freed from excessive taxation, they buy newspapers and radio stations, subsidise dubious political movements and personalities. They consider themselves wiser and nobler than people who do not know where to find fifty million dollars. 'They take all that money out of holes in the ground,' one newspaperman said to me, 'then think God has appointed them His prophets.' In this age of mass communications, some of them open to the highest bidder, great wealth can command more power than it could at any time since it ceased to equip and maintain private armies. Now our Wallensteins are nervous multi-millionaires barking instructions down the telephone to editors, radio commentators, public relations men.

From the Petroleum Club, which adjoins the hotel, we moved down into the banqueting room where the Association dines and meets. I was seated at the raised table for the speakers, but fortunately was not expected to speak. Fortunately, because I began to feel grumpier and grumpier. I hope my host, who meant well, will forgive me if I declare that these occasions represent American life at its deadliest. Everything is wrong. The dinner itself was bad: a first course of frozen fruit salad (and it is still frozen fruit salad if you call it 'fruit cocktail' and regard it, God knows why, as an appetiser); a miserable entrée that still contrived to taste sweet; then a dollop of ice-cream: a meal designed for a not very hungry child of ten. No drink, just gallons of ice-water. But is drink necessary when we meet to consider Foreign Affairs? In my opinion—Yes. Vast quantities of gin, champagne, hock, claret, brandy and vodka, all paid for by the silly sheep whose happiness, whose lives, are at stake in the poker game, have been consumed by the creators of this monstrous tangle; and we in our turn should not be asked even to contemplate it for half an hour on ice-water. Moreover, even when stupefied by food and drink, as I generally contrive to be, I find long after-dinner speeches hard to endure. Half-fed on nursery mush, icily sober, my chilled stomach appalled, every cell of my famished brain signalling distress, I was compelled to listen to these after-dinner speeches, mostly made by that type of middle-aged business-man who cannot leave anything out, in an anguish of boredom. I seemed to cross bare-footed all the frozen tundras of Siberia while the retiring president, the new president, the secretary, the treasurer, the chairman, went on and on and on; and if the General had led a flying column to my rescue I could not have greeted his opening words with more warmth.

His address on the situation in South-East Asia, obviously one that he had given many times before, was lucid and not unreasonable; but clearly it was based on the belief that no co-existence with Communism was possible, that we were already at war. He was no fool, yet it never seemed to occur to him that if American

generals move around in South-East Asia, a long way
from home, it might be as well if they have some simple
powerful ideas to sell to the South-East Asians. I am
nearly as anxious as he is that these people do not soon
find themselves members of the Communist *bloc*. I
believe the Communist arguments, appealing to a
nationalist or racial feeling that will soon be smothered
once it has served its turn, to be false and a cheat, just as
I regard Communism itself as a dreary swindle. But
half-bullying people is no use, it never works. Take
complete charge of them, or buy them off, or use greater
powers of persuasion than the other side. And, as I
suggested to him afterwards, when we had a brief talk,
a few essential freedoms and rights, not merely pro-
claimed but openly and definitely respected by our
governments, no matter at what immediate risk and
inconvenience, might help. (They would help the rest
of us too, for if we stand for freedom, let us enjoy the
freedom we stand for.) The General agreed, and invited
me to call upon him in New York; but he agreed so
quickly, so heartily, that I am afraid it only meant that
he had had a long day and would be glad to see the last
of us all and go to bed.

I went up to my bedroom too, to stare at the typewriter lent to me by the nice woman who ran the good
little bookshop. (She runs it no longer, and one clear
light has gone out in Dallas.) Later, when I returned
this machine, another nice woman, whom I had con-
sulted about hiring a typewriter for the rest of my stay
in Texas, insisted upon lending me her own private
machine, to take into the blue. As a man who has been
using and owning typewriters for about forty years, I

knew that these were no idle gestures of friendly concern: this was the real thing, so often discovered in the
American South-West, and never to be matched in our
colder and more cautious realm. Elizabeth McMurray,
Marihelen McDuff—I salute you, ladies—and pray that
no word of mine here will offend for even a fraction of a
moment. Remember that I too, as I hope I have proved
more than once, love the South-West, am nearly as
deeply devoted to it as I am to my own Britain. These
are great regions; they deserve the good life. And the
good life is in danger. Back then, ladies, to our typewriters.

Now I was moving round fairly confidently in 'Big
D.' as Dallas likes to call itself. Not a hundred-and-
twenty years ago, it was a trading post in a log cabin
beside the Trinity River; today its half-million inhabitants, with more money, material, space and vigour than
any half-million most of us know, are creating a pattern
of urban life for other cities to envy and to imitate. 'Its
Place In The Sun,' cried the *Dallas Morning News*, 'Gets
Bigger All The Time.' Fair enough. Not always in the
sun I moved like a bemused ant far down below its
'ever more imposing skyline', its 'impressive, restless,
changing, climbing silhouette. . . .' New and even
taller buildings were going up, as if the children of
giants were playing with Meccano sets. The forty-storey
bank building, which I had thought at first was made of
tin but is actually sheathed in aluminium (probably a
blinding spectacle in summer) was not quite finished,
and had already cost about twenty-five million dollars.
I read all about its 'formal dedication' after I had left the
city: four-thousand-eight-hundred celebrities headed by

Bob Hope had been invited; the dinner, in the huge Fair Park building, offered gold-coloured ice-cream as its dessert; there were free drinks at three bars 'stretching a city block'—quite a shindig or wingding, *yes*, *sir*! If the rest of us cannot build and celebrate in this fashion, it is not because we do not want to but because as yet we cannot afford it. Give us time. (And perhaps lend us Bob Hope.) What about a Fair Park of one-hundred-and-eighty-seven acres located within ten minutes driving time from down-town; top-ranking contests in basketball, baseball, ice-skating, wrestling, football, eighty movie theatres, seven radio and two television stations; and, if it nearly comes to the worst, seventeen hospitals? Culture is not neglected; there is a gallant symphony orchestra, a tiny theatre-in-the-round, some museums (including one for Health) and the Southern Methodist University. But rather too much is claimed for Dallas as a cultural centre; the oil tycoons do not seem to throw their millions in that dubious direction. The Public Library, I discovered, is one of the poorest in the country for a city this size; but then Dallas is expanding at a time when public libraries are no longer very important; probably the newest towns will not have libraries at all. Literature belongs to an age that is dying; to enjoy the poets, essayists, serious novelists, you need peace and quiet and an easy mind; already from the high towers above the plains of cement the doom of letters is being pronounced.

If you want to enter business in Dallas, to take your Cadillac with the rest along Elm, Main or Commerce Streets, you can choose oil, agriculture, manufacturing, banking, insurance and aviation. If something humbler will serve—bricklayers are paid $3.50 an hour, electricians $3.00, building labourers (a mixed lot, all colours) $1.45; and professors and teachers get by. There are also strangely confused and confusing vocations. A young taxi-driver, who lost me hopelessly one night going out to Lakeside, explained first that it was only his second evening with the cab, and secondly, to my bewilderment, that he was also a dental mechanic—and a dental mechanic in the Navy. He may have bought a booklet, widely advertised in the local press, in which 'the author gives a most astonishing formula for wealth and success, based on long misunderstood parables in the Bible', a booklet entitled *Get Rich In Spite Of Yourself*. This inland-city-naval-dental-mechanic-taxi-driver was richer by two dollars, by losing us both in spite of himself, but I felt that the money was well spent; I was in danger of taking this place and its people for granted. In my hotel, still as busy and noisy as ever, the delegates of the Southern Cookie Manufacturers Association had checked out, the representatives of the South-Western Shoe Travellers Association were checking in. Life, unlike so much of the furiously hooting traffic, was on the move. And where, I had time to ask myself now, did it think it was going?

3

Sandia Cave

J. H. TO J. B. P.

. . . Considering how vague my working plans are, I've launched them in an incongruously well-ordered way. Yesterday a nice woman I've made friends with here drove me out to the Sandia Cave, and of all the sites in America, this is the one which has given its name to the earliest known culture. I am hardly to be blamed for doing first things first in such a pedantic way, for, as you know, it was the planning of the railroad people rather than my own which took me directly to Albuquerque. Once here, it seemed the obvious thing to see this famous site before anything else.

Mrs. A. was having a permanent wave in preparation for some civic function, so we didn't start until well on in the morning; I spent some of the spare time in providing for a picnic lunch. The Sandia Mountains, a fine jagged range, are several miles away really, but in the evenings, when they turn the most ravishing colours (last night, powder-blue, fluted cobalt) they seem to make their redeeming presence felt everywhere in this rackety town. It may be an excellent city to belong to, but to look at Albuquerque certainly has need of some saving grace.

As we only knew that the Sandia Cave was somewhere along a road on the far side of the range we decided we needed further guidance and called on the Curator of the Coronado Monument, a prehistoric Indian ruin on the banks of the Rio Grande. He was supposed to know its exact whereabouts. As a matter of fact he didn't, but it proved an interesting encounter. We found (as one so often does) that we had chosen the one day of the week when the Monument is closed to the public, so we wriggled through the wild-west-looking gate of stripped branches bound with rawhide thongs and trespassed past ruins to the rough little adobe house where the Curator and his wife live—miles away from anywhere.

Then I had an experience which I am beginning to realise is quite a commonplace in this country: that of going into a house that looks wretched outside to find an enchanting interior. The Curator, naturally enough, is an enthusiast for Indian things (not only for things of the past, either; he left us to drive a sick Pueblo friend into hospital) and his house was full of choice specimens of their pottery, painting, basketry and weaving. I might have said alive with them, for it really is astonishing how much vigour they have. A fine Pueblo pot brings far more life to a room than a fire or flowers. I am becoming more and more excited as I discover how these things can annihilate all the expensive machine products of the age. Only abstract or near-abstract designs on objects of everyday use—yet how they cry out to one! I wish I understood how their own peculiar designs and styles crystallise in the imagination of peoples. But thank goodness that they do—or have

45

done. Do you think that any new ones are likely to come to birth in our kind of world?

The walls of the cottage were hung with Navaho rugs and tapestries—the nomadic Navahos being the best weavers, just as the sedentary Pueblos are by far the most gifted potters. Being old ones, red was the dominant colour and they glowed so richly that as I stepped in from the clear sunlight outside I had a sudden notion that this was how an insect must feel when it flies into a scarlet flower. When as a child I used to read about pioneers trading red cloth with Indians, I had no notion that the 'squaws' immediately unravelled it to make lovely materials of their own. There is a popular legend that they used the uniforms of arrow-shot red-coats, but I'm told in fact that it was nothing more romantic than red flannel.

We stayed for some time talking to the Curator and his wife. They are both in violent rebellion against ordinary American values and habits, raging against competitiveness, city life and the tyranny of machines. I can see that I'm going to meet a lot of such rebels over here; some of them neurotics, no doubt, but others just exercising a free choice.

We drove back across the Rio Grande and headed for the Sandias, knowing now within a mile or two where to look for the cave. The approach is through a small Spanish village, rather a pretty one with orchards still showing some autumn colours. After a steepish climb into the mountains we left the desert well behind and were in a forested canyon with limestone cliffs rising high above us. We crawled along, scanning the cliffs for a sight of our cave. It's very tiring to crane

46

upwards out of a saloon car, and the rocks were full of possible cave openings. At last we spotted the right one, and, as it was late, we decided to carry our lunch up there with us. The beer was heavy, and this little scramble up the side of the ravine made me feel the height for the first time. Albuquerque is getting on for six thousand feet, and I suppose by then we had reached nearly eight thousand. I puffed and gasped in the most shameful way—although Mrs. A. was worse, for she's fatter and smokes all the time.

The cave is a fine one as caves go, tunnelling far into the rock. But unless one is a child or a speleomaniac, there isn't a great deal to be said for caves once they have been excavated. Still, this one deserves a pilgrimage. When it was dug, in the late thirties, it proved to be an archæologist's dream site, as neatly stratified as a layer cake. On the top there was relatively recent stuff, sherds of Indian pottery set in a mass of bat and pack-rat droppings; it had some interest, however, for it included the bones of the ground sloth, which hairy beast had evidently survived up here until a few centuries ago. Below this came the remains of an Old Stone Age people (the Folsum) already recognised in this part of the world and thought to be its oldest inhabitants. So it must have been exciting to dig down to yet another, older, occupation layer with more food bones, flints and hearths. Here was the most ancient known habitation in America, and the flints were of an unrecognised type; among the animals which the hunters had killed and probably eaten were extinct breeds of horse, camel, bison, mastodon and mammoth. The new flints have been duly named Sandia points and the culture the

47

Sandia culture; the excavator dates it to about 25,000 years ago, but it may be rather later. Undoubtedly it corresponds to some part of our later Palaeolithic, the age of the cave-paintings and the last glaciation. It must have been a lot colder and wetter even in New Mexico, although of course it's too far south to have been glaciated. If the first human beings (Mongolians) came into America across the Behring Straits, they must have pushed down here surprisingly quickly. I suppose some day earlier finds will be made up Alaska way, but they haven't been as yet.

We picnicked on the rocks near the cave mouth, perhaps where the hunters may have squatted on a warm day gnawing hunks of mammoth. It was marvellous there yesterday. In the hot sun the pines smelt as good as frankincense and myrrh, and the little canyon was full of birds whistling and crying to one another. The ground fell away so steeply below us that our eyes were on a level with the tops of tall pine trees, and I could watch flickers, finches and tits feeding among the branches. The fire-colour of the flicker woodpeckers glowed through the dark pine needles. Can I possibly make you feel how nice it was there: the warmth, the resinous air, the bird calls, the sense of a sweet, private domain? Or how much I enjoyed letting myself lapse into it, float out on it, after so many days cooped up with noise—in New York, trains, aeroplanes?

As was only proper, I tried to imagine the lives of the cave dwellers. I wondered (in a visual sort of way) if they had driven the great elephants over the cliffs, for I couldn't see Sandia points killing them. On second thoughts, though, I recall a mammoth being found in

48

Arizona all stuck with Folsum points, which aren't much better. I pictured the nights when fires reddened the narrow mouth of this cave, and there were cooking smells and voices. There is something very moving in the thought of human voices in a world where there were so few, so very few, of our kind. A voice muttering in the wilderness. Probably they had poetic incantations and epic tales, but all as a part of the endless business of the chase. They wouldn't have wearied of hunting, anything else being inconceivable: *c'etait la vie*. What emotion the hunters must have known for the animals they preyed upon. In this place it wasn't difficult to think of the men and their quarry moving through the canyon together, both equally warm, living, alert and with the nerve current of the hunt running between them. *Participation mystique*, and hardly a twinge of human self-consciousness. Since coming here, I've seen paintings by a young Pueblo Indian of ceremonies where the dancers were wearing deer antlers on their heads and tails hanging between their legs. Exactly like the famous dancing Sorcerer, a palaeolithic cave-painting in France. I must try to see some of these Pueblo Indian ceremonies, because surely they must represent a survival of prehistoric life?

Perhaps because I've been moving about so much myself lately, I started to think about the Stone Age peoples trekking through the Americas. I find it hard to imagine what it was like to keep on the move with no general idea of one's whereabouts on a map: pushing blindly into space, generation after generation. We're so used to knowing where we are and where we're going. The Spaniards, and especially the Franciscans

49

and Dominicans, showed amazing guts when they opened up this region in the sixteenth century, but obviously deliberate exploring is different in feeling from this blind spread from the north to the south of two continents. A kind of somnambulism. The Spaniards had faith behind them, or the lust for gold and conquest; these Stone Age people had nothing but the Life Force to drive them from Alaska to Tierra del Fuego! I suppose they would have known their own hunting grounds far better than we know the Isle of Wight, but nothing fitted into a larger whole. There were no destinations.

Anyway, I'm very glad we went. I like visiting shrines, whether Dove Cottage or the Sandia Cave. . . .

—

New Names

·

J. B. P. TO J. H.

. . . I thought you ought to know about this as soon as possible, though naturally you can please yourself about making any use of it. But I have coined some new names, and from now on I shall use them. I shall do this not only for quick convenient reference but also to avoid suggesting, even to myself, that I am merely criticising America and not contemporary Western society in general. (Though America gave us the lead, of course, and is much further along. The rest of us, half sleep-walking, totter on behind.) First then—*Admass*. This is my name for the whole system of an increasing productivity, plus inflation, plus a rising standard of material living, plus high-pressure advertising and salesmanship, plus mass communications, plus cultural democracy and the creation of the mass mind, the mass man. (Behind the Iron Curtain they have *Propmass*, official propaganda taking the place of advertising, but all with the same aims and objects.) The people firmly fixed in *Admass* are *Admassians*. Most Americans (though not all; they have some fine rebels) have been *Admassians* for the last thirty years; the English, and probably most West Europeans, only since the War. It is better to live in *Admass* than have no job, no prospect of one, and see your wife and children getting hungrier and hungrier. But that is about all that can be said in favour of it. All the rest is a swindle. You think everything is opening

51

out when in fact it is narrowing and closing in on you. Finally you have to be half-witted or half-drunk all the time to endure it. So much for *Admass*.

In this empire are many kingdoms. One I propose to call *Nomadmass*. This is the land of the new nomads, dominated by the internal combustion engine. To enjoy it you must never want to get out of your car. So you have drive-in everything. But of *Nomadmass*, more later.* Another division I shall call *Hashadmass*. Here everything is turned into one tasteless hash. Whatever it takes is soon robbed of character and essence. It is full of Spanish, French and Italian restaurants that have long ceased to be Spanish, French or Italian—all just *Hashadmass*. It is like one of those Hollywood studio 'lots' that contain town halls, churches, mansions, saloons, all without interiors; odd bits done in plaster of New York, London, Paris, Shanghai, and Tombstone, Arizona, *circa* 1885. The difference is that *Hashadmass* is not intended simply to be photographed as a background but to be lived in, which is its tragedy. So, over here, what was honest and soundly-rooted in American life is thrust aside, replaced by a characterless mush of styles, made up of plaster, fancy costume, imitation everything. We have it of course in England now; it arrives with *Admass*. Probably most of the money earned in *Hashadmass*—the big money, I mean—is spent in the smaller but richer kingdom of *Luxad*. Here may be found Gracious Living, Casual Living, and soon any other kind of Living dreamt up by the copywriters. In *Luxad* you see yourself doing what you have been told is the latest thing to do, all unpaid actors in character

*See p. 156.

parts—Man of Distinction, Gracious Living Hostess,
member of Casual Living younger set, etc. So here
they are—*Admass*, the great empire itself, and the
satellites—*Nomadmass*, *Hashadmass*, *Luxad*. They have
almost a Biblical ring, these names, but those raging old
intuitives, the Hebrew prophets, would have made short
work of them—*Woe!*—*woe!*—*woe!* And to you if I
don't hear from you soon. . . .

c

Bandalier
Monument

.

J. H. TO J. B. P.

. . . I am beginning to understand how the parts of Indian history fit together. I ought to have known before I came, for there is a vast literature on the subject. But I don't altogether regret arriving here in open-eyed ignorance. The information one picks up for oneself on the spot is so much more convincing than any other—and remains so; it seems to go into a different part of the mind. What I've been made to realise most sharply is the strength of the tradition uniting the present-day Pueblo Indians with their prehistoric ancestors. Such little reading as I had done concerned Indian prehistory, just as the few plans I had made in advance were all for seeing cliff dwellings and other ancient sites. Now I've been forced to understand that it would be idiotic to neglect the Pueblos. I much prefer people who still have flesh on their bones.

I suppose I've thought of American Indians as having been harried from place to place until most of them lived round Hollywood waiting for film jobs. I admit I'm exaggerating, for I knew something of the Reserves in the South-West and have seen Hopis (who are a Pueblo people) and Navaho before. But I thought they were sweepings pushed into odd corners, their culture corrupted and all but gone. I failed to grasp that the Pueblos have been living in much the same region for about two thousand years, maintaining an unbroken cultural tradition for all that time. They still make and do many things as they did in the days of King Alfred. As my private symbol for this continuity I've adopted the *kiva*—a sacred underground chamber, whose sacredness seems to lie half-way between that of a church and that of the most exclusive Club in St. James's. But before you can get the point of this I must tell you what I've actually seen.

The other day when there was that public holiday, Mrs. A.'s husband was free and undertook to drive us to the Bandalier Monument, or more correctly, to the ruins of Tyuonyi in El Rito de los Frijoles. They asked if I would like to go by way of some of the Rio Grande pueblos, and I was very glad to say yes because I guessed this would take us away from the highroad and its traffic. It did: a few miles out of Albuquerque we plunged down on to what is called here a gravel road, something intermediate between the perfection of a 'black-top' highway and the crudity of the desert track which might be called a dust road or a mud road according to the season. This gravel road soon took us to a massive steel bridge over the Rio Grande (at this time of year a putty-coloured rivulet giving its bridges a look of megalomaniac pretentiousness) and then in a moment we were back in a more primitive world as we ran into the Indian pueblo of San Felipe. I don't want to sentimentalise these pueblos—they must be uncomfortable and mildly unhealthy—but I do like them so much. I suppose it is partly because they are true villages, while the motor-age has brought nothing to the South-West but slapdash little towns already plastered with neon before they've cut their milk-teeth as communities, and the highway settlements which are really just encampments of people out to take money off motorists by legal means. The pueblos are places where people live because their parents and grandparents did, because their sacred buildings are at the heart of them and their fields and orchards spread round about, and because all their tales concern the neighbouring rivers, mesas and mountains.

My first impression of San Felipe was of its lowness and compactness; a village very close to the earth of which it is made. The adobe houses conformed to an undesigned cubism, a composition of rectangular masses relieved by the lines of *vegas*. They are apartments rather than houses, for I believe each family normally lives in one room and these are fitted together snugly as the cells of a honeycomb. A single storey is usual, but sometimes there is a second, recessed to leave a most agreeable little colonnaded terrace where one can sit in the sun. Because San Felipe is right on the bank of the Rio Grande, it is set with huge cottonwoods; when we were there they were still in colour, seeming to hang like golden cumulus clouds above the low, flat roofs. In contrast with the cubical masses of the houses, were the little domes of the ovens which stood in twos and threes all about the village. A few were heating, with flames showing in their dark bellies and pinyon smoke swirling out in delicious clouds. This pinyon smell is as much a part of a pueblo as peat smell is of an Irish village, and to my nose even sweeter. The dun colour of the adobe is saved from dreariness by corn, chiles and the inhabitants themselves. Most of the corn was the ordinary yellow kind and flat roofs were brilliant with it, but the

Indians also raise red, black and dark blue varieties, and bunches of these were hanging from the *vegas*. Chiles, cunningly strung together, were looped in noble crimson swags across the house fronts. Here and there men and women wrapped in the usual bright blankets were sitting motionless on their roofs beautifully free from all activity. From behind they looked like little coloured tents pitched on the house-tops. There weren't many of them; on the whole, Indians like to remain indoors, so that the pueblos appear deserted when in fact the reverse is true. Yet one is half aware of them, of so many human beings clamped down close to the earth— as I walked the narrow, dusty alleys between the houses I seemed to feel their presence all round me. I saw the church, a whitewashed adobe pile with twin towers (very crooked) at the west end, each with a bell visible at the top and with a little blue-painted balcony running between them. Not far away, as I approached the plaza where they stage their dance ceremonies, I found myself against a solid, stone-built circular wall with a flight of steps leading to the top and the ends of a large ladder of unhewn trunks standing out against the sky. So far as I could see, the ladder led down into the heart of this strange-looking architectural drum. It was a kiva, and the ladder represents the rainbow, stairway of the Gods.

I don't think anyone could tell you just how the Indians relate Christianity to their own beliefs. Undoubtedly, though, the kiva overshadows the church in their lives, and I should say that they have succeeded in grafting Christianity as one branch on the spreading tree of the ancient faiths. On the other hand, I was told how when an enlightened anthropologist went to

Washington with an Indian deputation to plead some cause or other, and exhorted the court to remember that in a free country the Indians had a right to their own religion, the leading Pueblo indignantly insisted that he and his people were good Christians. The way of enlightenment is often hard.

From San Felipe we went on by desert tracks through other pueblos and in each I was impressed by the kivas. Two seems the usual number, one for each moiety or clan, but sometimes there are more and sometimes only one. They are used for initiations and other solemnities, for the teaching of ritual, for storing ceremonial gear and as male club-rooms. I liked to stand outside in the glare imagining the rich, fantastic symbols down there in the dark, where there had been so many secrets and so much emotion. I longed to go in, yet was delighted to know that all whites were forbidden. I must confess that by the time we reached Cochiti (famous for its ceremonial drums) in the flat afternoon light, the enchantment of San Felipe was wearing off. I noticed the messiness of the cattle pounds, the discarded bones, the bits of raw flesh and bloody sheepskins pegged up like laundry, the domestic popularity of old oil drums and petrol tins. The place had an air of arid desolation, and I wished that I, like the wiser inhabitants, were enjoying a siesta.

It was really only the time of day, always so dreary in the desert. After about another hour, during which I remembered how much I loathe motoring, the sun began to drop and my spirits to rise. We passed a magnificent mass of pink cliffs said to be full of the bones of dinosaurs which took refuge there when the surrounding country was inundated. Then the grim Black Mesa. By now we were on the highway which has been built to serve the Los Alamos atomic station and were climbing fast into the Jemez mountains. All the way we saw danger signs threatening death and destruction. As we twisted up the hairpin bends, great basalt caps hung above our heads and honey-coloured canyons opened beneath us, or sometimes we were looking back into the coppery haze of the desert we had left. What strange, cataclysmic country it is! Los Alamos and its sinister doings are perfectly in keeping.

The Bandalier Monument is in the bottom of one of the deepest canyons; there is a pleasant stream and an abundance of pine trees and aspen. Soon we were looking at the sad foundations of hundreds of little houses which had been built round an oval plaza—in plan exactly like that famous oval block of working-class flats at Leeds. Then we climbed up to the cliff dwellings where the Indians had piled up houses at the cliff foot and cut their small back rooms into the soft tufa. I went up a ladder to one of the highest of these burrows, a perfect lair with the whole of the valley framed in its round doorway. I looked down on the cellular structure of the ruined houses, thought of life going on there. It must have been a lovely place to live. A fertile, lonely crack among so much wildness. Do you think such communities felt their isolation? I doubt it. Not too much individuality and no sense of the map. I don't think we allow enough for the way in which knowledge can actually increase our fears.

It was evening; we were the only people in all this ruined city, which extends for miles along the cliffs.

The light was failing, but I was determined to reach the ceremonial cave which lies high up, just below the canyon lip. The way up was by means of rough ladders of the sort the Indians use, and have always used, in their houses and kivas. Although the bottom of the canyon was already dim, as we climbed from ladder to ladder we emerged into the light of sunset. Our faces and hands were ruddy in it, all such colours as there were burned with a last intensity, and there was some heightening of the atmosphere, a feeling as though the very air were charged. Mrs. A. and her friend dropped out of the climb (let me not deny that I was pleased. They had laughed at me for being quite normally dressed. Much good their western kit did them!) I was the first to step on to the cave floor, and stood beneath its wide, shadowy arch while the rosy light poured in below it. I moved softly, not wanting to disturb the evening hush, the expectation. Then I saw it. The ancient kiva dark against the sky, the same circular wall, the same pair of poles sloping up from the hidden chamber that I had just seen in the living pueblos. Knowing how visually minded I am, you can easily imagine the impact this sight had for me, the sudden joining of the hands between past and present. I squatted there, dusty as a miller, sitting myself so that the ladder poles made black diagonals across the flaming triangle of sunset that filled the end of the canyon. Indians must often have come here at this time of day, gone down through that hole in the kiva roof to dress themselves in masks, horns and skins before dancing on the cave floor or climbing secretly down the cliff to carry their rituals among the close-packed houses.

Actually Tyuonyi is among the later ruins, dating from the time when the prehistoric culture was already in decline. Still, this kiva was in use before any European except a Viking or two knew anything of America. The origin of the form is much older. The Indians of what archæologists call Basket Maker times (corresponding to our Roman and pagan Saxon centuries) lived in roughly circular pit dwellings, then when their primitive culture flowered into the full Pueblo cultures, as so often happens, the old form was kept on for ceremonial use and the pit dwelling became the kiva. There is no important break between the Basket Makers and the Pueblo, just as there is none between the pre-Columban Pueblos and their present-day descendants. At present there does appear to be a gap between the series of recognised Old Stone Age cultures (like the Sandia) and the Basket Maker, but new discoveries are made every year and I'm sure the gap will soon be filled. If so, then we have the spectacle of hunting savages creating what was a very considerable civilisation here in the South-West, and of course much higher ones in Central and South America. Did it really happen without any spark from the Old World? If it did, then it's enormously important. Man appears as a creature with an innate urge to develop urban civilisation, to build altars and temples and palaces. If I were an American archæologist I should think of nothing else but proving whether this is or is not the truth. I suppose everyone is terrified that when he's said it is, and made a great philosophical stir, then some wretch will find a site which proves a fine old influx of civilised Asiatics. But seriously, I can't think why people don't take more

c*

interest in this problem. Sometimes I think I'm the only person who really understands how important it is!

I've gone on much too long. You won't want to read all this stuff in your millionaire world. But please keep the letter—it will be my chief record. . . .

4

**Dance at
Santo
Domingo**
The moment the engine was switched off we could hear the drum. I was delighted, for we had come out to Santo Domingo with no more than a good hope of finding a dance in progress; the possibility of it had been whispered in my ear at the New Mexico Museum of anthropology, but, it was insisted, the news was both secret and uncertain. Now, however, there was no doubt; even in the distant corner of the village where we were parking our car the drum-beat dominated the bright sunny air relentlessly.

I was delighted, yet as we walked between the low houses towards the plaza, I also felt ashamed; yes, just a little ashamed. The Indians do not care for whites to attend some of their more purposeful dances and I am in complete sympathy with them: the moment a ceremony becomes a spectacle for gapers some of the good goes out of it. Yet when I heard of this one by the anthropologists' bush telegraph, I could not resist the lure, being too greedy of the experience. It was understandable. I had given a fair part of my life to prehistory, and here was my first chance to see a primitive people, miraculously saved for us out of the prehistoric past, performing such rites as I had often tried to imagine when confronted by their poor, lifeless remains. I had taken seriously the secrecy of my information; I had left behind my camera; I would try to enter imaginatively into the ceremony and not merely to observe it. These were the sops I threw to my conscience as we approached the plaza, our steps affected by the loudening drum.

It was a long rectangular space, the floor of trodden earth sunk some two feet below the rest of the village. The low adobe houses enclosed it on all sides and at the eastern end there rose the circular stone wall and ladder poles of a sacred kiva. The lines of dancers were still far away, and although the whole of the feeling and attention contained in that enclosure was turned upon them, it was the onlookers who, for the moment, filled my eyes with glowing colour. The long, south side of the plaza formed by a continuous line of houses had a wooden colonnade or portal in the Spanish fashion. There, throwing back brilliance for brilliance towards the streaming sun, were rows of Indians making a bank of colour like a late summer flower border. Down below under the portals were the women and girls with the tiny children and elders, up on the roof young men and boys; scarlet was everywhere, mingled with yellows, blues and dazzling pinks. The older men and women were wrapped in blankets of outrageous gaudiness; many grandmothers had them drawn over their heads and spread out round them; tiny children would peep out for a moment from among the folds then squirm back into the heat and radiance of these happy tents. Many of the younger people wore western clothes and the children jeans, but the colours chosen were so bright

64

and so distinctively combined that they were in perfect unison with their blanketed elders, and the total effect of the throng was wholly Indian. Among so many hues the warm brown faces and black, shining hair of the Pueblos stood out strongly.

They are not a physically commanding people like the tall, eagle-nosed Indians of the plain, rather they seem compact, rounded and calm, like the Esquimaux; there emanates from them not pride and recklessness but a softly-burning unquenchable confidence. When they have looked at me, I have always had the strongest sense of spirit withheld; even when turned towards one, their eyes seem sightless, perhaps looking inwards at the image of their resistance to the alien and unwanted. Yet they are always mild and polite.

I gazed in admiration down the long perspectives of the portal where the shadows of the posts fell brokenly across brown flesh and brilliant clothes. Here was none of the massed uniformity of a stadium crowd with its frightening rows of faces looking like the stacked products of a factory; some squatted, some sat, some leaned against the adobe walls; here and there on the roofs a well-grown youth stood consciously statuesque, hand on slender hip and leg advanced. Nor had they any of the tensity and excitement of a sports crowd; all, except the toddlers who dabbled quietly in their own various and messy affairs, were intent on the ceremony being enacted for them there in the centre of the square, but they were at ease—perhaps not relaxed, for the drum-beat held them—but very much at ease. Suddenly I noticed away to my left a grim old man, his long hair more grizzled than is usual among the Indians, sitting wrapped in his blanket, solitary on the kiva roof.

The dancers were coming nearer now, and the crowd fell back from my attention. They danced in four lines, two of men and two of women; young men who appeared to be conductors of some sort, stood at each end, and at right angles to the lines of the dance was the massed group of chanters, the drummer confronting them. While looking at the watching tribe I had been occupied with colour and mass, sun, shadow and attitude; now sound and movement had the power, with chant, drum-beat, rattle and dancing feet; the lines advanced, mingled and fell back, wave-like, with varying steps and rhythms which I felt but could not exactly apprehend.

They were splendidly clad. The women wore blouses made of satins and velvets, crude, but gorgeous in effect, below the ancient and traditional black dresses whose skirts glinted with little silver plaques. Above each ear was a rosette of red feathers and spanning their forehead a painted wooden frontal bearing such devices as formal flowers and butterflies; from below three tall red feathers fastened at the back of the neck, their hair fell in superb black cascades, often reaching below the knees. On some women it was rippled, perhaps after release from plaits, and on all of them it undulated softly with the movement of their dancing bodies. But more seductive even than the dense falls of hair were these women's legs; they were enwound to an immense thickness with bands of soft white buckskin, and peeping out from underneath, looking infinitely trim and tiny by contrast, their feet appeared in pointed white moccasins.

66

The men had a more barbaric air, with bare torso crossed only by white-beaded bandoliers, and knees, chins and hands painted a whitish grey. Across high cheek-bones and nose was a band seemingly sprinkled with mica which sparkled frostily below their dark eyes. Sprigs of green spruce, the traditional symbol of everlasting life, were bound tightly on to the bare upper arms with turquoise-coloured bands. Hung at their back was a fox pelt, its great brush tossing up and down with the steps of the dance.

The principal garment was a fine white cotton or buckskin kilt fastened with richly patterned sashes and silver-mounted belts. Below the whitened knees, scarlet garters and a ring of bells were worn over leggings and high-topped brown buckskin moccasins. There were more bells and more silver mountings on a sporan-like object that swung in front of their knees. All the male dancers wore the correct Pueblo hair-dressing with a fringe on the forehead, side hair cut level with the mouth, and back hair turned under and bound with cotton to make a stout queue reaching to the base of the neck. Fastened crossways on the top of the head was a coloured stick with a rosette of fluffy red and orange feathers at one end and a V of stiff, black and white eagle feathers at the other. All of them, and the women too, wore great numbers of necklaces, some chunky turquoise, some silver, and a few of them ending in the abalone shell pendants which are so ancient a form of ornament among the Pueblos. The men held a feathered stick in one hand and a gourd rattle in the other; the women carried spruce twigs. The total impression of so crowded a mass of details, of the thousand points of attention made by feathers, furs, turquoise, silver, sprigs, bells and brocading, was one of great richness, barbaric certainly yet with enough coherence and restraint to achieve the intricate beauty of a Maya carving.

There was nothing of African savagery in the dance. The rise and fall of its wave-like figures was controlled both by a feeling of solemn, thoughtless purpose and by the compelling force of sound. The drummer beat his hand on his huge, bright-hued cylindrical instrument, the singers repeated his hypnotic rhythm in a harsh perpetual chant, and the dancers not only returned it again with rattles and treading feet, but also with the multiple beat of bells, bandoliers and necklaces that rose and fell with the steps of the dance. The men skipped, each step lifting them clear of the ground but the women maintained a tiny, low step, cat-like, the little white moccasins under the soft white leggings never parting from the earth for a moment. So in their long lines the forceful brown feet and the little tripping white feet approached one another and fell back again always beating down, beating down, on the trodden earth of the arena. D. H. Lawrence wrote: 'Never shall I forget the utter absorption of the dance, so quiet, so steadily, timelessly rhythmic, and silent, with the ceaseless down-tread, always to the earth's centre, the very reverse of the upflow of Dionysiac or Christian ecstasy.'

I began to distinguish the larger pattern of the dance. The lines of men and women seemed to repeat the same series of joining and partings four times, and at the end of each movement the men raised and lowered their rattles with a fierce vibration that made a dying fall, a weird yet heart-affecting sound which is said to symbolise the fall of raindrops. After each movement the leaders, the dancers, the drummer and chanters all advanced several yards down the plaza before renewing the fourfold pattern of the dance. It was indeed a pattern of four times four; when the movements had been repeated for this number of times the drumming and chanting were worked up to an intense though never wild crescendo, and the final dying fall of the rattles was louder, more rending than before. Then the four lines of men and women fell into a single column which wound out of the plaza through one of the gaps between the houses and turned into the doorway of a two-storey house on the alleyway beyond. As the whole company tripped, still softly dancing, into so small a space, it seemed a miracle that the walls did not fall outwards; yet after the last chanter had entered, the sound of the drum and a glimpse through the doorway of moving head-dresses showed that the dance was being continued within. Soon the sense of confined activity, energy and heat, was like that of a wasp's nest humming below ground.

After a spell inside the house the compact mass reshaped itself into a column, and returned along the same route back to the plaza where the pattern of four times four was to be repeated; probably, though I am not certain, the whole dance would be complete when this largest pattern had itself been re-enacted four times. Some western people find this monotonous repetition unbearable; if they do, perhaps it is because they cannot rid themselves of the idea that a dance must be either a spectacle or an entertainment. Instead, these Pueblo dances are enactments, celebrations, no more to be censured for monotony than the perpetual celebration of the Catholic Mass.

One small but most happy change I did notice when the lines re-formed: a small girl and boy had now taken their place at the lower end. Both wore clothes identical in every detail with those of their elders and performed the steps and movements with equal perfection; indeed, the little boy in his eagerness and pride seemed even to outdo them in exactness and force. From afar the two miniature figures, their heads reaching only up to the waists of their companions, had the appearance of animated dolls drawn into the human dance. It was a glad as well as an enchanting sight, for it meant that an intricate ritual which had passed from generation to generation through the centuries was to reach yet another. In twenty years' time, it was possible to hope, these dolls might be leading the same dance in the plaza of Santo Domingo, maintaining at least one of those unique forms, peculiar to their own place, which are now fading so fast and leaving us so much the poorer.

The presence of these children, moreover, added a time factor to the all-inness, the pervading unity, which was what stirred me most in the performance of this November ritual. The participation of the new generation recalled the old, suggesting the aged men and women who had led these lines (perhaps even now in the mind of the grandfather on the kiva roof) and all their forebears stretching back into the prehistoric past. The dance itself had not greatly moved me, except to admiration; only the strange outcry of the rattles had taken possession of my feelings. But I was much affected by the sense of wholeness which dominated the arena where these men and women danced and sang before the intent eyes of their fellows. They danced for themselves and for the well-being of the village, they danced for the animals whose pelts they carried, they danced for the cloud expressed by the soft feathers, for the rain repeated by the rattles and by the swinging fringes of their sashes; they danced for the treasure of the earth shown forth in turquoise and silver, and, containing all, they danced for the enduring life of which the spruce twigs were the symbol. The words of the chant, the rhythm of the drum, every step the dancers trod and every pattern, colour and form of their accoutrement, spun out a maze of threads linking the actors with sun, cloud and earth, with village and fields and orchards, with one another and their ancestors and descendants. And all the threads wove together to make a picture of their desire for well-being and continuance. No one will ever be able to express this universal participation in words, for it is essentially a wordless thing. Yet even the outsider, the visitor, can share in it a little as he stands in this earthen place, enclosed by houses and a ring of eyes, watching it expressed in the being of the dancers and their dance.

Does reason say these rites are useless, the enactments of delusions? No dance has ever caused seeds to germinate, rain fall, corn swell and ripen, or the sun turn back. They are embodiments of the images of the psyche and cannot affect the physical world without. Yet undoubtedly as they spring from the psyche so they also satisfy it, embodying the promptings of the unconscious mind and the imagination. So celebration of such rites invigorates, brings confidence and wards off mental

71

ills; it suffuses with meaning a crowd of daily acts related to its purposes. It satisfies that terrible longing to do something to bring the desired to pass, when nothing can be done with hands.

These are reasons, justifications for a ritual which perhaps needs no justification beyond the fullness of its own existence. Yet in a sense it is already ahead of reason, having never left a position to which reason itself now returns. The dances express in the language of poetry the truth of man's unity with nature, the truth that science repeats to us, curing our delusions of grandeur. Yet because of their poetry they offer us visions for which science has no eyes.

When the dancers had returned to the house for a second time we wandered away from the plaza, exploring the alleyways beyond. Several ovens were alight, perhaps warming up for the baking of ritual breads. Then, towards the outskirts of the village, we came upon two stout old women who were using ladles to stir some substance steaming in large buckets supported over an open fire. A group of young women were standing near, most if not all of them in an advanced stage of pregnancy, giggling and chattering. Each one of them was carrying two empty bowls, fine bowls painted in black and red on white in traditional Santo Domingo designs but now somewhat darkened by heat and smoke. Presently they approached the cauldrons, and the old women ladled some of their steaming brew into the bowls, which the bearers balanced carefully on the palms of their hands and held out at arms' length while the steam swirled round them.

Before long the group broke up into smaller parties

that went off among the houses; we followed some of them, but never saw anyone show any interest in their stewed offal. I still do not know what they were doing, or if it had any special significance. Now we came upon the church, standing in a forlorn, dusty court enclosed by low walls almost outside the village on the side towards the railroad. This part of Santo Domingo is messy and run to seed, and it was obvious to contrast this drear isolation of the church with the neat, well-tended kiva there in the plaza at the heart of the village. The building itself, however, was quite attractive, whitewashed adobe with a gallery and other carved and painted woodwork enriching the west front. Above the gallery the villagers had painted a pair of horses, one black and white and the other brown, trotting towards each other in a most spirited fashion. I do not know what part they found to play in the Christian story, but they were attractive creatures and a testimony to the originality and independent spirit of the people of Santo Domingo. Going up to the west door, I found the jambs to be painted with small, bright flowers and butterflies of the kind that find their way on to the margins of illuminated manuscripts. It struck me that the whole of this west front, horses and all, had very much the flavour of European peasant art, utterly unlike the subtle native talent of the Pueblos. Here, round their mission church, the influence of Spain survives.

When we got back to the entrance to the church compound, two small girls with bright fringes above sulky square faces were waiting to waylay us with rather horrid little pots. They said they had made them themselves, but even if they had it was no credit to them. We didn't buy and felt rather foolishly aggrieved at this touting. Santo Domingo is one of the most conservative and traditional of all the pueblos; its dances and other observances are among the purest and best preserved. Yet it is the only village where I have been pestered to buy—and goods which are shoddily false. Perhaps because it is one of the largest of the pueblos it also has some of the poorest people.

As we returned to our car the drum was beating again just as it had been when we arrived. Probably it would go on for hours yet, and afterwards there would be feasting. I felt curiously limp and emptied out as though following the dance had taxed me more than I knew. But the next morning when I woke my memories had revived their colours, and as I examined them it seemed to me they offered some understanding of the ancient tribal life of my kind. Of life, as some would have it, before the Fall.

5

The Football Game at Fort Worth

In the phantasmagorial atmosphere of *Admass*, nothing can keep its true proportions, everything loses its real character. What should be solid and serious becomes frivolous and empty. On the other hand, what were once—and should be still—trivialities are magnified, blown up, painted over, given trick sound effects, until innocent, bewildered minds imagine them to embody the most stupendous ideas, the great realities of human life. Even the most cynical deceivers are themselves deceived on some other level. The money made by one conjuring trick is soon wasted on other conjuring tricks, rather more artful. Just as the nations, time after time, have been hoodwinked by their own false propaganda, in the end taking action along the lines of that propaganda and hurrying towards disaster, so men and women in *Admass* go running round and round in an ever-narrowing circle, begging one another to relax and to enjoy life but closing more and more avenues of escape into relaxation and enjoyment of life. What was once play is loaded down with yet more anxiety and responsibility. The week-end reproduces the anxious pattern, traced in acid, of the week.

75

Now, this being November, the college football season was at its height. There must have been a time, long ago, when colleges merely arranged some matches between their respective teams, and a lot of high-spirited young men, released from their studies for a few hours, went out to enjoy themselves. But now the college football season was at its height; and very high that is too, like the figures of attendance at the games themselves, like the investment in huge arenas, athletic directors and coaches and trainers, in equipment of every kind. Now at parties men got together in corners to thrash the subject to death; impassioned voices on the radio described last Saturday's games, speculated about next Saturday's games; presidents and deans of universities gravely compared notes, ventured prophecies; and in locker-rooms, scores of big-boned, heavily muscled lads listened white-faced while their football coaches, with tears in their eyes, implored them to remember what was at stake on the field, lashed them with bitter rhetoric. This indeed was their hour, and for most of them it would never return again; the rest of their lives would be one long anticlimax. And of course the newspapers were in there, battling. Above a photograph, the size of a small tea-tray, of four leather-armoured young men in a desperate tangle, a giant headline screamed *Ponies Snap Porker String*. And in letters not much smaller: *Longhorns Shade TCU Frogs*, and *Mustang Defence Spelled Defeat For Cinderella Hogs*. Yes, the season was at its height.

I had not attended an American football game since I saw Yale play the Navy, nearly twenty years ago. But on the Saturday I wanted to see a game, Dallas could not

76

offer me one of any size; I had to go to Fort Worth, where in fact the Longhorns shaded the Frogs, according to the headline. The morning was bright and warm, and I went to Fort Worth, through miles and miles of *Nomadmass*, by bus, a form of transport patronised exclusively by coloured folk and people well down in the lower income brackets. I took with me no prejudice against sport and games as such. In my youth I played games, and even won a few medals for sport; I once reported football matches; I have always enjoyed both playing and watching games; so nothing here is darkened by any introverted, egg-headed, thick-spectacled distaste for rough pursuits. If sport could escape the *Admass* influence—though none of the signs encouraged this hope—then so much the better.

At the bus terminus, such is the kindness of people in these parts, I was met by a professor whose team was playing that afternoon, a shy but very friendly man, accompanied by a very pretty little daughter, still at high school. Along streets so thick with traffic they were like sluggish rivers of gleaming painted steel, we drove out to a restaurant, *Hashadmass* Mexican, near the university campus and not far from the stadium. Most of the talk was between father and daughter, for it dealt with the problems of routes, traffic, parking. Where nearly everybody owns a car, preferably a new car two feet longer and one foot wider than the old one, such problems clamour for attention at all times, and on the day of a football game they are as urgent as fire alarms. It was not for me, without a car, an irresponsible rider in buses, to suggest that the terrible stadium-parking problem might be banished by our walking the half-mile there. I drank my coffee and lit my pipe, wondering idly to what frenzied final state, bordering upon immobility, the law of diminishing returns would bring all these car owners. Grateful for their kindness and hospitality, all I could do was to look sympathetic, murmur encouragingly now and again, and say nothing to disturb their concentration. In a year or two, I suspected, the girl would be driving this car because her father would have bought a new and larger one; and as fifty thousand other daughters and sons would by then have taken over the old family cars, and a hundred thousand other Fort Worth citizens would have acquired larger vehicles, all these route-traffic-parking problems would by this time be something like a nightmare. More and more millions would have to be spent on new highways and parking places; municipal traffic experts, already commanding high salaries in various cities, would be arbitrary dictators; more and more traffic signs and signals would have to be understood at a glance by the motorist; nervous breakdowns and ulcerated stomachs would be commoner than colds. And only lack of means, not any warning common sense, prevented the British, the Germans, the Dutch, the Danes, even the French, who ought to know better, from following this example. Even now they were worrying day and night how to catch up with this lunatic progress.

It was a warm afternoon, quite hot in the sun. Cars by the thousand, a grey-green tide, crept towards the stadium. Near the entrance to the main stand, I had to wait some time while my host found a place for his car. The daughter went off to join her sister, on the other side of the stadium, the open stand favoured by students. I watched the crowd pouring up the ramps, swarming along the galleries and up the flights of stairs. Programme sellers, newspaper lads, hirers-out of cushions, peddlers of drinks and peanuts, were hoarsely bellowing at us. The giant bowl, brimmed with anticipation, was humming away, already tuning up for its symphony of howls and roars. It was the same old atmosphere piled up, thickened but electrified, during this half-hour that always preceded the great sporting event, whether outside Chelsea's football ground at Stamford Bridge or outside the bullring on the edge of Mexico City; and though it did not matter to me who won or lost here, and I tried to feel aloof, my heart beat faster, my nerves tingled. These towering walls hiding the arena, these turnstiles, ramps, galleries, flights of stairs, the sound of the crowd already within, the sight of all the hurrying newcomers, the remote brassy music, the unresting harsh cries of the vendors, the whole concentrated expectancy of the afternoon, together create something that is immensely heightened and intense and yet dreamlike, banishing ordinary values, stirring and heating up a dark excitement, released from mysterious recesses of our being. However familiar it may be, it is still frightening, monstrous. If we remembered at these times, in this atmosphere, how apparently civilised Romans, learned senators, delicate aristocratic ladies, could accept without protest, could even enjoy, the elaborate cruelties of their circus, we would no longer feel surprise or be shocked, as we are when we are sedately reading the historians. So long as nothing was announced in advance, to be rejected in cold blood, I

79

would not like to say what a crowd, kept waiting in this atmosphere, heated in blood and brain, might tolerate tomorrow in an arena. I have sometimes been tormented by the fancy that if the future should prolong the lines of the present, if civilisation should mean organisation and not values, if sensation should become more and more blunted and some release had to be found for the dumb drilled mob, then the blood-stained games might once more affront the sun—and this time be relayed on coloured television for invalids, stay-at-homes, and children.

The professor and I carried our cushions to the top of the stand and then found our places among a group of his colleagues, of both sexes, belonging to the departments of Language and Literature. Nodding and smiling a welcome, Middle English, Romance Languages, Modern Novel and Elizabethan Drama, pleasantly acknowledged my presence, with that slight archness and hint of the deprecatory which scholars display when discovered attending some unscholarly college function. From this height, the whole stadium was spread below us, all open to our view. The scene had more colour than we find in our football grounds. The crowd opposite, mostly students in coloured shirts and blouses, looked almost like a vast heap of those tiny sweets known in my childhood as 'hundreds and thousands'. Two large students' military bands, one in orange uniforms, the other in purple, the colours of their respective teams, could just be distinguished, massed together, on the lower slopes, where the Sousaphones gleamed and blared. In the space between the touchline and the stand, there were cheer-leaders in white, men and girls, already beginning to signal to and encourage, with enormous rhythmical gestures, their obedient sections of students. One end of the ground, to my right, was dominated by an illuminated electric clock, ready to mark off every second of play. Above the crowd at the other end, lower than we were, I could see ranks of parked cars, extending apparently into far open country, glittering, glimmering, then fading into the haze, like some plague of grey and green beetles unaccountably stricken with death. Down on the turf a host of players, enough to make a dozen teams, all uniformed, leather-armoured, numbered, were throwing passes and punting the balls and loosening up. Other men mostly in white, not cheer-leaders but athletic directors, coaches, referees and linesmen, trainers and first-aid men, were gathering along the touchlines. From somewhere behind us, voices through loud-speakers, harsh and appallingly amplified, made announcements, called doctors to the telephone. The bowl, you might say, was busy.

The players ran off and cleared the pitch, to sit in a long row at the edge of it. One of the horrible voices announced that there would now be an Invocation by Dr. Somebody of Something Presbyterian Church. We stood up. Over the public address system came a very deep voice, which to my astonishment began by saying 'We thank Thee, Lord, for bringing us to our maturity——' but after that did not find anything else as surprising to say. This prayer at an end, we sat down. One of the bands began playing. We stood up again, this time facing the flagstaff, though I could still contrive to see, far below, all the men in white, the official athletic types, rigid in their fervent patriotism. The Stars and Stripes, surely the prettiest of all national flags, went fluttering to the top of the mast. We stood up again to hear the college song of the visiting Longhorns, from the University of Texas. And again for the college song of the home team, the Horned Frogs of the Texas Christian University, Fort Worth. We sat down, ready now for some diversion. It arrived. While the bands played and the cheer-leaders leapt and semaphored and the massed ranks of students rah-rah-rahed, the visitors' mascot, a Longhorn steer, a melancholy survivor of that old breed which the original cowboys of Texas had driven along the Chisholm Trail, went shambling round the field, no doubt wondering once again why it should have been robbed of its pasture for this loud indignity. It was followed by the home mascot, not a genuine giant Horned Frog—alas—but only a student in pantomime costume. This pantomime Horned Frog was joined by a pantomime Longhorn and then proceeded, amidst laughter and some organised cheering controlled by leaping leaders in white, to rope and throw it, thus deciding the game in advance by symbolic magic. The bands were still blaring away. The terrible voices behind me were still imploring doctors to come to the telephone. And two men in cowboy costume, behind the touchline down on the left, were inexplicably but startlingly busy, firing a small cannon. There was not, it can be fairly said, a dull moment.

The game began. I do not pretend to understand even the coarser of the finer points of this American college football, which must have been originally devised during an early revolutionary phase of American life, for like a revolution it is an odd mixture of secret plotting, with so many heads motionless and close together in the scrums, and sudden violent action. When either side pressed towards goal, we all stood up. The danger over or the prize lost, we sat down again. The enormous clock ran off the seconds when the ball was actually in play. It stopped when the game stopped. And the game was always stopping. Referees threw down little coloured flags; linesmen ran on, like half-crazed surveyors, with measuring equipment; trainers and first-aid men trotted up with water, sponges, liniment, perhaps disinfectant, brandy, antibiotics, blood transfusions, oxygen tents, God knows what; players came off, other players went on; three men in white occasionally turned somersaults; the cheer-leaders leapt and wildly gesticulated, the obedient fans noisily responded; the two cowboys fired their cannon. Meanwhile, the doomsday voices behind me were announcing the quarter-time and half-time scores of distant games. Nor were these figures regarded as a distraction, taking attention away from the game before our eyes. In the new *Admass* sporting life, these scores, so many figures on paper, are more important than actual games, the mere rough-and-tumble round the ball. A good *Admass* sportsman wants to know what is happening everywhere except in front of his nose. He attends one match to learn quickly what remote teams are scoring in other matches. And now, with the Horned Frogs ahead of the Longhorns, as hundreds of thousands of spectators were hearing elsewhere, the interval came.

I do not know what was happening to the players, who had now disappeared; they may have been having massage or electrical treatment, listening to a final appeal to their manhood by the coach, being photographed or interviewed; but I could not help remembering the football games of my youth, when both teams, having played forty-five minutes on end, and no substitutes allowed, never even left the field at half-time but stood about sucking lemons. But that was before football was big news, big business, big everything; before the sports editors and reporters and half their readers were in a permanent state of hysteria.

During the interval, while we recovered from the shocks and strains of the game, we were suitably entertained. A pretty girl who had been elected Miss Something-or-other was brought out to kiss a middle-aged functionary who had some claim to this privilege. Then the purple band, about sixty strong, marched on to the field, accompanied by drum-majorettes—every one a dish, as they say—who juggled with glittering batons. The orange band followed, also with delicious juggling girls, and performed a different but equally intricate set of evolutions, with never a man or a girl hesitating, fumbling, out of step; all drilled to a hair. The Prussian Guard itself never did better; indeed, never as well, for where were their girls? But that was not all. What are known as the 'card sections' now showed us what they could do. With each student holding up a large card on which there would be a letter or a blank, they began spelling out sentences for us to read and admire. It was all done accurately and briskly, on the word of command from the chief cheer-leader. Then the other cheer-leaders, making large sweeps of their arms in unison, would signal for and conduct their section's mass singing and organised cheering. No lack of organisation here. These were youths and maidens who, when they left college, would not find it difficult to integrate themselves properly in an industrious tidy community, almost instinctively rejecting whatever seemed radical and anti-social, not regular.

The game began again. The men in white ran on and off with their measuring equipment or first-aid kits. Players went off, players came on. Jet planes flashed a glance at us, after apparently ripping the old blue canvas of the sky. The monstrous voices roared out the half-time and three-quarter-time scores of other games. The cannon was fired at every touchdown. The tumblers somersaulted. The cheer-leaders continued their idiot ballet. The din suggested a war, the spectacle a circus. I kept glancing at the enormous clock, flashing the death of each second. Only ten minutes to go. I had had enough, and after hesitating a moment or two I said apologetically to my host that I should like to slip away but did not want to take him from the game. I never saw a man look more relieved. Out we went, to hear as usual the loudest and most dramatic roar of the afternoon just as we found ourselves outside the bowl. But my host still felt thankful. 'We shall have saved at least an hour,' he said as he started the car. I believed him, and would still have believed him if he had made it two hours: we seemed to be hurrying away from the automobile show of the century. A final roar from the giant bowl died behind us: the game was over. The afternoon was still blooming on the green lawns of the suburb,

D

but down in the city, which seemed almost quiet, they were switching on the neon lighting for the Saturday evening trade. My bus was not there at the terminus, but I begged my host, who had given me enough of his day, not to wait.

In the bus I gave up trying to read the paper-backed book I had with me; the light, dimmish within and flashing uncertainly outside, as we passed all the shops, bars, gas stations, illuminated signs, was not good enough; and there was too much stopping and starting and jolting. Coming to the end of a day when I had been around too long with too many people—and the bus was full of them too—I felt in fairly desperate need of a bath, a change of clothes, a short but strong drink, and at least half an hour of solitude and quiet. Lacking these, trying to close my eyes against all the flashing signs, joggled and bumped about, I could not properly sort out my impressions and marshal my thoughts, and was not happy with those that did turn out for parade. There was nothing much wrong with the actual game I had seen; probably the lads themselves, lost in their tussles, were not very different from what their fathers and grandfathers had been, trying for the same touchdowns; but clearly it was becoming more and more over-organised, moving further and further away from pure athletics and sport, crowding itself with more and more solemn supernumeraries, fancy equipment, nonsense; chiefly because now it flourished, immensely swollen, in the wrong atmosphere, no longer that of vigorous young males enjoying themselves and giving pleasure to their fellow students, but a perfervid atmosphere of huge crowds, big money, false standards,

86

hysterical publicity. What was good, and probably remained good, was buried under a mountain of rubbish: over-organisation on one level, hysteria on another. Even at play, *Admass* was at work.

6

**Problems
and
Machinery**

.

J. B. P. TO J. H.

. . . People load themselves with anxiety and grief because they will discuss their lives as if they were engineers on a job. 'Problems' for instance. The 'Marriage Problem'. The 'Parent-Child Problem'. Nice people talk like this and then worry themselves sick, for here are the 'problems' but where are the neat solutions, settling them once and for all? They forget that human relationships don't belong to engineering, mathematics, chess, which offer problems that can be perfectly solved. Human relationships grow, like trees; they can't reach checkmate in four moves; the language of gardeners and artists might help, certainly not the approach of mathematicians and engineers. But this is what happens to nice people in a mechanistic society. And when they have turned away in despair from these 'problems', they begin asking for more and better 'machinery' where in fact there cannot be any machinery at all. After so much talk of 'improved government machinery' you might think no human beings were involved at all, nothing but wheels, belts, pistons and cogs. We are told 'the

88

mechanics are faulty' when there is not a piece of mechanism in sight. (This last point is made in *The Age of Conformity* by Alan Valentine, a book I bought yesterday. Well-argued but in a muffled style, like a lecture delivered in a bale of cotton wool.) However, perhaps in a few years, after using more and more of this language, we shall be able to bring ourselves into line. 'When I give an order to a machine,' writes Professor Wiener, the Cybernetics man of tomorrow, 'the situation is not essentially different from that which arises when I give an order to a person.' Isn't it? You try me, Professor! . . .

Academic Life

J. B. P. TO J. H.

Late the other evening, too late for caution, I heard myself accepting an invitation, from a companionable professor I had met several times, to deliver a lunch-time lecture at his university. This morning I was taken at more than my word. The artful dog, after ringing me hastily, sent down in the middle of the morning a colleague—a handsome and intelligent woman—to take me out earlier than we had originally agreed, so that I could join him while he was instructing a group in Comparative Literature—whatever that is. There was no refusing this charmer, so off we went in her little car, a rarity among all these shining monsters. The university looked imposing, probably having had many of its large buildings presented to it by local millionaires. But these fellows do not like to waste money endowing Chairs or providing upkeep funds. The building we entered had marble stairs, but they were thick with muck—for lack of what my guide called 'janitor service'. The students, I gathered, were about to discuss Gide in their Comparative Literature group. We agreed that some of them might have been equally well employed cleaning the stairs. However, they were still at Proust when I joined them—some twenty untidy lads and wide-eyed girls. After I had been there about a couple of minutes—getting hot and sweaty in my thick English clothes, for it was a very warm little lecture-room—my professor friend, artful as ever, contrived by one cunning question to hand me the class for the rest of the session. I explained as best I could the Time aspect of Proust, even using the blackboard now and again; and if the youngsters were not interested, then they gave a fine collective performance. Some hundreds, plus a fair proportion of staff, came later to hear my talk on the Theatre, in a hall like an oven. I bounced around the platform for about fifty minutes, roaring, gesticulating and sweating hard; and the response seemed to be genuinely enthusiastic. I did make some points worth making and new to them; the rest, no doubt, was so much showing-off. My professor and his colleagues told me that here, if necessary, was another career. *God forbid!*—I told myself. For by this time I had been entertained in the Faculty Club, in a basement among steam pipes and about as cosy as an improvised officers' mess. Lunch, with no drink of course, consisted of tuna fish, looking like little globes of wet cement, half-drowned salad, and some sort of ice-cream stuff—disgusting. How could girls and lads, coming to college from distant oil towns and remote ranches, learn about civilisation from men and women who accepted without protest such a dreary mockery of a club? No wonder so many of these instructors are underpaid and bullied. Or that civilisation decays and *Admass* grows unchecked. Here in academic life, or what passes for it, there are now too many defeated men. Nor are we at home much better—with the new and deliberate loutishness among so many of the younger lecturers in provincial universities, with Fellows of ancient foundations offering to perform monkey tricks on radio and TV, all succumbing to *Admass*. Dons are

91

narrow and arrogant in the wrong places and at the wrong times. We need some brilliant and bitter scholars, disreputable in the eyes of newspaper proprietors and business men. Youngsters smell defeat at once. The stuffed shirt or the anxious conformer never takes them in. They arrive at college hoping for genial madmen who don't care a damn, fellows who will clarify their young dreams and then pass out lasting ammunition to defend them. I argued down there, among the pipes (steam, not tobacco, though mine was out and alight), against the courses of 'Creative Writing', so popular in these places. How can it be taught? And if a man knew enough about it even to pass on a few hints, would he submit to having his wine taken away by some board of Methodist or Baptist elders, and eat wet tuna fish in a basement? . . .

Road-makers

J. H.. TO J. B. P.

. . . . I have just arrived at a little place called Cortez after the longest drive I have ever made in my life. I was driven by Miss B., a Real Estate agent who told me even before I left La Fonda that she was in her seventieth year. This boast alarmed me for a moment, knowing the journey ahead of us, but I needn't have worried for she drove over three hundred miles through mountains without turning a hair. Imagine an English woman of her age achieving this! On the other hand of course, Miss B. would be quite appalled at the idea of walking a mile or bicycling at all.

Most of the way we were on first-class black-top roads, and this saved me from real fright when I watched the needle creeping up above seventy and staying there. In one or two stretches, though, the highway was incomplete and bends and over-steep gradients were being ironed out. In spite of myself, I can't help enormously admiring the way Americans tackle road-making. You'll understand why I say 'in spite of myself'—I'm speaking as a pathological hater of motor-cars and their effect on the countryside. But it really is impressive to see the boldness of the highway engineers and the colossal mechanical power they can command. Where we should set to work with a grab or two and a fine old steam-roller (with the brass horse I loved in my childhood still prancing on the front) and take years, the Americans mobilise a force of bright yellow, up-to-the-

D*

minute giants which seems to me at least as numerous as an entire armoured division, and finish the job in a matter of weeks. To remove some quite mild bend or climb, they won't stop at battering down the end of a rocky mountain or blasting through it down to the very roots. They go at the work in the true heroic manner as though they were fighting dragons or defending their loved ones from dishonour. Fearful steel teeth tear at rocks, vast shovelling jaws scoop up the hard desert soil and hurl it afar, gigantic knives grind along levelling all before them. And constantly battalions seem to break away, wheel round and then hurl themselves back into the fray, their spiked tracks turning square miles into a ravaged battlefield. And all the time hundreds of lorries come and go and concrete mixers gaping like the several mouths of hell churn and spew.

Down here, where a few more roads are still needed, one sees all this as the last great surge of the frontier spirit. But of course it's really exactly the same man-can-do-it attitude which has created New York and is still raising those magnificently defiant bridges over the East River. Sky-scrapers, bridges, dams, railroads and highways—it's a marvellous acceptance of the challenge of this savage continent. Miles away from the things I naturally care about, but I do respond to it. I suppose if I had a brilliant American son I should want him to be a civil engineer, while in Europe I'd long for him to be an artist of some sort. When the English were at about the present American stage of development we prided ourselves as the modern Romans in law-giving and Empire-building. The Americans certainly have the inheritance as engineers. Although they must have gone about it more soberly, I should think that the legions drove their roads straight through forests and over hills in just the spirit of these peak-capped and gaudy-shirted navvies hurling their yellow monsters against all resistance. It may be that such masterful ways breed too inflexible a habit. When I see the adobe villages of the Pueblos lying low a mile or two off the highways and think how these Indians, who have always been the quiet ones, the ones who would bend paths round obstacles, are also the ones who survive and flourish, I wonder whether maybe they will still be there when highways are crumbling and bridges falling down. It's unlikely, but not impossible.

Already there are disappointments. For instance in the hope that perfect roads would reduce accidents. Do you remember how in Arizona it was the straightest, levellest stretches which had the main crops of those sinister little white crosses put up to mark fatal crashes? One dies so easily at a hundred miles an hour. Then in this part of the world I've noticed how the very same people who rejoice at being able to do a journey in one morning which before would have taken three days, groan and complain when they find their favourite scenery spoilt and Indian villages and ruins seething with tourists. . . .

Santa Fé

J. H. TO J. B. P.

... Since last I wrote I've had time to be horribly disappointed by Santa Fé and then to discover a new kind of liking for it. Obviously it was stupid of me to expect an old Spanish town, but I must confess I did. Knowing something of its early history, and seeing references to the Governor's Palace, the cathedral, the 'Oldest Church' and the plaza at the 'end of the old Santa Fé Trail' I had allowed myself to hope for the sort of beauty we saw in Mexico—perhaps a Spanish colonial palace and some fine touches of baroque among the churches. What dreadful disillusionment I was preparing for myself! My first surprise, though, was to learn that the Santa Fé railway doesn't go to Santa Fé. So I had to travel from Albuquerque by Greyhound bus (unexpectedly steady and comfortable) and approach my 'old Spanish town' as part of a stream of traffic on a double-track motor highway. Though some of the desert scenery en route had been at its best in the evening light, the approach to the city was simply a large slab of your *Admass*. Hoardings, motels and trailer courts, filling-stations and bungalows for mile after mile. At first view, the centre of the town didn't seem much better. The State building as large and commonplace as it could be, the 'Oldest Church' strikingly new, and the cathedral a weighty pile of false Romanesque (it was in fact built in 1869 by Archbishop Lamy, Willa Cather's hero). The shopping streets

96

seemed almost as shoddy and neoned as Albuquerque's, and the plaza was crammed with traffic and marred by modern shop fronts. I took a taxi from the bus-stop to my hotel, the famous La Fonda, only to rob myself of another illusion. Like the Alvarado, it is a Fred Harvey establishment, and I'd read of its distinction, intimacy and charm. Someone quite sensible had said it was the most enjoyable hotel in the States. I knew that it was an imitation Indian building, but these can be agreeable, and I'd dared to hope for something small and quiet with the atmosphere of an old-established hotel. I believe it had these merits once, but now it's been enlarged out of all recognition—and ruined. Outside it is a shapeless dung-coloured pile of sham adobe covered with queer, meaningless nobs and stumps. Rather like a poorish sand-castle already blurred by the sea. Inside I found the usual bookstalls, gift counters and a vast Spanish-Indian curio shop; the foyer was swarming with officers, business men shoulder-slapping and handshaking, and a few rather sad and exhausted tourists. A large board announced the conventions and fraternity meetings to be held there. Among all this, two or three Pueblo Indians were sitting about in dark corners mutely offering jewellery and bits and pieces of weaving for sale. They looked morose and full of hate, as well they might be. By the time I had drunk a dilute martini and eaten a dull and expensive dinner, I was thoroughly cast down.

But since the first sad evening Santa Fé has steadily redeemed itself. People have been extraordinarily kind. The place abounds with artists and craft-workers. I read in a magazine that the Americans claim to have thirteen times as much mechanical power per capita as any other country: well, Santa Fé must have at least thirteen times as much artistic power as any other American city. There is also an abnormal number of art photographers, anthropologists, poets, historians and cranks. All of them, of course, have been attracted here by the lure of Indian and Spanish culture. It is easy to laugh at them as arty-crafty and absurd and to argue that by swarming here they may be helping to kill the thing they love. Still, their own work apart, many of them have in fact done splendid work in aiding the Indians to defend themselves against white encroachment, in recording their lore and ritual and in spreading some understanding of what is valuable in Indian ways of life. Also most of them are charming—the kind of people one can have real talk with at a first meeting— and their houses are often delightful. I've already discovered that the cultural life of the town is mainly run by New England ladies, formidable characters whose upbringing in the sterner intellectual and moral disciplines of the East enable them to take the lead here. They establish and run museums, organise Indian Associations, and are to be found controlling committees and lectures. (A lecture has been announced on 'The Lion-Dog in Chinese Art', absolutely *everyone* seems to be going!) Some of these ladies have money, some haven't, but all are full of energy and on balance have done a lot of good. The relationship between the Spanish-Americans and the 'Anglos' is not happy; naturally the Spanish feel that they are the ones who belong, and resent being dominated by the invading hosts of American culture, commerce and tourism.

While getting to know people, I've been led into the nicer parts of Santa Fé. There's a pleasant walk among the cottonwoods by the tiny (and now dry) Santa Fé river; I like the long line of portals on the north side of the plaza where there are amusing little shops, and some of the older residential roads, still unpaved and countri-fied, hung with weeping willows, would be quite charm-ing if there were no traffic to raise the dust. Here, at the back of the town and on the fringes of the Sangre de Christo, there lingers a trace of the city I had imagined. There are genuine old adobe houses and others in the more formal Territorial style, suggestive of a rustic Georgian. Then I've been driven out to houses perched on the foothills which fully justify the modern craze for adobe architecture. Their low, flat shapes look just right on the desert knolls; they're solid, comfortable and perfectly adapted both to sun and cold. The view from them over the Rio Grande valley is quite staggeringly beautiful, especially at sunset—a vast bowl of iridescent light with the far blue cone of Mount Taylor lifting above the mountain rim.

Yes, I think I shall enjoy Santa Fé. I shall try to keep it as my base for visiting the Mesa Verde ruins, even though they are hundreds of miles away in southern Colorado. Only heavy snowfalls could stop me from going, for I believe them to be the finest prehistoric ruins in the United States. This will make an excellent base, too, for seeing more modern Indian pueblos, and, if I'm lucky, ceremonial dances. Perhaps you might join me here when you're through? I must just tell you of one comic incident. The other morning when break-fasting in my room, I decapitated my egg only to find it totally raw. I sent for another: raw again. Then I learnt that they were being 'cooked' in some automatic gadget ... I asked would the chef please use a saucepan and his own watch. If anyone here knew my prejudices, I should think this affair had been personally arranged to give me pleasure. . . .

7

Mesa Verde There had been clouds on the mountains when we reached Cortez, and before falling asleep I heard the rustle of snow-flurries on my window. In the morning I looked out, fearful of seeing a fall heavy enough to block the roads up to Mesa Verde. Instead, there was no more than a decorative dusting of snow on the higher slopes, the sun was shining and the sky had returned to its clear brilliance. True, it was freezing hard, but there was no wind: it was a sharp, enticing day for an expedition.

From the little town of Cortez we were looking on to the loftiest side of the Mesa Verde, for while the whole tableland rises from the surrounding plains like a precipitous island from the sea, it is gently inclined towards the south. Thus the score of deep and narrow canyons dissecting the plateau all run from north to south, their whole fanlike system joining at last with the valley of the Mancos river which curves round the eastern and southern sides of the Mesa.

Miss B. and I breakfasted at a steamy little restaurant called The Place, before setting off at high speed across the plain. On the steep northern scarp of the Mesa a hard cap has held beneath it an immensely high pinnacle

of rock which commands the approach and the entrance
to the National Park. As we pulled up at the gates with
this rocky tower standing out against the blue about two
thousand feet above us, I had a sense of seeking entrance
to a vast natural fort, a stronghold fit for giants.

The road needs many detours and hairpin bends to
get it up the northern face, and that morning it was
everywhere frozen and snow-encrusted; although the
surface itself was excellent, large stones and small
boulders were inclined to slide down on to it from the
heights above. I had already discovered that Miss B.
had only one weakness as a driver—this was her
tendency to swerve whenever she looked away from
the road. Unhappily, the views as we climbed were
strikingly lovely, and Miss B. naturally wanted to enjoy
them. I am a cowardly passenger, for ever imagining
the most horrible pictures of tearing flesh and breaking
bone, and during that cold early morning climb I was
more cowardly than usual. Soon I was passionately
absorbed in an idiotic form of magic, staring at the road
ahead with ferocious intensity as though I could hold
the car on it by an optical magnetism. When at last we
reached the tableland above, with no misadventures
beyond the slightest of skids, I had missed most of the
views; nevertheless, perhaps because the few glimpses I
did allow myself were etched into memory by the acid
of my fear, I can still most vividly recall them. From the
lower slopes the beauty of the scenery lay in the contrast between the tawny-coloured plain spreading below
us, with its patterns of cultivation and miniature towns
and villages, and the craggy mountains beyond where
the snow lay delicately, picking out every detail of

precipice and crag. Then, as our own height increased, the foreground began to be filled with tossing miles of dwarfish forest, dark green pinyon broken here and there with larger firs, part of the Mesa Verde itself, a world set apart far above the now distant plain. That was the value of these impressions: they brought home to me the isolation of the Mesa and the extent to which the ancient Indians who dwelt here were set apart in a separate realm of their own—and to that extent must have felt both 'chosen' and secure.

When Basket Maker Indians first settled on the Green Mesa nearly two thousand years ago they were still probably semi-nomadic hunters with little dependence on agriculture, and living some part of the year in caves. But as their farming improved and corn and squash cultivation became more important they and their descendants came to live in open villages on the mesa top. The National Park authorities have excavated a series of these settlements in such a way that a con-scientious visitor can progress through them in chrono-logical order as though reading a text-book of Indian prehistory. This I did, moving from ruin to ruin, all of them pleasantly set in small clearings among the woods. Beginning with a shallow, roughly circular pit-dwelling, approached through an ante-room, which dated from about A.D. 600, I was led by winding pathways to a second, perhaps a century more recent, where the pit was deeper, the ante-room now a ventilating shaft, and a bench-like construction ran round the wall about three feet above the ground. At a still later site the wooden poles which originally supported the thatched roof of the pit-dwelling had become stone pilasters rising from the bench, and in the floor was a small, stone-lined hole, the *Sipapu*, or symbolic entrance to the spirit world. I had, in short, walked from late Basket Maker to early Pueblo times and seen the former dwelling-house turn into a kiva, no longer an ordinary home but at least in part a ceremonial chamber and private club-room for the men. Meanwhile, what had been little store-rooms, set above ground near the pit-dwellings, were enlarged and improved into wood and adobe houses, rectangular and joined together in rows. As the Pueblo culture ripened, the kivas reached their full development, the domestic architecture became far more ambitious; houses were stone-built in excellent masonry and might rise to two or three storeys. So by the century following the Norman conquest of England, pueblos with apartment houses and kivas had been brought into being; in spite of upheavals among the Indians themselves and the coming of Spaniards and Americans, they have been built and inhabited ever since, here in the land of their origin.

Probably Basket Makers and Pueblos themselves invented none of the new techniques. The idea of agriculture, of the bow and arrow, of pottery-making and house-building, may all have come to them from without, indirectly from the flourishing civilisations of Mexico. Yet it was evidently only the idea that was foreign, no practical farmer or craftsman came to live among them and teach them the new skills. Sometimes, perhaps, they only heard of the new inventions by word of mouth, and sometimes saw them as finished products, but always they had to perfect their own forms by slow experiment. This is shown in the pottery, where the first pathetically crude vessels of the late Basket Makers grow into the lovely Pueblo wares, and shown also in the architecture, nowhere better than here at Mesa Verde where in one short walk one can see the improvements achieved by many generations.

During the twelfth century the Pueblos of the Mesa Verde were thriving, and as their number increased they built more villages on the mesa top and brought more and more land under cultivation. Then there was a dramatic change in their habits. The villages were abandoned. The people moved down into the canyons, dragging their house stones with them to build fresh pueblos in the wide caves and smaller crevices of the sandstone cliffs. This abrupt descent may have been forced upon the Pueblos by some threat—perhaps war-like tribes of Comanches or Utes had pushed south-ward among them—but as it was made at the height of their cultural pride, the new cliff-dwellings in the shadowed depths were finer, and far more strangely impressive, than the old villages built beneath the sun.

I left the latest of the mesa-top sites and went back to the car where Miss B. was patiently reading. We drove along through the low woods at the stately pace pre-scribed by the regulations; all seemed quiet and mono-tonous, the level plateau unbroken. With the sudden-ness of most delight it was there before us. We were at the edge of a deep canyon—the earth had opened before us. The upper parts were vertical walls of sandstone, banded buff and brown; lower down, these broke into steep slopes dark with vegetation. This natural grandeur so suddenly revealed was marvellous enough, but there, opposite to us on the far side of the canyon, was a hanging city, a little pale gold city of towers and climbing houses filling a vast oval hollow in the rock. The dark points of the pines rose up to its foot, the immense black shadow of the cave roofed it with a single span, but the fronts of houses and towers were in bright sunlight, all their angles revealed and the doors and windows showing as jet-black squares. It was like an intaglio sharp-cut in an oval bezel. The limestone rose sheer above it to meet the forest and then the unbounded blue. It looked so infinitely remote, there across the gulf, so remote and serene in its rock setting, that it seemed like some dream or mirage of an eternal city.

In truth it was neither very fine nor very ancient. Salisbury Cathedral had already just gone up when it was built. Yet there was something in its emptiness, its serenity, its fastness in the rocks, that lifted it above such calculations. Perfect, inaccessible, unchanging: so it seemed in that first, distant view.

We drove on to the National Park headquarters and museum, where we were received by the Ranger in charge, an archæologist who has lived for many years on the Mesa. We were all very kindly entertained to lunch by his assistant, a tall spare woman, also an archæologist, who took us back to her cottage in the Rangers' compound. Here in a pleasant little road entirely hidden from sight among the pines, the National Park officers have houses where, if they wish, they can live all the year round. Our hostess had furnished her sitting-room in the usual Indian style, but her bedroom had the air of a New York-Parisian boudoir with its looking-glasses and quilted satin. I found it rather touching that this lean woman in her severe uniform should have made so feminine a room out in the wilderness; afterwards, when I thought of the cliff cities folded in their canyons, I found I also recalled this unexpected satiny boudoir in the cottage among the pines.

It was agreed that we should go to Cliff Palace (as the pueblo we had seen is popularly called) in the afternoon: it faces west, so in winter this is the best time for visiting it. I set out with the Ranger, realising how fortunate I was to have come at this season when I could have the ruins to myself, for he told me that in summer they conducted parties a hundred strong. Skirting the lip of the canyon until we were almost above the ruins we went down by the same track that the Indians had used when going to and from their fields on the mesa top. It was very narrow and twisting, sometimes no more than steps cut in the rock, and just before we reached the ruins we squeezed through a crack in the cliffs which must have made a perfect defence point, easily held against all comers. In another step or two we were approaching the north end of Cliff Palace, and its two hundred houses, twenty-three kivas, three square towers and single round one, were stretched before us, filling the whole length and height of their enormous cave. The place was smaller than it looked from afar, the houses a little rougher and less complete, yet in another way it was even more impressive than I had expected. Although I knew that these cliff dwellings had been built up beneath a natural vault, I had supposed they would project beyond it into the open canyon; instead, the cave was deep enough to hold the entire city; when I stood on the wall of the foremost kiva, still the great, low-pitched arch of sandstone curved between me and the sky.

Small though it had been, never many more than two hundred houses nor so much as a thousand inhabitants, it deserved to be called city. The towers, the density of the houses, the boldness with which they climbed to three and even four storeys, all suggested a city in miniature. Just as European peasants will claim the last possible inch of a mountain valley for their fields, so these Pueblos had made use of every ledge and crevice for their buildings. Even a fissure running high up along the back, too narrow for living-rooms, had been walled in and used for storage places and turkey roosts. The houses were excellently built in evenly squared masonry, while inside most of them were plastered and painted in red and white; the ceilings had the pine-log rafters which are so often imitated at Santa Fé. The windows were few and very small, but as the doorways were raised three feet or so above the floor level, they served also as windows. These could be closed with carefully shaped slabs of stone. So the houses were snug and dry, and must often have looked very attractive with gaily decorated walls and fine pottery and blankets, but they were terribly small—smaller even than is usual in the ancient pueblos, for the cave space was limited. So the kivas must have been needed not only for secret societies and their ceremonials, but as refuges where the men could escape from their crowded homes to talk and gamble. Yet in fact the congestion was not serious. People lived very much out of doors (still with a roof over their heads) lighting their fires in the open courts and, inevitably doing most of their work there. Though few of them were high up, most of the kivas were ranged along the front of the cave, and when they were roofed their flat tops made an agreeable terrace. It would have caught all the sun; it commanded the best view both of the city behind and of the canyon in front; and in winter it would have been warmed from below, for the men kept good fires going on the kiva floors.

Now, however, the line of kivas stood roofless and I walked along the walls looking down into the perfectly circular rooms below my feet. With no more than elegant variation in proportion and in the number of pilasters, all were the same, all showed the ventilator shaft with its own opening above ground, the raised slab or baffle to prevent the descending air from blowing across the fire in the central hearth, the *Sipapu* between the hearth and the far wall, and the encircling bench supporting the pilasters—which would, in turn, have supported the roof. Once, perhaps, these chambers were plastered and covered with stylised paintings, scenes from the tribal myths such as I had seen restored in the kiva of the Coronado Monument. Once, more certainly, the bench and the recesses above it would have held the superb masks of the Katchinas, the divinities who were also ancestral spirits, masks with inscrutable but not savage faces, painted in black, white, red and turquoise blue, ruffled with feathers, beaked, eared, or crowned with horns. There, too, would sometimes have lain all the gear of the lesser members of the society, their head-dresses, gourd rattles, necklaces, aprons and sashes.

As I stood staring down into the bare stony wells trying to waken them to barbaric colour, I looked up to see a chipmunk poised on the farthest wall, its tiny body standing out against the sunny vacancy of the canyon. These creatures, quick and darting as lizards, must have come to the city when there were lively little children here to tease or feed them, must have nibbled among the scraps left behind when the last Pueblos trailed sadly away, and visited it through all the centuries when it was deserted. As this particular chipmunk stood undulating from nose to tail as though charged by an electric current, it seemed to me well suited to be a messenger, like the squirrel Ratatosk who carried messages up and down that tree of life, the great ash Ygdrasil.

As far as I can judge, the Pueblo Indians who lived in the Mesa Verde during the thirteenth century had developed as good and satisfying a way of life as any primitive people are likely to do. Admittedly, I am basing some part of my judgment on the evidence of the modern Pueblo, but I believe this to be well justified, for not only do the inhabitants of several of the present-day pueblos (Santa Ana, Santo Domingo and Sia, all Keres-speaking) claim to be the descendants of the Mesa Verde people, but there are countless similarities in things large and small to prove that the Indians are still astonishingly faithful to their ancient traditions. Indeed, where there has been change it must certainly have been for the worse. The thriving cultivators of the Mesa Verde, though they had failed quite to achieve the civilisation of their southern kinsmen and neighbours in Mexico, had advanced far beyond most primitives. In their heyday they must have known dignity, have lived on their mesa confident in the rightness of their ways and the benevolence of their gods.

Their descendants, after defeat and repression, are still threatened by an immeasurably more powerful material culture. Things that seem good among them today are likely to have been better when America belonged to them.

I think many Western people would now agree that the Pueblos were wise to vest all property in the women. Houses and land belonged to the community, but they were assigned to the women and were handed down from mother to daughter, remaining with the same household for generation after generation. Furthermore, though the men and boys were the cultivators and owned corn, beans and squashes while they were in the fields, once the harvest was gathered, that too came into the possession of wives and mothers.

This did not lead to a monstrous regiment of women, for much power within the household was in the hands of the owners' brothers and other male relations, but it did, I think, mean that the Pueblos recognised woman's practical capacity, her ability to run the affairs of every-day life in a seemly and traditional way. Equally it recognised man's passion for the theoretical, for intellectual and spiritual exercise. Thus, women built and owned the houses, while men were responsible for the life of the sacred kivas.

On marriage, men naturally went to live in their wives' houses, and all children were born into their mothers' clans. It would be his mother's brother who would undertake a boy's education, first teaching him the general lore of his people, then introducing him to his own kiva where he would be given instruction in the secrets of the men's world and be initiated into his

uncles' society. Once they had outgrown the cradle-
board which flattened their heads for life, little children
were allowed a life of play till they were five or so,
after which they were expected to begin to learn adult
ways by imitation of their parents. They were seldom
punished, but if they were it was most likely to be by a
threat from the masked Katchinas who seized persist-
ently naughty children and terrified them into virtue.

All members of the same clan ranked as brothers and
sisters and could not marry; a prohibition which must
have been one of the few frequent sources of unhappi-
ness in Pueblo life. However, it was not too difficult
for a youth to direct his desires more wisely, and for a
marriage to be arranged to everybody's satisfaction.
While love-making before marriage was not encouraged
and adultery disapproved, divorce was left to the free
decision of the heart and mind. If a husband felt the
marriage to be hopeless he gathered up his possessions
and returned to his mother's house; if the wife despaired
of it she put the man's belongings on the doorstep and
he had to accept the verdict whether gladly or in sadness. Yet the ideal of marriage was high and generally
maintained. In the charming Hopi story and poem *A
Woman Mourns for Her Husband* (who had been killed by
the whites), after an account of the woman weeping in
her loneliness, unable to eat or sleep, these lines appear:
'Husband and wife talk together to relieve their
thoughts. Then they will forget their trouble. But
when one's husband dies there is no happiness.' It is
often hard to see why primitive peoples are so-called.
It is worth mentioning the end of the tale, for it shows
how in spite of their simplicity and naturally poetic

outlook, good sense and sincerity are respected among these Indians. After a full year of wretchedness and mourning, an uncle says: 'It is all right, niece, do not cry. It cannot be helped. It is ever thus. Do not think of where you come from, but rather look forward to where you are to go. . . .' The young widow was ready for the advice, she cheered up and was happy again. Excessive mourning is always deplored by the Pueblo, for it is said to make the dead suffer in the depths of the spirit world.

The ideal of behaviour was good humour and conformity at home, and peace abroad. The Pueblo claim never to have made war but only to have defended themselves if attacked—and in their world there could be no difficulty in defining aggression. A Zuni recalls how when he was a boy his grandfather counselled him 'to keep bad thoughts from his mind, to face the east, to look to the bright side of life and to show a shining face even when unhappy'. Precocious and gifted boys and girls, though there were plenty of opportunities for them if they behaved discreetly, were nevertheless held back and discouraged. It was bad form, and worse, to be far above the rest.

This ideal must greatly have eased the running of pueblo affairs. Disputes were brought before a council of chiefs (or priests), heads of secret societies and elders meeting in the appropriate kiva. Everyone spoke for as long as he wished and was listened to attentively; at the end of the proceeding, which might last for hours, the Town Chief gave his binding verdict and it was announced to the whole community by the Crier Chief. That was the end of the affair.

HUNT LIBRARY
CARNEGIE-MELLON UNIVERSITY

The insistence on modesty and conformity must be seen as an aspect of the religious ideal of harmony, fertility and continuance, in which the Pueblos seem to have had much in common with the old Egyptian concept of *ma'at*. Certainly like the ancient Egyptians they had established an exquisite harmony between man, nature and divinity. It is impossible to distinguish between religious and secular life for they were interwoven as warp and woof. Not only were there the great communal festivals of the revolving year, for sowing, growing, harvesting and turning back the sun, but simple everyday acts had their rituals and observances; there was continuous traffic between natural and supernatural. Before a woman would begin her potting or house-building, she would use prayer sticks and other means to secure divine sympathy; so probably would a man before starting to weave a blanket and for every act of tending the plants which he cultivated with so passionate a devotion. Before each of the two meals of the day an offering of food was made to the spirits with a spoken prayer; young children were not weaned until they were old enough to perform this universal grace. Nothing better shows the symbolical nature of Pueblo life, the impossibility of separating any one part of it from another, than the simple rituals of birth. While she was pregnant the mother would carry a perfect ear of corn to secure physical perfection in the child, and would wear loose, unfastened clothes to facilitate its birth; another whole ear was laid beside the newborn baby. After a few days, perhaps ten, the grandmother or other woman sponsor would take up the child and the ear of corn and set out with the mother

114

to greet the sunrise. The two women would make a
straight track of sacred meal to signify the way the new
human being was to live in order to satisfy the gods and
his fellow mortals, then hold up the little brown body to
the rising sun and speak a prayer both generous and
hopeful.

Now this is the day.
Our child,
Into daylight
You will go out standing.

. . . . . .

May your road be fulfilled.
Reaching to the road of your sun father,
When your road is fulfilled,
In your thoughts may we live,
May we be the ones whom your thoughts will embrace
For this, on this day
To our sun father,
We offer prayer meal.
To this end:
May you help us all to finish our roads.

Although the Sun Father was worshipped as the great
cosmic power, Pueblo religion was mainly directed
downwards towards the realm of the Earth Mother, the
realm that was reached by way of the *Sipapu*, the home
of the spirits whence the newborn came and the dead
returned. Yes, the Earth Mother presided benevolently
over the endless cycle of birth and death. The Katchinas
who dwelt down there in her spirit world were the
ancient and great ancestors who in former times used

themselves to visit their descendants, but who now would do no more than possess the living men who impersonated them. Still, however, they were well-disposed to the living and brought them clouds and rain. The recently dead, too, were friendly; true, they had to go down through the *Sipapu*, but they still thought of those they had left behind and could hear all they said. They were allotted different tasks in the underworld, but most often and most happily they were sent up as clouds and so enabled to bring rain to the living who longed for it so much.

Earth and the female principle were honoured, for in them were enthroned the fecundity of all things which was the Pueblo's greatest desire. Pueblo dances, nearly all their rituals, were directed towards it, recognising how in this principle, animal and plant life, women and the earth itself, were at one. It was the principle of completeness and continuance in contrast with the masculine ideal of unique perfection. That for the Pueblo the goddess was (and still is) almost wholly beneficent is further proof that with them individuality and the assertive ego were but little developed. For when they grow in strength, then the sky god of the masculine principle waxes with them, while the Great Goddess begins to show the malevolent qualities of the feminine; she becomes the devouring unconscious seeking to pull back the climbing intellect into her realm of darkness. It is said that one reason why the Pueblos could not readily adjust to Christianity was because of its sky-directed worship. Nor did they find it easy to tolerate the thought that the dead who had returned to the universal home should be punished or rewarded.

Life in the rock-fast city and its neighbouring villages was normally a good one. It had the mixture of the practical, the sensual, and the poetic which we have so largely lost. From first waking when the light touched the canyon wall opposite, there was much to be done, but not too much. The simplicity of possessions and clothes had its own form of labour-saving, leaving more time for talk, idleness, craftwork and ritual. Almost every day the women would have to fetch water, grind flour, and prepare the one big meal of the day which families took together in the late afternoon. Parties of friends or women of a household would go down to the dammed water pools in the canyon floor or to the perpetual spring at its entrance, and wend their way back in line, big jars balanced on their heads. Corn was ground on sloping millstones permanently set in stone troughs, these handmills being installed in special rooms where several women would work together, kneeling side by side. These were quite strenuous but not disagreeable tasks; when one has taps and ready-made pastry what is there better to do? Sometimes there would be clay to be dug and prepared and pots to be shaped, painted and fired; sometimes outings to collect wild onion, juniper, beeweed, pinyon nuts and other wild herbs and fruits to enliven their cooking. Then, as well as such everyday chores, there were everyday pleasures: gossiping with neighbours when the whole world was next door, dropping in for snacks and to inspect new babies neatly mounted for display on their cradle-boards. No one had to work or idle imprisoned within the walls of a lonely house. (Who does not understand the sudden success of our communal laundrettes?) When the men were either up on the mesa or down in their kivas, the women could feel the whole cave was theirs, they could see all that was going on, and feel a vast sense of possession over all they saw.

Nor was life less well suited to the men. On most days they had to go up to their fields to clear, to weed, to press down the seeds, thin out the corn plants, pick off insects, scare away birds. Yet the truth is, they went up more often than was needed, for they enjoyed such husbandry, as well as its material rewards. As for the life of the kivas, it must have approached the male ideal. The men and youths could climb down into their warmth and privacy to talk, trade possessions, or gamble for them, in addition to the more solemn business of learning, rehearsing and enacting the rituals of their secret society. No man's club in the world, I think, could rival this combination of social cosiness, secrecy and high ceremonial.

As well as the pleasantly monotonous tasks and the everyday pleasures, there were the stirring seasonal activities: the winter deer-hunting and long journeys after buffalo, the summer trading expeditions for turquoise and salt. Then, too, there were the many festivals; best of them all, perhaps, the feast of the green corn. On that day every fit man, woman, and child went up to the fields carrying food and drink; then hundreds of corncobs, still young and tender, were roasted in the open and feasting was kept up late into the night. At last, gorged, everyone took the cliff path homeward by the light of the full moon.

One other aspect of the experience of these people deserves reflection. They lived in the heart of what they knew best; further from home their knowledge grew more and more tenuous, and of the great outer world they knew nothing at all except what their myths suggested. That is to say, they were familiar with everyone who lived in their own city, they heard news of all who lived in the canyons of the Mesa Verde, even of the odd characters who, one imagines, may have chosen to live in some of the tiny single dwellings squeezed into remote crannies in the cliff face. They had trodden every acre of their island-like home and knew where to find its plants and animals. Then beyond their protecting and defining cliffs and scarps, they heard from time to time of the fortunes of the friendly villages on the surrounding plain, and had plenty of rumours of the movements of enemy nomads. Finally once or twice a year they had tidings from the places a few hundred miles away where parties regularly went for trading and whence traders came to them. Beyond that were the unknown and the imagined. I do not know whether this is a better way of knowing the world than our curiously diffuse and scattered one; certainly it is easier, more conservative of effective energy, and less disturbing.

Judged by any standards, this life of the prehistoric Pueblos was good in its order, its effortless communal living, in the good relationship between parents and children, men and women, and in the strength of a shared poetic symbolism that charged every act and every possession with meaning. It was good in its near self-sufficiency which gave no opportunity to an unknown 'them' (whether bureaucrats or foreigners) to upset one's life or rob labour of its rewards. It was good almost beyond our understanding in its unity and its consistency, in being a life in which action fitted exactly with belief.

It was bad in that it was sometimes too harsh, with winters full of suffering and summers haunted by fears of drought. It was bad in that while there were no human 'they' to tyrannise and interfere, there was a constant fear of supernatural hostility and of discovering death-dealing witches even among one's friends. But these were minor ills; chiefly what was bad lay in the mirror image of what was good—in the conformity, the lack of enterprise and of privacy, the suppression of individuality. For us of the Western civilisation the central criticism must be that it lacked greatness and genius; the individual was smothered in the tribe, the tribe in the slough of tradition.

Yet today when we seem to be completing a circle, or rather another loop of a spiral, when the Renaissance pride in great men seems to be giving way to mass cultures, when even in the United States itself competitiveness is changing to the ideal of the regular fellow, and children are given good marks for conformity, we cannot condescend towards this 'primitive' people. For certainly the tribe is to be preferred to the crowd. If we are not bitterly to regret our lost innocence, our oneness with nature, the gods and each other, we must serve with all our might the cause of great men and women and their service to consciousness. So it seems to me.

One of the strangest things in the history of Mesa Verde is the manner in which it was abandoned. The Pueblos lived in their cliff dwellings for hardly a century before they left them for ever. They went, perhaps by stages, to the banks of the Rio Grande where we can find some of their descendants and very many of their traditions in the modern pueblos. Why they went no one is agreed. There was a long drought at the end of the thirteenth century which might well have accounted for it, but elsewhere other Pueblo peoples are known to have been on the move when there was no drought. The hostile tribes who drove them from the mesa tops might have increased their pressure, yet there is absolutely no sign of sacking or massacre among the cliff dwellings.

On the contrary, before they were pillaged by their first modern discoverers, Cliff Palace and the other pueblos showed every sign of having been left quietly and in order by a people who hoped one day to return. In its obscure and humble way, it must have been one of the saddest exoduses in history when the peaceful people, who had put so much trust in their gods and their own ways, had to give in, to trek down the canyons leaving not only their little golden city and beloved fields, but also the setting of their life-giving legends and the familiar places of worship.

Our drive down was very easy, for the snow and ice were melted even on the northern scarp; I was free this time to enjoy the tossing miles of forest, the tawny plains, the mountains, now lilac freaked with white. When we were down and driving hard to the east we looked back to see the Mesa fading with the evening light. There is a song from the Rio Grande pueblos, a lament:

My home over there, my home over there,
My home over there, now I remember it!
And when I see that mountain far away,
Why then I weep. Alas, what can I do?
What can I do? Alas! What can I do?
My home over there, now I remember it.

I do not think it was a lament for Mesa Verde lost, but how well it might have been!

8

Saturday It was a very long Saturday night,
Night that one. I must have walked out
in Dallas of my hotel bedroom, a room
designed to be walked out of, just
after seven; and I did not return to
it until sometime between two and three in the morning.
The fact that I can remember everything worth remembering—not only the events themselves but also what I
felt and thought about them—proves that I inherited
more than broad vowels from my West Riding ancestry,
from grim moors and even grimmer mills. Saturday
night, the young Public Relations man told me at lunch,
some days before, was the Big Night in Dallas. Could I
take it, if he showed me round? I could; I did. He was a
nice lad, who had come down from New York to do his
Public Relations, whatever they are (and perhaps my
Saturday night was part of them); he had published a
novel, which I read afterwards, late at night in Houston,
and saw it as a fine start for a lad in his early twenties;
and throughout that long evening he alternated between
being a Public Relations man (let us call him P.R.)
showing me round, and the fellow novelist he felt he
was at heart, anxious to exchange opinions about books

and writers, opinions that need not concern us here. Our tour of the 'night spots' was to begin at Fair Park, on the edge of the city, so we did not meet down-town at my hotel but out at his house, not far from the Park. There I met Mrs. P. R., a delicate blonde, rather fine-drawn and anxious, and the baby upstairs, and the little boy downstairs, who told me, not too severely, that I was a fat man, and an elderly baby-sitter with one eye already fixed on the television set. When we left in the car, Mrs. P. R. announced that baby-sitting had given such women a new interest in life, as more than one had told her: it added something to their pensions or small incomes, brought them into family life, showed them little darlings they could cherish, and so on and so forth. I agreed with all this. I might know how restless and wakeful American children could be, but this was not the moment to air that knowledge. We were already roaring down the boulevard, out for a Big Saturday Night in Big D.

Culture claimed us at first. This was at my request. In the Fair Park is the little theatre-in-the-round, directed by Miss Margo Jones; and I had often read and heard about this experiment. Both in America and in Europe various plays of mine have been presented 'in-the-round'—that is, on circular or almost circular stages, without scenery, and with the audiences seated as they are in a circus; but I had never seen any of these productions, never even visited a playhouse of this sort. I like experiment in the Theatre, and was prejudiced already in favour of this particular one. It cut down costs, banished all the *chi-chi* of *décor*, and might help the good actor. Moreover, I was tired of sets, tired of canvas, paint, counterweights, impossible windows, doors that would not open or would not shut, tired of trying to light actors against highly decorative walls. So it was at my request that we began our evening at this theatre-in-the-round, though I had been warned that this first production of the season, a new comedy, was below the theatre's usual standard. The place itself was tiny, seating about a couple of hundred, and, in my opinion, much too small. The audience was too close to the players, who had to use the same entrances. Indeed, after the play had been going about twenty minutes, I saw what looked like a most promising new character, the best so far, making a leisurely entrance, only to realise that he was actually a late arrival in the audience. I began then to imagine a play for this sort of theatre in which characters who at first seemed members of the audience gradually took charge of the action. The comedy we were seeing badly needed some such development; it was a mournful little patchwork of familiar theatrical scraps. The only new and surprising line in that first act came from an elderly character, calling on the family, who said: 'This is the first time I've visited with Presbyterians—socially.' There may have been other and rarer gems in the later acts, but we did not stay to admire them. As we left I wondered why Dallas, so rich, so confident in its claims to be a centre of culture, allowed this tiny theatre to operate, as they say, 'on a shoestring', when so many millions could be spent on other things.

Even on steak, for example. I am as far removed as possible from the kind of man (not to be trusted) who does not know what he is eating. I like food, and do not

E*

merely consume it but take some interest in it, even away from the table. This may explain why I do not understand Steak Worship, which has now spread from America to most parts of Western Europe. None of the famous old gourmets like Brillat-Savarin or the great chefs ever displayed any particular passion for steaks. In my youth they were associated chiefly with the lower class of commercial travellers, who tucked into their regular 'steak and chips' at tables crowded with bottles of sauce. In those days, and indeed right up to about 1940, steak was merely one robust masculine choice among many. (The old-fashioned eating places for men were called 'chop houses'.) But then, as meat became scarce in Britain, our dreams were haunted by the archetypal symbolic Steak, imported, if only as an image, from America, which had never quite freed itself from a pioneering frying-pan idea of food; one may realise this from ten thousand signs across the continent, the 'Chicken Dinner' being only excelled by that supreme feast, the 'Steak Dinner'. So, as *Admass* closes round us all, the Steak reigns unchallenged. If a good *Admass* man does not order a steak, either he is not hungry or he cannot afford the price. (It was an advertising expert, a creator of *Admass*, who declared, when questioned about his method, that he did not try to sell the steak 'but the sizzle'. And all the steaks have been sizzling ever since.) *Admass* types who have spent the whole day in an armchair, merely lifting a telephone, will then order steaks that would daunt a six-foot navvy. There may be symbolic magic in all this. You become a he-man by eating like one. Losing by day the self-respect that belongs to manhood, you hope to restore it at night by chewing a steer's hindquarters.

A steak at the club I was taken to, after the theatre, cost $5.50, without anything else, with hundreds of thousands of beef cattle all round us. I was glad that I was not a steak man. It was a pleasant club, with some sedate dancing in the centre of the dining-room, but that night there were too many large dinner parties being held there, probably ordering $5.50 steaks by the dozen, the coloured waiters in their red coats looked harassed, and the small table specially put up for us was much too small for comfort. I forget what we ate and drank, but I know that we did not linger over the meal. We motored down-town, to arrive where a doorman in a convict dress, black-and-white stripes, ushered us into a crowded, smoky pandemonium. The name of this joint was *Cell Block* 7. There was no dancing, no food, no cabaret. People sat at small tables, closely packed, drinking beer or the liquor they had brought with them, and shouting at one another through the din. This was created, unceasingly while we were there, by a jazz band —the *Cell Block* 7 boys—who were also wearing convicts' clothes, with battered black bowlers on the backs of their heads. Now and again, one of them would clutch the microphone and bellow incomprehensible lyrics into it; but most of the time they simply banged away at the piano and drums, blasted away in a frenzy through trumpet, trombone, saxophone, until the deafened customers rose at them with applause and shouts. I do not know whether it was good jazz or bad (or even jazz at all); I seem to remember my friend P. R. bellowing that it was only fair; but the sheer noise produced by those young maniacs (one or two of them, I was told, students from the university) would have blasted the ear-drums of a mammoth on heat. That smoky hot room shuddered with sound. It was like being in a brass foundry adrift in a hurricane. No talk was possible, only a desperate exchange of roars and shrieks. Sometimes I joined in the applause, not because I thought there was anything worth clapping, but just to be able to make a noise myself too. Total insanity, one felt, was just round the corner. As the trumpet player collapsed, the trombone man, a shambling fellow with glittering eyes, would lurch forward and lift his menacing horn, while the rest of the striped *Cell Block* 7 inmates nodded away, wearing the blank grins of imbecility. Not that there was any genuine idiocy up there on the platform, for after all these boys were being paid to do in public what they were always ready to do for nothing in private. It was not they who handed out dollars for the privilege of sitting uncomfortably round little tables and being deafened. And they were having a fine old bang and blast, doing themselves, no doubt, a bit of good. What we thought we were doing, I do not know. But this, I was told, was one of the favourite night spots of the young in Dallas. Here perhaps, forgetting that they too might accumulate 263 million dollars like Mr. Hunt of Dallas, they sit and dream the hours away. And unless they happen to be deaf, this must take some doing. Unlike Mr. Hunt, however, they will not be haunted by fear of all those Reds in Washington. They are probably not afraid of anything except silence.

Our next spot—was it Abe's Colony Club?—was the type of night club that has been seen in hundreds of Hollywood films. (There ought to have been a gangster

proprietor sitting, poker-faced, behind a desk somewhere, attended by a thin gunman and a big fat ex-pug,
all waiting for Humphrey Bogart.) It had a small dance
floor surrounded by tiers of tables. The floor show was
on when we arrived. It consisted at that moment of a
comedian who had obviously taken out his teeth in the
hope of being funnier. As we were taken to our table,
he began wildly gesticulating and thrashing around,
giving one of those 'impressions' of rustics that are
based on no observation whatever and suggest that the
performer has never been outside a city all his life. He
was a hard-working comic, far too industrious and con-
scientious to light up anybody's Saturday night: he
would have done better as the foreman of a small
struggling factory. But when he went, we sat up expec-
tantly, staring through the blue haze. Like wintry
thunder and hail before the daffodil, a roll of drums
brought us the dazzling flower, the downy ripe fruit, of
all darkened niteries and dimmed hot spots. We were
looking—and here I quote—at that lovely headliner who
is one of the fastest rising stars in the exotic field, who
can best be described in one word—*Wow!* (Who would
not pay the minimum cover charge to look over the
fence into that exotic field and cry *Wow*?) Has she
gained a wide following among convention goers? She
has, and you have taken the very words out of my
mouth. Can she always be relied upon to do a real gay
bit of entertaining? She can, and you are putting it
mildly. Let us give her a great big hand, folks.

For a minute or two, our lovely headliner merely
offered us some faint notion of a song and sketched a few
dance steps. Only her radiantly confident smile was

really with us. This was mere teasing. Her own particular field, the exotic, was still out of sight. Not by this parody of a dance, this ghost of a song, had she gained a wide following among convention goers, solid men loaded with Scotch, rye and bourbon. This was not one of her real gay bits of entertaining. So the applause she asked for, and received, was not by way of thanks, it was so much encouragement. Then at last, still murmuring what was left of the song, still hinting at those dance steps, her smile more radiantly confident than ever, she began to dispose of various gauzy wisps of costume, revealing more and more of that body, firm and golden-tawny, which, as we had been told, had transformed her into one of the fastest rising stars in the exotic field, a field now blossoming before our entranced eyes. No convention goers were with us, crying their wolf calls in chorus, but such manhood as we possessed brought the palms of our hands together; and as we applauded, wisp after wisp fluttered down, veil after veil was lifted. Slim legs were bared; neat rounded thighs, a small inviting waist, all for our leisurely inspection; and then at last, just before we might have yelled like hungry babies, there emerged out of the blue haze, like twin full moons in a summer night, the rarest and most succulent fruit of the exotic field, and breasts naked as Eve's bloomed, dazzled, tantalised. Solidly there for one glorious moment, real and breathing and warm, was the Pin Up Girl of a million adolescent dreams. A chord in C Major, a final roll of drums—and she was gone.

Good-looking girls who have slender and almost boyish figures, with no pelvic breadth to suggest maternity, the ancient fertility of Earth-and-Mother

130

goddesses, yet proudly, insolently, carrying breasts that are exceptional among young white women, are now the favourite erotic symbols of *Admass* men. They are seen everywhere, in night clubs like this one, in films, in advertisements, and above all in the little magazines, reproducing 'art photographs' and offering more sumptuous specimens for private sale, that lie thick on the news-stands, where boys and men starved of sex buy them by the hundred-thousand. And all this, to my mind, is only further proof that *Admass* is a society unhealthily dominated by the masculine principle. But its maleness, no longer balanced and nourished by the feminine principle, no longer rooted in Earth, has something stale, almost rotten and perverted, poisoning it. There is here no true feeling for Woman herself. These over-emphasised breasts and undeveloped hips do not belong to, never suggest, man's mate, his companion along the road from the Old Stone Age. It is not the time-old simple healthy lust that is roused in this exotic field, far removed from the meadows where many a wide-hipped country lass lost her virginity. Woman has not changed; these girls merely have an unusual physique and cannot be blamed for taking advantage of the fashion: it is men—the patrons, the customers, the fans—who have changed. There is in them now, it seems, still a famished and frustrated baby, never finally weaned, still eager and hungry for the breast. So this exotic field has a secret no press agent will reveal: all its straining curved silk, its bulging sweaters, its 'thems and thoses', its melons and globes and moons, so generous in their promise of lactation, are not luring the customers to bed but making them leap up in the cradle.

131

But that is only one side of the picture. What about the narrow-hipped boyish figures that support, so inadequately, those magnificent bosoms? Surely no mothers there? No indeed; they do not belong to essential Woman, brooding, fertile, deep-rooted; they represent Woman in her new aspect, away from her own ancient realm, all the smart hard girls who may compete with men but do not challenge and reject the values of the society that men have created: they symbolise what is left, sadly diminished, nearly impotent, almost a freak, of Eros in *Admass*.

The floor show over, dancing began. My host and hostess had met friends, and now I found myself dancing with a pleasant young married woman. I am no ball of fire on the dance floor; my style is a sedate version of what was going strong about thirty years ago; but like all heavy men who happen to have a sense of rhythm I can at least give my partners an easy if not an exciting session; and when the hour is late, the dance floor dimly lit, not too empty, not too crowded, this style of mine encourages fairly intimate talk. So I told my partner that I had often wondered what women felt about these strip-tease acts. I had often seen them, I told her, at burlesque shows, almost exclusively patronised by men, and, often with some astonishment, at large 'stag' parties arranged by and for middle-aged professional men. But in night clubs, where men brought their own women, I said that I thought it odd that one girl should be brought in to undress herself. What did she feel about it? After a little hesitation, my partner declared, with some heat and obvious sincerity, that she detested strip-tease. She didn't see why one sex had to go through

this sort of performance just for the benefit of the other
sex. If there had to be this kind of thing in public, then
she would rather see something downright obscene
between a man and a woman—and have done with it.
Then we said no more on this subject. But as we continued dancing and chattered away about other things,
I told myself there was more in this protest of hers than
the obvious resentment of a young wife who had just
seen her husband stare goggle-eyed at another woman
baring every charm. That was there, of course, but
with it was a deeper and more impersonal resentment.
Here was yet another protest against a society in which
masculine and feminine values were not properly
balanced, harmonised. Strip-tease or equivalent antics
existed of course in older societies, where feminine
values were still deeply-rooted, but they were offered to
men on the loose, having a break from domestic life,
knowingly playing truant. But a society in which a man
takes his wife for a night out and they pay extra, out of
their common stock of dollars, to see another woman
undressing herself, is a society on which the male has
completely imposed his values, and all talk of its being a
matriarchy is nonsense. No doubt there may be something pleasing to feminine vanity in the idea that the
evening's great treat is the uncovering of some woman's
body; but even this is a perversion of essential femininity,
which must regard this impersonal show of a body, not
truly erotic because outside any relationship, as so much
male absurdity, no better than childish peeping and
sniggering. At home this young wife and her friends
might assert themselves freely, ordering their husbands
to do this and not to do that, with a boldness that

would astonish, let us say, a young woman of Southern Europe, who might easily be envious of such boldness, freedom, assertiveness. Yet these in truth are mere compensations on the surface for what has been lost on more profound levels, showy victories that conceal terrible defeats inflicted upon Woman herself by the organisation and character of this society, in which she is compelled to appear not as her true self but as the reflection of man's immature, half childish, half adolescent, fancies and dreams. Victorious woman forms a lasting relationship with a mature man. Defeated woman strips and teases.

There were other night clubs still open, though now it was getting late, but we decided to end our tour at the social club to which I had been taken occasionally for cocktails. In the dim bar, the only room open now, the grand piano supported a thin table-top shaped like itself on which the remaining members, in a haze of whisky and sentiment, could put their glasses and elbows. Their voices were uplifted, irregularly and draggingly, in the more popular choruses of the last thirty years, those ditties that at half-past one in the morning, after much drink, forgo any gaiety they originally had to steep the reveller in sentimental melancholy, in regret for all the lost golden years. We had professional assistance. A hard handsome blonde, conscientiously rounding off the act but bored with it all, played the piano, while the choruses were led by her male partner who had a small microphone. He was considerably older than she was, wore a velvet jacket, and had one of those soft monkeyish old pro faces that are both strangely young and yet horribly old, faces never seen on ordinary men, faces left untouched by common experience but oddly moulded by years of false feeling, grimaces and grease paint, softened by innumerable sessions with cold cream and towels; we can find them anywhere backstage, yet they are as far removed from any face in the street as the faces we see in fourteenth-century pictures. Smiling a little crookedly, blinking, as if sentiment might soon bring tears, he sang into the mike his laments for lost farms, Dixie, old Ireland, anything. These two, like so many I had seen and heard that night, worked hard but had no real talent. They entertained without art. Talent always delights me, and the absence of it, in places where we have some reason to expect it, always makes me feel dissatisfied, bored, depressed. And while drink may sharpen and illuminate any delight, it also deepens and darkens my dissatisfaction, boredom, depression. So I was about to say that I must go when my friend P. R. caught sight of the little plump Mexican, who, it appeared, sang to his own guitar accompaniment in the dining-room upstairs. The dining-room was closed now; nevertheless, P. R. said that I must hear some of these Mexican songs. He would persuade the singer (a good friend of his and not a man who would want to go home, even though it was two in the morning, leaving a patron hungry for his music) to perform for us somewhere in the club, if we could find a place out of hearing of the piano, the amplified voice of the entertainer, the lugubrious chorus of old Tin Pan Alley hits.

We went upstairs and sat in a corner of the deserted dining-room, with its chairs piled on the tables, one small light burning, all forlorn, chilly, smelling coldly of

the night's dishes. There was as much romantic atmosphere as there is in a garbage dump. As I tried not to
yawn, I marvelled at the naïve enthusiasm of P. R. and
his plump little Mexican. The little man might be good
at his own time and in his proper setting, but not here,
not now. And I was wrong. (Unlike many writers and
all politicians and editors, I am often wrong.) For the
next quarter of an hour, while we huddled there and he
plucked at his guitar and softly sang one little song after
another, the warmth of the earth and real life upon it
came through to us; in the soft husky voice, the quick
hands, was talent; in the songs and their accompaniment
was art, unpretentious, humble, but authentic art; and
across the long desert of the evening we came at last to a
little water and things growing and green, a glimpse of
flowers and fruit. This little Mexican, like his songs,
was still remembering and being nourished by a life
before and outside *Admass*. Perhaps soon he will be a
Big Success, one of the ornaments of *Hashadmass*, no
longer Mexican nor yet truly American; and then all the
organisations, the machines, the instruments, will
multiply and distribute him, and he will be able to do a
thousand things he cannot do now. But will he be able
to bring warmth and life into a cold empty dining-room
at two in the morning? When I returned to the lobby of
my hotel, it had finished with one day and not begun
the next, and so for once was almost deserted and dead
quiet. If we do not soon restore and increase that
warmth, cherishing life again, how long will it be, I
asked the four elevator shafts, before we seem to exist
for ever in cold empty dining-rooms and it is always two
in the morning? The face of the coloured elevator girl,

136

when she finally opened her cage, looked a yellow mask of boredom or fatigue. I did not put the question to her. 'Eight, please,' I said, and went shooting up out of my Saturday night, ending it, you might say, with an exclamation mark.

9

*Musicians,
Novels*

.

J. B. P. TO J. H.

. . . Though I had announced firmly I wanted to attend the opening concert of the Symphony Orchestra, I got landed with one of those confused and maddening evenings of telephone calls, improvised arrangements, too many drinks on an empty stomach, much rushing round in cars. Finally I ate only half a dinner, very late, and arrived at the concert hall only in time for the final item, Mahler's First Symphony. The strings were quite good, the others—in Walkley's favourite phrase—as God made them. I was taken afterwards to a party for the members of the orchestra and their wives, a packed affair, with much simpler food and drink than the oil people lay on, but altogether far more enjoyable. After about an hour of it, I suddenly asked myself why, after so many parties, this one was so enjoyable, and then I realised I was among musicians, with far more capacity for enjoyment, give or take, than businessmen, bankers and lawyers. Their women much happier too, all alive in a world they understood. One of the players—I think he may have been the leader—asked me about Max Beerbohm, whose work he collected and loved; and then told me he had a duplicate set of one series of drawings and offered to give it to me. I felt I had to refuse but was touched by so generous a gesture. He wasn't tight—only expansive, probably after the night's ordeal, and merry, open-hearted and open-handed. As elsewhere, a lot of these instrumentalists, though American citizens, had come from Europe, probably in the 'thirties, and were still in spirit outside *Admass*. Later, unable to sleep (the hotel noisier than ever), I read about some other musicians, in a paper-backed novel about Tin Pan Alley and Broadway. Here was *Admass* at its worst, a commercial jungle, described by a man who obviously knows all about popular song-writing and publishing. He contrived a happy ending, for business reasons, but clearly did not believe in it. The hell along the way was far more convincing. I keep reading what I call these 'documentary novels', which have little or no literary merit, but do offer glimpses of strange worlds, taking one behind the scenes in popular entertainment, advertising, business. When these writers are not reporting—and then they are at their best—they keep going with bleeding raw lumps of sex. What they can't do, not being real novelists, is to suggest ordinary life going on, all that lies between professional or business crises and melting blondes taking off their clothes or angry blondes putting them on again. (Most of them hate women. But then the dislike and the distrust of Woman pervade contemporary American fiction.) All these horrible little behind-the-scenes worlds belong of course to *Admass*—unlike the symphony orchestra. True, some of these writers may have turned to authorship because they have failed in the activities they describe. But mostly there is more than sour grapes here. Genuine indignation or contempt comes through: another rotten slice is being condemned. This is my last day here. They robbed me of some sleep last night, but I am glad I met the musicians. . . .

Motels

.

J. H. TO J. B. P.

. . . I have just had my first experience of a motel. After driving past so many hundreds, laughing at their fantastic names and fantastic architecture, at last I know what it is to drive in, pay one's money and take one's key. Miss B. had been told that the San Juan was a good place, and I'm sure it was. The architecture vaguely Spanish Colonial. It wasn't at all badly done, but several dozen flatlets and a large car park can't really amount to a *hacienda*. Your *Hashadmass*, I suppose, though a fairly pleasant example of it. My room was larger than I expected and well furnished; there was a hot and cold shower with the usual plastic curtain bubbling with fancy fishes. This was all admirable, but of course quite expensive. I'm not sure it wasn't more satisfactory in the old days when motels were austere but cheap. After all, if one is camping by the roadside, why not do it with proper lack of style? I soon realised the first great drawback to motels. No sooner had I showered myself, changed, and begun to feel human again, than we had to get back into the car (drawn up right against the bedroom door, stinking like anything) and drive off in search of a restaurant for dinner. Dinner itself was disturbed by the knowledge that as soon as it was over there would be the smelly car once again and the long drive back to the motel. Feeling sickish, I went early to bed, slept for a bit, then woke up to the real joys of motel life. Freedom to come and go at all hours is the great advantage of these places. Therefore motor-cars come and go at all hours, but it is not an advantage to those staying. The walls are very thin and the noise and fumes murder sleep. Yes, the walls are very thin, and before long it was the couple next door who were enjoying the advantage of going at all hours. I suppose it might have been even more trying if they had been quarrelling or making love, but I must say I found their loud laughter, sudden violent exclamations and prolonged thumping of luggage not at all what I wanted at 3 a.m. I began to wish we were staying in that Wig-Wam motel we saw in Arizona. Do you remember? Each flatlet was a massive concrete cone painted with scalps and totems and the cars stood about among them. It wasn't much like an Indian camp, but at least the concrete walls must have been thick, and a concrete wigwam being circular is bound to be detached. I slept again and when I woke a general roar of internal combustion engines on all sides warned me it was time to get up. Then the full distress of my situation came home to me. I'm not one for breakfast in bed, but I do like to be able to take it quietly and even privately. We were going to have breakfast at an Air Port. Read those words again and ponder on their full horror—adding 'ten miles away'. Breakfast at an Air Port ten miles away. The choice before us was either to get up, pack, and load the car (with no drop of tea or coffee to make such activities tolerable) before driving to the Air Port or to drive straight there knowing one would soon be returning to pack . . . Miss B. chose the second, and I'm a child in her hands over these practical arrangements. I shall never know which of the alternatives would have been the worse.... Either way, it is horrid stepping more or less straight from bed into the atmosphere of a garage.

I know all this is exaggerated and absurd. The San Juan Motel was a very decent and well-run place. The trouble is with me. It is too late now for me ever to accept a motor-car as an extension of one's body and personality. That is what most people down here do, and as they spend a good deal of their lives in the things, may well have been conceived and even born in them, it is perfectly natural and right. Granted this unity of man and machine nearly all the horrors of a motel cease to be. But, as I say, I'm too old to adjust. Motels are not for me. I'd rather wake on a cave floor and reach out to fry an egg on a hot stone—or so I imagine as I've never had to try....

American Girls

.

J. B. P. TO J. H.

... Last night, at supper, I was put beside a mother and daughter. The girl was seventeen, looked about twenty, and was quite delectably pretty—a flashing dark little thing, beautifully shaped and very much on display. She was clearly out of temper at first, probably because there were no boys fussing around her, but after a little encouragement she soon began to talk. Should she go to London or Paris? Should she do this or that? All vague and rather childish stuff. There is something appealing and pathetic about these pretty eager creatures. (Do you meet any? And do you feel as I do about them? Making some allowance of course for sexual prejudice, hardly conscious, on my part.) What touches me is their naïve feeling that everything is possible, their mixture of confidence and ignorance. They flutter about trying to decide between a dozen worlds of art and adventure they imagine to be open to them. They have visions of lovers, of which one just gets a glimpse, that it would take half a dozen first-class men, of widely varying types, to satisfy. All the possibilities, they feel, are opening out for them. Whereas, in truth, everything is about to close in on them. Much of the later dissatisfaction, aggressiveness, secret bitterness, must arrive with the belated realisation of this. They expect too much. They get, in the end, too little. The glittering treachery of *Admass* life. The masculine principle,

144

rampant. The terrible *impotence of power*, unable to create and sustain the real life Woman needs. An existence without symbolism, the extra dimension; blunted sensation; everything inside dull and monotonous. A woman I met at the university—early thirties, attractive, well-educated, happily married and with two fine children (I met them and the husband, afterwards, over a drink), with everything going well—took me about in her car, yesterday afternoon, exploring a stretch of *Nomadmass* just outside the city. We roamed around, chattering away. But when the great gold afternoon, high above the trim clutter of bungalows, bars, shops, began to fade, and she was driving home, both of us quieter now, rather tired after so much dullish sight-seeing, suddenly, without a word of prompting from me, she turned and looked at me sombrely—we were waiting at a traffic stop—and said: 'Tell me—what's wrong with all this?' And let nobody try to persuade me she was making conversation, posing the prize question. She was embarrassed, hating to put the question to a visitor (she had always lived here, and so had her husband; both of them local patriots); but she wanted to know. And probably the flashing, dashing, What-shall-I-decide-to-do moppet I met last night will soon want to know. . . .

10

The Basket Maker's Sash While I was in New York I went into a Fifth Avenue store on some trifling business. Probably to buy nylons. Whatever it was, a mission slight enough to allow me to go about it in a state of non-attachment and not as a questing beast. It was quite a good store, a place where one could easily spend a lot of money. I exchanged the icy grey air of the street, where the wind ravaged one's very soul, for the brilliance and intense heat of the shop. My features, still in deep freeze, rapidly oozed a waxy surface sweat as I launched myself among the counters. As is usual with such shops, this street-level floor was entirely given over to the lesser goods of life, including those puzzling displays of 'Gifts' which seem to have been distinguished as a separate category of merchandise only because no one could be expected to want them even as a gift.

There were counters beyond counting, but still there were not enough; the approach of Christmas (no more than two months ahead) had brought out fleets of trolleys to add to the congestion in the thronged gangways. These, the light skirmishing forces of commerce, each fancifully disguised as something other than a trolley, were employed to show some special line, some novelty or sudden bargain.

On this single sales floor out of thousands in New York alone, there were so many objects that to list them would fill an encyclopædia. I was among ladies' accessories; I should estimate two acres of them. There were things to go on women's feet, legs, thighs, waists, busts, necks, arms, hands and fingers; things to hang in their ears or stick in their hair. There were things to make their nails and lips every shade of red, their lashes and brows every shade of brown and black, to make their faces white, pink, apricot or dusky, to make their eye-sockets grey, green or blue. Things to make them smell and not smell. Stockings whirled in enormous cart-wheels or glimmered on transparent, bodiless legs; gloves were massed in dense rosettes; scent sparkled in glass renderings of crowns, top hats, opera glasses and cowboys; hundreds of silken scarves spouted from a fountain; thousands of handkerchiefs filled the heart of a golden flower.

Like one corpuscle in a bloodstream, I was carried along the gangways where women were in that stage of shopping intoxication when they would hardly know what or for whom they bought. I myself felt drunken from an excess of goods, and like all the intoxicated found myself staring at the details of things close to my eyes. I saw patterns of triangles, rose-buds, pine-cones, masks, derived at many removes from Cubism, from Romantic ideals, from the Orient and Africa; I was startled when suddenly confronted by a spiral design first seen on a megalithic tomb among the green plains of Ireland.

As I waited the quarter of an hour which is the normal time needed for making a simple purchase in a New York store, I drifted into a vision. I saw, as though in parallel and opposed mirrors, endless streams of little figures hurrying to and fro to make all these things, to make the machines to make the things, to keep accounts of the buying and selling of things, to supply and take back money for the sale of things. . . . In all this, never one instance of direct imaginative creation or of a human being making something because he wanted to, wanted it, and knew how.

I like museums, but as my husband and most of my friends loathe them I can approach them with a fairly open mind. In this particular museum I felt happy and tranquil. It was a small place, exceedingly well done like all National Park Service undertakings. In deftly lit openings some of the finest handiwork of the prehistoric Indians of the region was on show; decorated baskets, painted pottery, some textiles, and necklaces and pendants made from shell and coloured stones. There were also displays of the simple equipment used for grinding flour and preparing food. All the finer exhibits seemed to enjoy a quiet life of their own, standing in their cases with calm self-assurance, breathing soundless communications through the glass. I moved at once to a rather narrow opening which I could see contained something quite out of the ordinary. There, as elegantly displayed as they could be in the most exclusive boutique, were six woven strips, their ends sweeping down in long, graceful fringes. In perfect condition, they were found in a dry cave above the little mining town of Durango, where they had been

148

lying for some fifteen hundred years. These strips had been fashioned as belts, or more properly as sashes, for they were easily long enough to go twice round the waist, while the fringes must have been intended to hang free at the wearer's back, as do the wider sashes of the modern Pueblos. The colours—off-whites, buffs, browns shading towards black—were soft and harmonious, the texture soft and rich. A few were plain, but the rest bore beautiful designs, either enriching the whole surface or confined to formal borders. All possessed what we now call 'quality' to the very highest degree. They could not be said to have the hundred million dollar look, for they looked, quite simply, unobtainable.

The sashes were woven by Basket Maker Indians out of the hair of their dogs, the only domestic animals known to them. They must have used them to gird up the deerskin and rabbit-fur robes which they wore against the bitter winter cold. (In summer they preferred to go naked.) At this time, just about the years when the Romans were abandoning Britain, the Basket Makers had not long raised themselves from a life of nomadic savagery. A few rudiments of civilisation had come their way. As well as being skilled in basketry and weaving, they knew how to cultivate maize, and some of the more progressive seem to have been experimenting in house-building. Even then, however, they lived in a way which we should consider beggarly. Caves were their usual dwellings, they had no bow and arrows to help them in their hunting, but, like the Palaeolithic hunters in Europe, relied on the spear thrower. As they were also without the art of potting, the women had to employ the tedious method of dropping heated stones into baskets of water if they wanted to vary their cooking from the usual roast.

The Basket Maker 'standard of living' would, I suppose, fall below anything our economists could calculate, yet when these poor barbarians wanted something to tie their flapping robes, they made sashes lovely enough to rouse my twentieth-century lust for possession. There would be nothing of their kind half so good in New York, London or Paris. If a great dress designer saw one, I believe he would be inspired to create a model for its display.

How truly wonderful it is that a people living without so many of the things we regard as necessary, always uncomfortable and often in danger, should gather the hair of their dogs and weave sashes whose length, cunningly twisted fringes, and, above all, whose fine patterns, so far outshone the dull forms of necessity! The making of patterns is a thing we take for granted, yet surely it represents one of the least explicable urges of our kind? As I looked at that show-case and thought of the Indians carefully selecting the hair of white dogs, of brown dogs, of blackish dogs, and then tiring eyes and fingers to produce these harmonies of line and colour it appeared to me hard indeed to explain. Where did the patterns come from, charged with emotional force to make a woman living as humbly as a badger give hours to their expression? We know how the forms of weaving modify designs and how tradition comes largely to control them, but what gives them birth? How do they arise in imaginations that are the product of endless generations of animal life among

mountains and forests? We do not know. That is where
sociologists and their kind are at their most misleading:
for them everything is conditioned, everything determined by one's parents, one's fellows, one's education.
For the Basket Maker weaver there was no compulsion;
merely the gift and the desire.

I left the sashes and went into the Pueblo room where
the air was lively with the zebra-sharp patterns of the
pottery. I came to a halt before a case in which two
large, pumpkin-shaped vessels were displayed; they had
been found in kivas, and the fact that they were made
for sacred use must explain their surpassing excellence. I
have spoken of zebras in connection with the brilliance
of the black and white painting, and having once thought
of them must say that the full bodies of the pots were as
taut, as evidently swelling with life, as the barrel and
flank of these most decorative beasts. As for the designs
painted in black on a white slip, they were masterly. On
one jar a motif recalling a stiff, fierce tropical flower
appeared against a delicate chequer-work background;
on the other, a simple step pattern was most ingeniously
composed into a banded ornament of force and originality. It is extraordinary that such symmetry and
balance of form could be achieved by a woman shaping
clay with nothing but her fingers and a pebble, far more
extraordinary that such intricate and extensive designs
could be painted freehand on to curved surfaces by a
woman who guided a yucca-leaf brush solely by the
image carried in her mind. Yet at the same time it was
the slight, intuitive deviations from exact regularity
which gave these pots the additional strength and
rightness of things shaped by hand.

Perhaps the artistic skill of the prehistoric Pueblos is less remarkable than that of the Basket Makers; they were further away from bare savagery and already architects and town dwellers. Yet their talent as painters of pottery is another manifestation of the same mysterious urge which showed itself in the sashes. As soon as the latest of the Basket Makers had fumblingly learnt to fire pottery they began to decorate it, and within a few centuries their descendants the Pueblos had brought the designs to perfection.

I have long thought the sudden emergence of man's artistic powers in the superb animal art of Palaeolithic Europe to be the most unexpected event in all our history. Yet in truth these abstract designs on things of everyday use are at least equally astonishing. One can understand the emotional inspiration of the animal art even while one marvels at the brilliance of its execution. It is harder to see what lay behind the decorative art of such primitive peoples as the ancient American Indians.

It is, of course, highly individual. It is easy to tell the handiwork of one potter from that of her neighbours, of one pueblo from all other pueblos, and of this one people from other peoples of whatever age and place. I believe that in the decoration of surfaces only the Celts have ever equalled the Pueblos and their even more gifted cousins of the North-West Coast. One of the few purely happy forms of historical thinking is to contemplate the infinite variety of decorative arts coming into being here and there but by no means everywhere throughout the world, developing, perhaps becoming part of a great culture and enriching the dress, the furnishings and architecture of civilisation, then dying back, plant-like. One can turn them over in one's mind as a miser handles his coin: the stiff elegant patterns of the Egyptians and Greeks, the exuberance of the floral patterns of the Central European peasantry, the weirdly contorted animal form of the Anglo-Saxons and their northern kin, the formal splendour of Persian design. When all are told, they make no mean part of the wealth of mankind.

Yet still we understand so little about their origin, how they are born in all their beauty on the waves of time. Some designs, certainly, are symbolic. The undulating line, for example, which appears on one of the Basket Maker sashes may have represented flowing water and hence fertility, while the fringes symbolised rain, as they do for the modern Pueblos. Even where there is a symbolic meaning, however, it may often have followed the creation of the design, coming into being only as the human mind played over created form, seeing likenesses and giving them significance. We can be sure that if we were clever enough to be able to distinguish all the tangible elements contributing to a decorative art, the materials and techniques available, the practical and spiritual needs of the people, the influence of the land with its forms and colours, and the contributions of individual genius, still we should be far from comprehending its genesis.

What is certain is the power and indestructibility of true products of the imagination, however simple. As soon as I stood in this little museum I found I was comparing the world it represented with that of the New York store. Here, a few things supremely satisfying to those who made and enjoyed them, because they expressed something in the being of the makers, of their tribe and its tradition. There, a vast welter of things expressing absolutely nothing but cash value, jazzed up with scores of corrupt decorations plucked senselessly from their living contexts. If some of the Pueblo pots and Basket Maker sashes were displayed on one counter of that store, then all the products of mass production and cultural scavenging would become virtually invisible, falling out of sight like dead leaves. These objects made by Indian women living obscurely among the mountains of Colorado, would stand in New York regnant, seeming to show a confidence in their own existence and its power to command admiration and feeling.

I have to be severe with myself. I know that I should feel frustrated, cut down, if I had to live in a pueblo with a few possessions such as these. I know, too, that a greater degree of social organisation and technical skill has been needed to nurture the highest genius and human achievements. There could have been no Dante or Leonardo among the Indians. Nevertheless, I am truthful when I say I would rather share in the life of a pueblo than in that of any of the little scurrying robots I saw in my vision. I believe it to be not only a happier life, but one more worthy of our kind.

On every hand the development of the imagination is threatened by mass production at its most corrupt— whether it is by words, by visual images or by the deluge of goods. Sometimes I fear that life on the imaginative level may be slowly stifled. Already in our western civilisation, poetry, once open to all, has become inaccessible to most people. Will it soon be dead and the other arts dying? I am inclined to be over-satisfied with myself as a person of sensibility and imagination, yet as I took my last look at the Basket Maker sashes, I knew that if I wished to communicate with some woman of fifteen centuries hence I had no means so sure and true as the Indian who addressed himself to me by means of dog's hair and rough hands.

11

Lay Sermon to Nomadmass Between Fort Worth and Dallas there is a fine stretch of *Nomadmass*, though I have no doubt there are equally fine stretches of it elsewhere, especially in California. At each side of the road for miles and miles there are trailer courts, motels, gas stations, second-hand trailer and car dealers, 'super-markets' offering packaged and canned foodstuffs, bars, eating places with quaint names, *Pig 'N' Loaf* or *Chuk Wagon*, but all serving the same tired food, drive-in restaurants, drive-in movie theatres, possibly drive-in banks and drive-in drug-stores (I saw these in Houston), radio repair shops, thickets of television aerials. This is the land of the new nomads, folks for ever on the move, either because they are restless and do not know where to settle or because they are living on pensions or income from savings and prefer to keep on the move. They live in trailers or drive from motel to motel, the tuneless gipsies of the machine age, wandering month after month, year after year, in *Nomadmass*, the long thin empire of the internal combustion engine. Here people must mostly serve themselves, as in the 'super-markets', but the automobile is waited on like some divine

Pharaoh, for as soon as it arrives at a filling-station there are young men, so many acolytes in spotless white robes, to attend to every need, to anticipate every want. The most expensive advertisements in the magazines are pictures of families standing round new automobiles and gazing at them in a trance of ecstasy, with visions of *Nomadmass*, where you need hardly ever get out of your car, beginning to dawn and sparkle in their eyes. If you live in *Admass* and cannot aspire to *Luxad* or superior *Hashadmass*, then you dream of the day when you will be free to roam in *Nomadmass*.

Yes, the *Nomadmassians* can go where they please, with a whole wide continent to play with, but nothing except the dust on the roads and the temperature can change very much, for they are always in *Nomadmass*, part of that long frieze of trailer courts, motels, gas stations, neon signs, always driving in or driving out, eating and drinking the same things, watching the same television programmes that tell them to eat and drink those things. A man is free at last of the office or the warehouse, draws his pension, and off he goes, with his smiling wife. A youngster is bored with Main Street and the old bunch there, throws up his job, buys a bigger car out of the money his aunt left him, and off he goes too. Two women teachers pool their savings, buy a trailer, leave their class-rooms for ever, and drive down the road into the blue. Their grandparents left their homes to break the prairie: these go to break the monotony. But unless they are fairly clever, determined, courageous, they will arrive in *Nomadmass*.

It is good for people to travel, to leave their homes now and again and discover how other people live, to spend their days in wildly unfamiliar surroundings, their nights under strange bedclothes, to make every meal an experiment, to sit behind exotic drinks and listen to foreign tunes and unimaginable lyrics, to try to understand alien habits, customs, values, to be half-repelled, half-enchanted; and then, with bursting bags and memories, to find themselves back home once more. But this is the opposite of *Nomadmass* life, which offers movement without any essential change. It is a street three thousand miles long. At each end are the same cigarettes, breakfast foods, television programmes, movies, syndicated columns, songs and topics of conversation. You burn a hundred and fifty gallons of gasoline to arrive nowhere. You are never really at home nor away from home. You neither cultivate your own garden nor admire other people's: the gardens have gone. So has the Past, for everything here is brand-new, just unpacked from the factory, with gadgets replacing old skills, endless entertainment and no art, filled with the devices of second-rate men and utterly removed, perhaps for ever, from the noble passions, the tragic insights, the heroic laughter, of great minds. Ten miles of it will not show you a bookshop. Books belong to yesterday. *Nomadmass* is nearly tomorrow.

Between Fort Worth and Dallas, however, the prophets have not been entirely banished. Religion of a sort, chiefly manifesting itself in sects unheard-of elsewhere, has not lost its hold on the Texans, who put long lists of places of worship in your hotel bedroom, fill several newspaper columns with advertisements of services, and maintain some little chapels among the

Nomadmass filling-stations and trailer courts. Near these chapels on the highway are posters and signboards bearing Bible texts, competing not too hopefully with the advertisements of gasoline and breakfast foods. One of the largest of these, catching my eye as I passed originally in the bus, repeated the ancient warning: *The Wages of Sin is Death but the Gift of God is Eternal Life.* There it was, the old growl of thunder, with miles and miles of *Nomadmass* on either side of it. And considered simply as one advertisement among many, the boldest, the most astounding, on view. What was stale orange juice as against fresh orange juice, ordinary gasoline as against gas-with-a-tiger-spring, bad breath as against sweet breath, compared with this threat of Death and promise of Eternal Life? Either this was the biggest and most impudent lie along the road or a statement that reduced all the others to the most trivial twaddle. A choice not between Bing Crosby and Alan Ladd, Camels and Luckies, Shell and Esso, but between Death and Eternal Life. *Yes, sir!* And let nobody imagine I have quoted that text in order to jeer at it. I believe it to be true; though the largest and most astonishing claim made along that shouting highway, it was the only one I believed to be strictly true. I was delighted to see it there, bang in the middle of *Nomadmass.* Even in the old-fashioned world outside, we need that sharp reminder. In *Nomadmass* I felt it ought to have been repeated, in larger and gaudier lettering, every mile or two. At the same time I could not help suspecting that the people who put up that bold notice did not know what it meant. If that is too strong, then they did not know what meaning a passing stranger might discover in it. And as these people were clearly ready to preach a sermon at me, I will now preach one at them: *Lay Sermon for Nomadmass*.

My brothers and sisters—and brothers and sisters you are, though I no longer drive a car and you do hardly anything else—let us examine this text: *The Wages of Sin is Death but the Gift of God is Eternal Life*. A big bold statement, unlikely perhaps to win friends and influence people in the ordinary way, better left unsaid by the keen salesman or ambitious junior executive, but with something fine and challenging about it. Straightforward too, up to a point, but past that point, at which we dismiss the ancient world of prophecy and doom and shining miracles and begin to consider our own world and our lives in it, we are compelled to ask some questions. What is the Sin whose Wages is Death? What is the Eternal Life that is the Gift of God? Why does God give it? And why should Death follow this particular Sin? I shall be told that no particular sin is meant, just sins in general—murder, theft, fornication, drunkenness, playing cards on Sunday—perhaps playing cards at all. It is the old story. Wrong-doing is punished. Virtue will be rewarded with everlasting life, perhaps in a *Nomadmass* with millions and millions of miles of gas stations and trailer courts and motels and drive-in movies. But many people, most of them the very sinners who ought to be punished, would prefer death. So what they ought to be given—and serve them right—is everlasting life, time going on and on and on and on. Meanwhile, this prospect is beginning to alarm, perhaps appal, many of the virtuous, ready to receive God's gift, for they too would prefer death.

And now, with the punishment becoming a reward, the reward turning into a punishment, we do not know where we are. Yet the text still stares us in the face: *The Wages of Sin is Death but the Gift of God is Eternal Life*. Could it mean something quite different?

I suggest, dear brothers, that it could: I believe, dear sisters, that it does. And in order to understand its meaning, we do not need to reach an agreement about the mysterious hereafter, nor try to furnish and decorate the mansions of Heaven. Observe the present tense of the statement. There is no 'will be' or 'shall be' about it. All is happening now, not following the Day of Judgment. We are considering ourselves as we are, not trying to guess the motives and actions of celestial police and magistrates. We are all the characters necessary, and the scene remains here in *Nomadmass*, with the usual incidental music of motor-horns and juke-boxes. God is not about to intervene, either to punish or to reward. His gift simply Is: we receive it by recognising it for what it is. And what is this 'eternal life', which our text places in such contrast to 'the wages of sin'? Well, it is not everlasting life—with time running on and on and on. That way lies lunacy. Eternity is not unending time. It is outside time. It involves another dimension of things. If we think of time as a line, then eternity is a plane. Life in time is existence along the one-way track from the cradle to the grave. Eternal life has some freedom of movement away from that one-way track. It is different in quality from life in time. It offers a different sort of psychological experience. As soon as we cease to believe in eternal life, in *being* as opposed to endless *becoming*, we

161

think that the happiness we crave can only be somewhere further along the time-track, so we drive on and
on as in *Nomadmass*. Here and Now can never do it,
we must arrive at There and Then, which become Here
and Now again, and once more rejected. (So, feeling
cheated, we denounce all the other people, the revolu-
tionaries, the counter-revolutionaries, the government,
the opposition, the reactionaries, the radicals, the reds,
pinks, blues, anybody, anything.) But eternal life is
always a new and heightened experience of Here and
Now. Nor is it necessary that we should be saints,
mystics, the profoundest of philosophers, to know something of that experience. All moments of noble living,
the ecstasy of love, the compassion and understanding
that enter into every genuine personal relationship, the
creation and rapt appreciation of great art, the adven-
tures of the mind among significant ideas, even an
amazed wondering about ourselves, all demand this
unknown dimension, this timeless being. Every greatly
heightened state of consciousness involves eternity.

The more we are enslaved by time, behaving like a
hen hypnotised by a straight line drawn before it, the
more remote we are from this eternal life. We are
rejecting God's gift, the higher level of being. We are
turning away from God. And this, surely, is the Sin in
our text, the Sin whose wages is death. Not the breaking
of any familiar code of ethics is being condemned here.
What is threatened with death is a certain way of living
that already has death mixed in it. The sin that banishes
a man from eternal life and pays such deadly wages is the
sin, which may breed many other and more familiar
sins, of narrowing and blunting consciousness. The

sinner here may be a man who has a dull and cloudy
mind and makes no attempt to clear and brighten it,
never tries to think for himself, to feel keenly and
freshly, to enlarge and heighten his experience. The
death which is the wages of this sin is not simply the
grave, the end of man's time. Men who respond less
and less to life, behaving more like automata than living
spirits, are dying every day, and may be dead in the
spirit long before the earth is shovelled on their coffins.
Even to reply more and more feebly and grudgingly to
the challenge of the senses is a form of dying. This does
not apply to the deliberate ascetic, who is most sharply
aware of his senses while doing battle with them. A
hermit in the desert, tortured by visions of women,
feasts and wine, is more vitally sensuous than the
average man-around-town, probably lost in a glum
routine of sensuality. It is the man whose sensibility on
all levels is becoming more and more blunted who is on
his way to death. The slave of automatic reactions, no
longer sharply aware of real life and indifferent to most
of its possibilities, incapable of a new thought or fresh
feeling, bankrupt of rich experience, such a man exists in
a world that is rapidly diminishing and growing greyer
and dustier. He might almost be said to be walling
himself up. He is paying himself the wages of this sin.

Now I believe, my friends, that it is possible for a
man to live anywhere and yet avoid this sin, accept
God's gift of eternal life; we need not all be like Words-
worth's skylark—

Type of the wise who soar, but never roam;
True to the kindred points of heaven and home!

163

and indeed the poet himself enjoyed travel and movement, as so many of us do; and I am far from suggesting that we should imitate those Orientals who save their souls by squatting in jungle huts or desert caves. Nevertheless, we shall do well to examine *Nomadmass*—and the *Admass* out of which it sprang—in the light of our interpretation of this text. Unless we know for certain that we have exceptionally powerful characters, tempered by a long arduous training of the will, we shall be foolish deliberately to pile up obstacles to our progress. Few of us are saints and heroes. We are common weak men. So we must ask ourselves if what he finds in *Nomadmass* encourages such a man to avoid the sin, to accept and cherish the gift. Will these almost endless rows of filling stations, motels, trailer courts, juke-box bars, drive-in restaurants and movie theatres, radio and television sets, always the same everywhere, inspire a man to live adventurously and nobly in the spirit, in the timeless part of himself, or will they fasten him into routine, turn him into the slave of time, and so offer him the wages that are death?

Here I would ask you to beware of false prophets and those smooth preachers who will interpret the ancient wisdom falsely. All, I repeat, is Here and Now. If we reject eternal life today and tomorrow, next year and the year after, though we may refrain from murdering our relations by marriage, reject the advances of the auburn-haired woman in Joe's Bar, sing hymns every Sunday and drop the price of a rye-and-ginger-ale in the collection plate, there will be no free motel awaiting us in the fields of Paradise. There is a queer hard saying that we never see along the road: *Let the dead bury their dead.* And if you lived where they come shambling and mumbling, how many Zombies would you ask to stay with you? Why should God throw open His shining courts for the dullest of His creatures? They would not even know where they were. They would still be going on and on, round and round, in time. In *Nomadmass* you can go further and further; *Admass* shows you how to go faster and faster; but where in all this is eternal life? So now I declare it is useless to spend time and money putting up such reminders of ancient wisdom unless they are accompanied by warnings against *Nomadmass* and *Admass*. You can enjoy what they have to offer, for what it is worth, or you can turn to religion, but you cannot do both at the same time. If *Genesis* is right, then the Tower of Babel is still wrong.

So beware of false prophets. Regard with the profoundest scepticism those 'religious personalities' who have made themselves so much at home in *Admass* and know how to make use of all its devices. They have elaborate public-relations organisations, a fine microphone manner, a television programme, a useful tie-in with the popular press and the films; but the truth is not in them. The religion that comes out of ballyhoo is not true religion but so much sentimental juggling with symbols, once potent, that have lost their real meaning and force. They do not denounce, but encourage by their example, an existence that is essentially irreligious, rooted in the belief that God has no gift for men. For Time is the master of *Nomadmass* and *Admass*. The timeless soul has no status there, eternal life no real meaning. Every man recognised as a noble spirit—and we are not entirely beyond such recognition or we should be lost indeed—has refused to accept *Admass* without strong protest, is for ever rebelling against it. On the other hand, men not yet automata who do accept it, with the intellect if not with the heart and the whole mind, pile up in secret such frustration and despair that no enterprise is for them too menacing, lunatic, desperately irreligious; they plan total destruction, the suicide of a whole society and every man, woman and child in it. Let the hydrogen bombs fall, the very earth rot with biological warfare! Yes, yes, my friends, this may never happen; we are not yet committed to turning our world into a smoking ruin; *Admass* and *Propmass* may exist peacefully side by side. But to do—what? For there still remains the other death, the wages of the great sin, the death by inches that comes from the refusal of God's Gift of Eternal Life. And now, dear brethren of *Nomadmass*, you may drive in or drive on: my sermon on the text you showed me is ended.

12

Houston . . .
·
J. B. P. TO J. H.

. . . I arrived here early yesterday afternoon, the train rocking quite violently as if to remind me that this is the second largest port in the U.S. It is bigger than Dallas and supposed to be much rougher and tougher. Somebody up there told me that a Gracious Living sort of woman arrived in Houston and asked where she could find a nice restaurant, with shaded lights, wine, soft music: 'Sorry, lady,' said the Houstonian, 'this is strictly a whisky and trombone town.' They all warned me in Dallas I wouldn't like it down here. But so far I prefer it. This hotel, which has a fabulous history (of which, more later), must be at least four miles from the centre of the city. Quite comfortable, expensive but not outrageously so, and much quieter than the one in Dallas. Near-by are gigantic new hospital buildings, largely the gift of the local multi-millionaires, who believe in health as well as in themselves and Joe McCarthy. If they also believe in the arts, they do nothing much to help them. The Contemporary Arts Association here is an excellent little society, offering its members all kinds of advantages (but of course only if they need some art in their lives),

but no millions come its way. A nice woman connected
with it—a friend of Paul Horgan's put her on to me—
ran me round the city this morning, and just before
lunch we went to a show run by the C.A.A. in their little
centre, a small but not unattractive hut-like place. The
show was of fairly recent purchases by local people,
fairly impressive, though the names were generally
much better than the works themselves. They included
Bracque, Dufy, Epstein, Paul Klee, Leger, Matisse,
Miro, Monet, Diego Rivera, Rouault, Matthew Smith,
Utrillo, Van Gogh, Vuillard, Jack Yeats. There were
voting cards, for your three preferences. I voted for the
Vuillard (a beauty), a Utrillo (only fair but at least not a
fake), and, to please the nice woman, an American
water-colour (not bad, though) she had lent the show.
There was some interesting local work, but as usual it
lacked individual style. Too many of these painters,
you feel, never worked anything out for themselves but
went straight from their art schools *non-stop* Picasso.
We had lunch at some club on the edge of the city—
charming surroundings, excellent food and service.
They do this kind of thing far better than we do, and it
is their own, not copied from anything elsewhere, no
Hashadmass. But this noble sun of late autumn must
help; by this time at home we have had the heart rained
out of us, all creative zest water-logged for months and
months, perhaps for ever. I have been invited to attend
the annual masked ball of the Allied Arts (of which the
C.A.A. is a member society), also the inauguration of a
new television programme, Channel 13. The car fuss
and worry are even worse here, where everybody owns
a car about eighteen feet long. If only 20,000 owners

are moving around, they take up 360,000 feet of road at the very least. So the parking problem darkens these glorious days for them. With the result that there are now drive-in banks, drug-stores, laundries. I saw a drive-in bank. You open the window of your car, push the cheque through a slot, beneath a very thick sheet of glass behind which the cashier sits; you talk through microphones; it is banking in science fiction, with branches on Mars and Venus. A drive-in *Eats* place I saw only served three kinds of food, and you have to ask for 'a wheel', 'a hub' or 'a spoke'; probably so your mind won't wander from automobile problems and responsibilities. Not having any, I enjoy these strange sights and the friendly people and the magnificent November sun, great father of us all. . . .

**Deserts
Compared**

J. H. TO J. B. P.

... At close quarters I don't find the desert here nearly as fascinating as it is in Arizona. Perhaps this feeling of mine is partly a resistance provoked by the official State slogan:— *New Mexico, Land of Enchantment*—which even appears on the number plates of all motor-cars. I find this perpetual self-advertisement of towns and states and countries almost as embarrassing and disagreeable as it would be if individual men and women indulged in it. Of course we do just the same thing in selling the beauties and virtues of Britain over here, nauseating stuff, but I don't think we stand for it on our own doorsteps. I believe it to be subtly bad for pride, and for a true love of one's place. It undermines its reality, rather as the flashing and whirring of cameras destroy the reality of ceremonies; everything is reduced to a show, for spectators, for tourists or whatever it may be. But to return to the *Land of Enchantment*, I have quite definite reasons for setting it a little lower than Arizona —in the detail of its deserts. For I'll gladly allow all the high claims for its landscapes. The colours, the contrast between desert and mountain, the quality of the evenings, one could truthfully praise them in language enthusiastic enough to satisfy even the Bureaux of Commerce. But if you walk out into the desert and try to enjoy what is near at hand it is really rather dull and unattractive. There seem to be fewer birds and reptiles

and small, varied plants; nor have I met any Jack rabbits
loping among the scrub. Certainly there are hardly
any cacti, and that is what I miss most. Not only the
saguara, those giant and noble vegetables, but also all
those different stumpy, drum-shaped ones that you find
in Arizona, sometimes tiny, close-to-the-ground little
morsels, sometimes like huge hassocks set with spikes by
a nightmare practical joker. Then the prickly pear, and
the inflammable cholla—strange serpentine masses of
spines, yet harbouring the soft body of the cactus wren.
Yes, I think that is the thing which delighted me most in
Arizona, the odd yet inevitable communities of plants
and creatures. Best of all the saguara community, which
includes two kinds of flickers that cut their nesting holes
in the body of the cactus, and the diminutive elf owl that
contrives to nest on the spiny summit. How delicious
to be an owl with a nest on the top of a slender column
held up twenty or thirty feet towards the stars, able to
slip off it and go hawking the great fat-bodied moths
that fly around your tower. (What a pity New Yorkers
can't do this from the top of their skyscrapers—a perfect, Goyaesque scene!) Now I've made myself think
about it, I realise that nowhere else out of England
have I felt so much a part of the country as I did there
at Wickenberg when I went stalking cardinal birds with
our camera or just daundering about the edge of the
desert. But here it wouldn't be possible to enjoy such
doings, for there seems to be nothing but miles of sage
brush, which may look fine in the mass but is infinitely
dreary when you're among it, or the usual small conifers
growing out of bare rock and grit. Nor do you ever
seem to get here that savagely blue sky of the Arizona

mornings; the blue which is so strong, so plangent that it strikes the eye almost like a red. A perfect back-cloth for the cacti, which have, I suppose, the simplest, most violent, of all vegetable forms.

Well, here we have Indians instead of birds and cacti. If you say that it's a shocking give-away of my attitude towards them when I refer to them as part of the flora and fauna, I'm quite prepared to defend myself. It's because they're so close to the country, because they've forged every piece and pattern of their culture out of it, that they have the power to attract us. The cardinals have somehow sucked their scarlet out of the desert, the saguara built their slender frames; the Pueblos have won from it their designs (which master birds and plants, water and mountains), their dances and poems and tales. There's something wrong about this? Certainly, there's always something wrong in our concepts about ourselves, but there may be less wrongness in this unified view of existence than in many others. However that may be, I'm prepared to swear that the Indian way of living is better than passive participation in *Nomadmass*, makes them more confident, more potent as human beings—perhaps even happier. . . .

Noise

J. B. P. TO J. H.

... I envy you the quiet. If there were an instrument for deadening sound, working like a juke-box but in reverse, I would spend all my loose dimes and quarters setting it in motion. There is in these cities a growing fear of silence, out of which might come strange and frightening whispers, the muttering of outraged gods. It is not enough to have the unending roar of the traffic, the hootings of impatient drivers, the screams of police and ambulance sirens, loud enough for an air-raid. More noise must be turned on if there is any threat of quiet. Most of the taxis down here are like our radio cabs in London, but the voice of the distant operator, calling cabs and giving addresses, is always left turned on, to disturb you throughout the journey. Maddened by one such hoarse monologue, I asked the driver if he really had to listen to it, and he replied, obviously surprised by the question, that there was no reason why he should. 'Then please turn it off,' I told him; and more astonished still, he did. There were only two of us sitting in the parlour car of the train between Dallas and Houston. The radio was on when we arrived, and for an hour I endured the false smooth voices of the men doing the 'commercials', the synthetic high spirits of the programme announcers ('all having fun'), the automatic applause of the studio audiences, trying all the time to read or to enjoy the autumnal majesty of the Texas plain rolling by; but

173

finally I asked the other man if he wanted to listen to this radio. He replied with some emphasis that he didn't. 'Then let's have it turned off,' I suggested. And we did, and then had more attention for either print or plain. At the end of a hot afternoon and much sightseeing, you go into some huge dim bar for a beer and some conversation, and at once the enormous juke-box, as loud and glittering as the organ of a merry-go-round, shatters the peace of the place, probably with the compliments of the proprietor, who feels you would hate to talk without an accompaniment of saxophones and trombones. And in many of these bars there is a device on every table, another triumph of misapplied ingenuity, that enables a customer to start up the juke-box (but not stop it, alas) without leaving his seat. (We shall have them in London as soon as we can afford the dollars to import them.) Then, the other night, I accepted the invitation of a pleasant intelligent young man (with literary ambitions) and his pretty wife, to dine with them and 'have a nice quiet talk'. But no sooner had we taken our martinis than he began playing records of Caruso, Chaliapin, and assorted coloratura sopranos, against whom we had to shout at the top of our voices, like men exchanging news in a cyclone. I stood it as long as I could, and then apologetically suggested we should either listen to the music or dispense with it and try some conversation. But then it was too late to repair the evening, which had brought us neither that nice quiet talk nor some satisfying music. You may say that the young man had no fear of quiet but merely wanted to show off his high-fidelity reproducer and his records. But if so, why did he try to talk through their performance? No, I am afraid that for all his literary ambitions, and his genuine sensitiveness and intelligence, that young man was only another victim of the great phobia—the fear of that background of quiet which might begin to suggest the unknown dimension, the doors silently opening in the deep of the mind. There are hundreds of religious sects and cults in these parts, advertising themselves everywhere as if they were tooth-pastes, but not one of them hoists on the roadside a sign that reads: *Be still—and know that I am God.* . . .

Largest Cafeteria

J. B. P. TO J. H.

... There is a place down-town here that advertises itself as 'The Largest Cafeteria In The World'. This morning, towards lunch-time, I went to have a look at it. If there is a larger one, I don't want to know about it, let alone go and look at it. This one is in a basement underneath a big store. You go down escalators, packed close. Below, there was what looked like an enormous steel tunnel—fine for an air-raid shelter but no treat as a prelude to lunch—and it cannot have been more than about eight feet high, and jammed with hungry people, queueing for something, though I couldn't see what. I decided this crammed tunnel was quite enough, but couldn't get out. The escalators behind me only came down, nothing in sight went up, back to daylight and sanity. Then a man told me the exits were on the other side and that I could edge my way past the waiting crowd. Which I did, finally arriving where the tunnel opened out into a gigantic steel cave, with lighting coming from the low ceiling, still only about eight foot. Here I could look down four 'serving lines' (their name for them) vanishing into the gloom. Hundreds and hundreds of people were taking trays and then slowly moving past four lines of waitresses who dumped things on the trays: a conveyor-belt system of food service. I never discovered where these people took their loaded trays because they vanished clean out of sight. I never found

176

out what they were eating and drinking because it was impossible to tell from where I was standing, and to go nearer I would have had to jump the queue. If there had been fewer customers I'd have lunched there myself, but there was too big a crowd. No doubt the food is fairly good and very cheap, otherwise so many thousands wouldn't pack in every lunch hour. But I'd rather stand on the pavement and eat a sandwich than lunch in that underground termitary. And, thinking it over, I'm not sure it follows that the food is better or cheaper down there than it is elsewhere. It may be the sheer size that attracts so many people. Size does, you know, and that is why one sees so many advertisements of 'the largest'. But what is the attraction? A really gigantic cafeteria, shop, or hotel, has all manner of horrible disadvantages, consuming time, energy, patience. The greater the quantity of food that has to be prepared, the less flavour and character it has. The larger the shop, the harder it is to find what you want, the slower and more complicated the service. And when an hotel is a giant warren, it takes you a quarter of an hour to find your room. Why, then, this appeal of bigness? Is the mass mind of our time ready to overlook all these disadvantages because it feels more at ease (in its desire to destroy individuality) when it is half-lost in some vast enterprise, some fantastically elaborate piece of organisation? Does it feel uncomfortable now in a small establishment, where human values still have to be recognised? Is the big one preferable because it is more like a machine? How the Communists would admire this Houston cafeteria! Just their tank of tea! Probably the Russians are just completing a much bigger one—all steel and concrete, deeper still and with more escalators, eight 'service lines' with waitresses made of synthetic rubber, and the same dish every day. . . .

**Resistance
Movement**

·

J. H. TO J. B. P.

. . . Do I meet lovely young girls who are appealing and pathetically confused? you ask. No, I don't meet lovely young girls in any state of mind, and indeed very few young girls. I am meeting people who are reacting against the people you are meeting—that is at least roughly true. As I told you, I came across a few in Albuquerque, but here there are far more of them; Sante Fé might be said to be their capital city. I've already given you some idea of the kind of people they are, though since then I've met yet another poet (wisely married to a richish wife) and two charming women, retired from running a first-class girls' school somewhere in New England, whose horror at the advance of *Admass* is at least as great as yours. The point is, are all these nonconformists doing any good here, or are they simply a prosperous kind of Displaced Person? Can it ever be right to fly from your own culture and try to find nourishment in others (Indian, Spanish, Chinese)? I think you'd say no, that even your confused young lovely was in a stronger position, but I'm not so sure. For one thing I'm peculiarly bound to think it worth while to discover, record and protect primitive cultures, as so many people here are doing. Then I'd say that, unlike the characters you're meeting, most of them are happy—or if unhappy, then in a sufficiently conscious and elaborate way to enjoy it a little. But more seriously I'd argue that they

179

are doing good simply by setting the example of standing out against *Admass* and the rest, spending their
money in ways that accumulate enjoyment of life and
refusing to be rushed into competitive consumption.
They are individuals flying their own colours and not
so much Displaced Persons as members of the Resistance. The only reason why I don't fully agree with you
when you say that Britain and Europe would have just
as much *Admass* life as America if they could afford it,
is because I'm convinced we have far more people like
these who are deliberately holding out against it, or
openly rebelling. And their ideas do spread. I've met
very ordinary people in other parts of the country who
say, 'I've come to believe the Indians have something
to teach us' . . . and silly as this sort of thing can be
made to sound, it's worth while if it sometimes checks
compulsive talking or the idea that a good man must
work frantically for as many hours as he's awake.

Perhaps I'm in danger of forgetting one very good
reason for living here which requires no solemn dis-
cussion. A lot of my friends, like ourselves, have come
down here to enjoy the sun. I'm going out into it now;
so wonderful to know that it's always waiting for you.
I enclose a sun prayer from the Havasupai who live a
bit further west, by the Grand Canyon. I'm quite ready
to endorse even the last line—provided you will soon
come and join me again. . . .

Sun, my relative
Be good coming out
Do something good for us.

Make me work,
So I can do anything in the garden
I hoe, I plant corn, I irrigate.

You, sun, be good going down at sunset
We lay down to sleep I want to feel good.

While I sleep you come up.
Go on your course many times.
Make good things for us men.

Make me always the same as I am now.

13

Taos and Progress

The magnetic power of an extraordinary individual can profoundly affect a place or a stretch of countryside. Long before I clearly understood where it was (I believe many English people suppose New Mexico to be a part of Mexico) I had my own imagined picture of Taos and a great desire to see the original. This must be true of hundreds of thousands of people in every part of the world who began to read D. H. Lawrence when he was already dying or dead. His power was great enough to endure, and so it is that since his death we have all come to know about the three women of Taos, who are given force to live in our consciousness very largely by their association with him. The *tres matres*. Strange that they should have incarnated the myth of that ancient trinity proper to the chthonic religions which Lawrence himself had preached.

Now I was to meet one of them. Already I was grateful to Dorothy Brett for her recommendation of the little restaurant in Spanish Taos where I was eating quite the best meal I had enjoyed since leaving New York. A trout perfectly cooked, a salad perfectly appropriate, and a glass of decent wine. Near me in the low, small room was an Indian, who, I assumed, had come from the pueblo which lies about five miles from the Spanish town; he sat rakishly, perhaps in the attitude of a man not brought up to tables and chairs, but ate deftly and with attention. Just as I was finishing my meal, I felt a slight stir in the restaurant as someone entered through the door behind me. I turned quickly, and there she was—one of the three tutelary goddesses of Taos. She was very thickset, though her stockiness looked as though it were partly due to many layers of clothes worn below the rug-like overcoat. She had young blue eyes in the rosy face of an elderly woman, and her white hair was all but extinguished by a many-coloured turban glinting with metal thread. Her personality had the weight and density of her body; perhaps it had not always been so, but now she appeared to me to possess the combined authority of her upbringing in an upper-class English tradition and of her lifelong reaction from it. When I praised the lunch, she told me the place was run by Indians, which I had not known.

In the early twenties Lawrence spoke of 'Taos village . . . a Mexican sort of plaza—piazza—with trees and shops and horses tied up.' Now the pretty plaza was congested with cars and its portals thronged with people, but as we reached Dorothy Brett's house we drew clear of the little town and were in sage brush desert, the yellow flowers of September now a withered grey. But the desert was not allowed to be monotonous, for close at hand were the climbing summits of the range of mountains which rises at the back of Taos pueblo as the Sangre de Christo rises behind Santa Fé.

The house was in the usual adobe style, only a little higher than is normal, to accommodate a studio; on the closed doors of the garage the Brett coat of arms was boldly emblazoned in a manner and colours unexpectedly in keeping with the desert beyond. Frieda Lawrence's present house lay among some trees just across the highway; she herself, perhaps the best known of the *tres matres* had, to my great regret, gone south to winter in Texas.

Dorothy Brett pointed northward to the slopes of the mountains where a patch of pink showed in a clearing among the pine forests. 'That is the Lawrences' ranch,' she said. I looked, seeing something quite different from what she saw. For me there was the tiny pink mark and a cloud of images picked up from letters and essays—the best defined, of Lawrence milking a black cow. She must have seen the whole ranch in detail, including her own cabin, and all the memories centred there; she had in fact lived at Questo far longer than the Lawrences, staying there often during the time when year after year they hoped to return and did not.

I approached the pueblo with that stupid, inevitable fear of disappointment which long expectation instils. The sun was brilliant; a wind blew a white mane of cirrus clouds from the mountain crests: the whole atmosphere was extraordinarily lucid. A few old Indians loitered at the entrance to the trodden space separating the two blocks of the village, and some very small children were playing by the river that traverses it. Otherwise no one, and I kept from my thoughts my knowledge of the thousands of tourists who invaded this tranquil space in summer. The northern house group stood solidly before me, like a stack of building blocks made by a child with a genius for design and right proportion. The angular pile was tawny-coloured, its cubical construction heightened by strong shadows and relieved by the bold shadow-stripes of projecting *vegas* and of the ladders which marked a zigzag climb from the first storey to the two tiny houses forming the fifth floor. Set in the tawny walls were many turquoise painted doors and window frames and a few of pure cobalt blue. What gave this irregular step-pyramid of houses its great charm and effectiveness (making it eclipse the similar pile on the south side of the river) was the relation between house-pile and mountain-pile behind. For just as the pale adobe stack rose step by angular step to its cubical apex, so the rock-pink and pine-green mountain rose crest by rounded crest to the exalted but still gently curving Pueblo Peak, sacred mountain of the Indians.

As I stood admiring this curious piece of counter-point, a woman came out of one of the houses and walked across my foreground; she wore white buck-skin leggings and moccasins, a scarlet dress and a flowing purple cloth over her head. Fortune was kind, and I not disappointed.

As soon as we arrived, Dorothy Brett had been claimed by the old Indians, all of them her friends; she had changed into a coat made from a bright red Indian blanket with a bird design spread across the shoulders; in this and her glinting rainbow turban she made a fine spectacle where she sat on a bench in animated talk with dark and wrinkled elders. I left her among them, and went off to saunter round the village; because of its monolithic structure there are none of the interesting alleyways of the Rio Grande pueblos. Taos impresses in one blow, and has little more to offer. I noticed only that the beehive ovens were the smoothest and most perfectly shaped I had seen, smooth and perfect as eggs, while the Christian cemetery (an unusual feature, I think) had a pitiful air of ruin and desolation, the adobe looking as though it was being eaten away by termites. I crossed the wooden bridge, where small jet-headed boys were dibbling in water and mud just as brown- and tow-headed boys do elsewhere, and approached the south apartment house. I did not go far, however, for I soon encountered roughly written notices politely asking visitors to keep away from the precincts of a kiva.

I saw very few people, yet there are not far short of a thousand Taosenos and it was unlikely many of them would be out in the fields. The little cubical mountains must have been full of flesh and blood. I believe, however, they would not be found right at the centre, for those now deeply buried, dark and airless cells have become uninhabitable; most are said to be store-rooms crammed with rubbish—perhaps among it, who knows, relics which archæologists would give much to possess. Archaic though it is in form, this village has only been on its present site since the struggle between the Pueblos and the Spaniards in the late seventeenth century; before that most bloodthirsty and destructive time it stood a short distance further upstream.

Taos is a mixture of the archaic and traditional with the new and changing. Even before great numbers of

whites were attracted there, this most northerly of the
pueblos was very considerably influenced by the Plains
Indians from beyond the mountains; here more than
anywhere else the Pueblo culture has been permeated
by this foreign element. Then, during the present
century, every temptation to corruption has come the
Taosenos' way; first an artist colony, then the great
Lawrence legend and a highly organised tourist traffic.
They could not escape it altogether; some shoddy stuff
is there on show, conducted parties are taken round
the village, there is a tariff of charges for photographs,
and some, even, of their festivals are in danger of becoming displays. Yet in many ways the Council of
Elders has shown itself exceptionally conservative, and
the genuine life of the Pueblo is holding out against
tremendous odds. At Taos no one is allowed to sleep
away from the village, there is no electricity, and the
introduction of a piped water supply has been pro-
hibited absolutely. The Council says that natural water,
their free, flowing Taos River is a holy thing and must
not be confined to man-made pipes. When, as a result
of soldiers returning from the last war, some house-
holds made moves to adopt plumbing, they were ruth-
lessly expelled. To rationalists this may seem simple
folly, yet probably the Council showed instinctive
wisdom. Water and the ideas connected with it runs
through the whole fabric of Pueblo religion as is shown
in many rituals, in their poetry and in a host of symbols
on their pottery, in their weaving and in their ceremonial
dress. To approach the subject merely hygienically, to
have allowed the pipes, would probably have been to
have admitted the thin end of a wedge which in time

would have split their whole culture. It is not possible to be reasonably religious. I think that Simone de Beauvoir showed a very misplaced Gallic cynicism when she suspected the exclusion of whites from the neighbourhood of kivas to be part of a deliberate policy to attract tourists by false mysteries. The integrity of their religious life, its inspiration of their whole existence, is the inner power which has enabled the Pueblos to hold out against all the forces of alien religions, commerce and wars. And in defending that integrity, sworn secrecy has been one of their most useful weapons.

In the early days after the Spanish conquest the Franciscans, often good and always courageous men, made resolute efforts to save Indian souls by conversion; the Indians complied superficially, numbers were baptised, but always below the surface they held out. The leader of the murderous Indian insurrection which broke out in 1680 came to Taos and there talked with three gods who had taken up residence in a kiva; their instructions to him were to restore Indian life to the ways of the ancestors, to lead it back to the original purity of the days when men first came up through the sacred Lake Sipap to people the earth. This sense of the 'ancestral ways' seems never to have been lost. Thus, in spite of the force behind the Christian missions the Pueblo have in general adopted only those parts of the faith which are in harmony with their own. The Virgin Mary and the Saints were easily accepted for they were like their own Katchinas in being human beings who had acquired divinity; yet they have never, it seems, really agreed to monotheism or doctrines of heaven and hell, while the concept of a sacrificial redeemer has meant little to them; in spite of the long contact with Spain, blood-splashed crucifixes are rare in their churches.

If the Pueblos' resistance to Spanish conquerors and missionaries was remarkably tenacious, the stand they are making against Americanisation is really astonishing. Until recent decades American policy was to lead them as quickly as possible towards the American way of life; there were instances of children being carried off to boarding schools under military guard. Similarly their arts and languages were discouraged in the schools. Now all this has changed, the value of their native culture is recognised and self-government has been encouraged—even while they have been recognised as citizens with full voting rights. But from other directions the threat has grown more severe, for now it works through temptation rather than force. The new admiration for the Indians has led to the tourist invasion—at its most forceful at Taos, but enough to be extremely corrupting at all the pueblos. Anthropologists, too, have done something to make the Indians self-conscious and to undermine their natural acceptance of their faiths. Finally, now comes the temptation of big business and its millions. The Indian Reservations of the South-West consisted very largely of some of the worst land in the New World, but of late, ironically enough, it has proved to contain mineral wealth. Oil has been found in the territory of the Navaho, the Pueblos, nomadic neighbours, and partly because of their footloose and reckless ways and love of intoxication, still more because of their more individualistic social system, some have allowed their new wealth to change them. Now, uranium is turning up in the

Pueblo lands; prospecting permits have been granted at
Laguna, Zuni, Acoma and Jemez, and will probably be
sought elsewhere. It is too soon for confidence, but it
looks as though these cautious and conservative
villagers are going to hold out even against an avalanche
of dollars; owing to their immemorial custom of communal ownership the moneys are put into tribal funds
where they may considerably improve the material
conditions of the Pueblos, but need not destroy their
culture.

The symbol of Pueblo resistance through the centuries
is the kiva, the earth-fast sanctuary of an earth-regarding
people, the secret place where they are safe from all
intruders. In these kivas which they have maintained
for fifteen hundred years, each with its entrance to the
spirit world of an essential chthonic religion and with
its rainbow ladder for the ascent of the gods, the
Pueblos have initiated fifty generations of their boys
into tribal membership, handing on to them the accu-
mulating riches of their religious lore. There, dance
steps and movements, ritual observances of all kinds,
have been taught; the words of very many long chants
and litanies have been memorised. The kiva is, in fact,
the perfect focus for an underground resistance movement.

Yet secrecy has spread far beyond it. The Pueblo
have used this most effective weapon at every level of
existence. The wiser anthropologists have learnt to
ask very few questions in order to avoid either lies or
silence in reply; the less cautious and many other
enquirers have probably been greatly misled. One
story shows how even small children have been in-

structed in secretiveness. 'A supervisor, visiting a schoolroom in Santo Domingo, inquired gaily: "And what did you children have for breakfast this morning?" The class leader . . . hissed a swift incomprehensible phrase, undoubtedly the Keres for "Clam up!" Not one word could be got out of any of them. What would have been merely an adult's stupid condescension to white children was inexcusable prying to the little Pueblos.'

So, having something to hide, a complete and consistent culture, the Pueblo have hidden and maintained it. Certainly, as they took sheep and cattle, portals, beehive ovens, silver-working, saints and other things from the Spanish, so now they take many material goods and a few habits from the Americans; there are college students and returned soldiers who have forsaken or are even actively hostile to the ancestral ways. Even with these, westernisation may be very thin, as a friend of mine discovered when she had befriended a high-school teacher. This Indian appeared to have gone further towards the West than most of his kind; he even wore an American overcoat, a garment very few of them are willing to adopt. He wanted to do something to show his gratitude and affection, and so asked my friend if she would like to see his fetishes, evidently his most important possessions. He told her that his were very ancient and efficacious fetishes given to him by his grandfather, who had turned up a jar full of them with his plough. He had put them on the shelf in his bedroom where they still were, he said, but one night he woke up to hear them dancing together. He was quite sure they were about to leave him, to return perhaps to the spirit world, but when he woke in the morning to his joy he found them still on the shelf.

All in all the resistance of the twenty thousand or so Pueblos against the power of the vast nation in which they have been incapsulated is astonishingly effective. As the action of the Taos Council in banning piped water and electricity shows, it is conscious and deliberate. Those who maintain it are willing to practice self-denial and turn their feet from the ways of easy acceptance. It has also been in part selective, foreign goods and ideas that can be digested into the body of their own life are allowed. It is an intelligent (if in origin largely instinctive) resistance to the easy ideas of 'progress' which is of peculiar interest in the United States. I have found that this word 'progress', so exalted in the nineteenth century, is rapidly assuming a doubtful or even an evil meaning for many Americans. Again and again in the South-West I have heard people say in hopeless dejection, 'You can't stop progress can you?' as they gazed at hoardings and filling-stations or experienced the destruction of some long cherished beauty or quietness.

Is it so hopeless? Are we in truth so little masters of our own discoveries? Certainly we can't go back; when I look with admiration on what is good in primitive life I am not so inane as to imagine a return to it to be either possible or desirable. But can we not, like the Pueblos, make some conscious refusals? Only, if like them, we have something coherent to defend. Surely it must be our individuality, our freedom of mind and experience—and with them the surroundings in which they can prosper: peace, privacy and some loveliness, whether natural or of our own creation.

Most people tell me that the Indians cannot hold out much longer. Another generation at the most, they say. I am not so sure. There is in the world today some spirit rising against the huge forces of uniformity. Who a century ago would have imagined the revival of self-consciousness among the Welsh, the renewal of their language and literature and of their desire for self-determination? But if in truth the Indians must lose their struggle—and I know it is very likely—then I pray they may become whole-hearted and active Americans. What I should hate would be for them to make a show of what has been the living reality of their religious life, like the poor creatures I saw dressed up and going through sad, meaningless antics in the hotel at Grand Canyon. That is why I rejoice when the Pueblos turn blank or hostile faces towards me, when they prohibit photography and keep their dances secret; when they retreat down their *kiva* ladders. Admiring their peace-time Resistance Movement, let us defend the Western mind against its iron children the machines.

14

Inauguration of Channel 13 On Saturday, the 20th of November, 1954, a new television programme, Channel 13, KTRK, was inaugurated in the city of Houston—and I was there. Two of my new friends, a delightful couple, were acquainted with one of the directors of this enterprise, and he had given them tickets for the inauguration ceremony. There was to be a select party afterwards at the Rice Hotel, to which we were also invited. This was an Occasion—the newspapers left one in no doubt about that—and I was very glad to be in on it—on a pretty high level too, for our tickets, of purest white, not coloured like those issued to the three thousand decent but not noteworthy citizens, admitted us to front seats among directors and stockholders and the more important pressmen; and the party, as I have already suggested, was only for the elect. Anybody who does not accept this as a great Occasion is left trembling before the sharp and searching horns of a dilemma, for if you do not believe that the opening of a new television channel is important, then you must consider our society to be dithering on the edge of imbecility. Please yourself, but you must believe one or the other. Here is no minor pursuit, no hobby for a few, nothing like amateur book-binding, breeding tropical fish, learning commercial Spanish. Millions of money, billions of hours, are devoted to television. The children cannot be dragged away from it; their elders stare at it until their eyes ache. Whatever else this age may be, it is the age of television. Food, furniture and clothes are advertised and displayed as suitable accessories to the enjoyment of television. Its little lighted screen, the magic window in millions and millions of homes, can immediately bring fame and fortune, even great political office, more power than Aladdin found in his lamp and his ring. For making a single appearance on a television programme, one of our singers or clowns may be given more money than Shakespeare, Rembrandt and Beethoven together earned during all their lifetimes. One conclusion or the other, then: either we are drawing nearer to collective idiocy or the inauguration of KTRK, Channel 13, was an important public event, a solemn Occasion, worth describing in some detail.

We drove through the dusk and quiet of my friends' suburb into the roaring and neon-bright centre of the city. Our expectation was clouded with some anxiety, for the Saturday night traffic was thick, the terrible parking problem loomed ahead, and we knew that we must not be late at the Music Hall; we had been warned that the doors would be closed, and all late arrivals locked out, once the proceedings were being transmitted. (It is one of the difficulties of our *Admass* life that while we are always being told to relax we are also always being warned that any relaxation will be

fatal to our hopes.) But all was well. Careful planning—
and where would we be without it?—was triumphant
again. There was a moment when the parking problem,
apparently beyond all solving, darkened the city's
blaze, but then some inspired cell in my host's quick
brain twinkled in the gloom, a possibility became a
certainty, the car was securely disposed of for a few
hours, and we used our legs—one of us not without
relief—to take us the last few hundred yards. There,
with all its doors still open, was the vast bulk of the
Music Hall, holding three-thousand-five-hundred people.
Big as it was, accustomed as it was to Occasions of all
kinds, nevertheless this Music Hall was excited. You
knew at once that here was an Occasion. Ticket-
holders were besieging the entrances. A crowd without tickets, names or faces, one of those *Admass* swarms
that never fail these events, heaved and surged beyond
the lighted and guarded spaces like waves from some
dark anonymous ocean. In the foyer, all chatter and
last cigarettes (*No Smoking in the Auditorium*), bright
eyes and mink, ushers separated white from coloured
tickets. I was given a celluloid button to wear in my
lapel. It bore the symbol of Channel 13, a black cat for
luck, to defy any malign influence that number might
develop. I am a superstitious man myself, knowing so
little about this strange universe that I never reject any
possible clue to its behaviour, but as I was born on a
thirteenth day I do not consider this number unlucky;
moreover, I am no button wearer; so I promptly gave
my black cat to a small boy, for having been a small boy
in my time I knew that much might be accomplished, in
the magical barbaric world of small boyhood, by the

owner of several celluloid buttons. I was now a guest without a button, was spotted at once, and given another, which I presented to the next small boy I saw, who was delighted to receive it. By this time we were inside the hall.

Outside, the excitement had been loose, unfocused, like a warm wind out of the night blowing round the building; here in the packed auditorium the atmosphere was tense; we might have been looking for our seats inside a bomb about to explode. We found ourselves, as the little girl said, 'in the importance'. Only two rows ahead of us were the directors and chief stock-holders of the new company, all middle-aged men in evening clothes and wearing white carnations: a solid study in black-and-white of prosperity and enterprise. Their womenfolk sat all together behind them, in the row next to ours; and I thought at first rather wildly—for I am immediately responsive to atmosphere—that this segregation might have some religious significance, the men having to keep themselves free of taint and unspotted during the ceremony; but later I saw that the men occupied one row so that they could file out to-gether, as we shall discover. An unusually large orches-tra had been crowded into the band pit. The conductor, wearing earphones, was bobbing up and down, all anxiety. On the stage itself and in the aisles close to the orchestra were men with microphones, men with spot-lights, men behind television cameras, men carrying flex of all kinds, men with stopwatches, men who just shouted at other men, busy platoons of technicians. Outside the proscenium arches were several television sets, and high on one side a large screen on which the

programme could be projected. All this complication
was necessary, for the performances on the stage were
to be transmitted, and in addition the Channel 13 studio
was to be used, chiefly for filmed material; so that when
nothing was happening on the stage we could look at
the screens at each side and view the items from the
studio. Again, if we preferred it, we could discover on
the screens the very performers, brought to Houston
at gigantic expense, who were there on the stage. We
were simultaneously at both ends of the communicating
process, where it went in, where it came out. Sitting at
ease, there we were, in the new wonderland, some of us
only two rows behind the stockholders, the men whose
money was about to work this miracle. Why, I had only
to push aside two of their wives, make a very long arm,
and I could have plucked one of their white carnations.

Time rolled away its minutes, flashed by its seconds.
The moment, sharpened to a heartbeat, was rushing to
meet us. The host of technicians passed from a frenzy
of activity into a frozen agony of anticipation. Earphones were adjusted, watches stared at, hands raised to
give the signal at the exact fraction of a second: all as if
a hydrogen bomb were about to be exploded. In more
than one stomach there the acids of anxiety and apprehension were eating into the lining, the ulcers were well
on their way. And for what? I reminded myself how
in my time I had been behind the scenes in many a
theatre, opera house, concert hall, where supremely
difficult, famous, noble works were to be offered audiences of notable distinction, and how the people working there might have been more than alert and eager,
sometimes perhaps on edge, but had shown nothing of

this agonised preoccupation with the smallest divisions of time, this racking anxiety not to delay the programme for half a moment. But such is the idiotic spell of mere size, the evil sorcery of multiplication, men will now torture themselves among the split seconds so that masses of the idle-minded shall not be kept waiting, not for five blinks of an eye, for their trivial entertainment. These men become the galley-slaves of time all for the benefit of millions who only want to kill time. There is some false addition here. A million lost minutes seem a disaster, a disgrace, because they appear to make a total of six-hundred-and-ninety-four days and ten hours, wasted and gone. But these days and hours do not belong to anybody; no possible achievement has been lost with them. All we have is a minute's idleness, so much chattering, yawning, head-scratching, thumb-biting, multiplied by a million. There is nothing here worth the sacrifice of any man's digestion and peace of mind. But we swarm so thickly and feverishly now that we allow ourselves to be humbugged and bullied by numbers that mean nothing, by idiotic bigness. No wonder, I told myself, we are already half out of our minds and may soon be blasted out of our bodies.

The last second was split. The orchestra blazed into triumphant sound. Channel 13, KTRK-TV, was born into this world. The voice of some solemn high priest of TV dedicated the Channel 'to service'. I was sorry to hear it. I am no cynic but I am always suspicious when I hear people talking about 'service'. When advertising men get together and are still fairly sober, they talk a good deal about this 'service'. But there it was. And now on the stage were some dancing girls

199

dressed as black cats, hard-working girls but no treat
for any balletomane who might be with us. On one
side, rather awkwardly bunched together, was a vocal
chorus, all wearing that oddly severe virtuous look
which seems essential to women who have been
divided into sopranos and contraltos. The black cats
danced as best they could, the sopranos and contraltos
mouthed some mysterious lyric, the orchestra fiddled
and boomed away, and the television cameras moved
around ponderously like curious visitors from another
planet. Some tremendous master of ceremonies, booked
at vast expense, had failed us because his plane had been
held up somewhere between New York and Houston;
so his duties were taken over, admirably too, by the
tenor late of the Metropolitan Opera House, a large
genial fellow with one of those flat dark Irish faces, a
broth of a boy at either the singing or the talking. All
the performers he announced, asking for and instantly
receiving our applause, were, like himself, star turns.
The first of them was an extremely handsome platinum
girl dressed in bright green; a smiling and cool card of
a girl who pretended in song to be devoured and devas-
tated by passion; an accomplished torch singer whose
torch burned without heat. We could glance away
from the pale gold and emerald figure, alive and charming, on the stage, and see her on the screens as she would
appear to all the distant viewers—flickering in black
and white, an unattractive image. There was also a
mezzo from the Met, a darkly blooming Italian type,
cajoling and deeply feminine to eye and ear, who like
the tenor, with whom she later sang a duet or two,
wasted a magnificent voice and years of training on

popular rubbish. All this no doubt was part of the 'service' of the new Channel, a guarantee that it would keep faith with its mass audience, hiring for them at any expense the best voices to sing the most foolish songs. There is something almost vindictive about this aspect of cultural democracy: it bribes such fine singers to leave their opera houses, to desert the genuine culture that nourished them, so that they may serve whatever brand of treacle the mob currently prefers. In *Admass* the crowd is no longer asked to make some effort, to get out of its armchairs and try to climb a little; it stays where it is, yawning and twiddling its thumbs, and everybody and everything that might have brought it richer experience, new life, are delivered to it down on that level.

There were two other acts. One was a pair of exhibition dancers, a tiny woman, like a graceful puppet, and a small but chunky man, who went through every step with enormous care and concentration, as if he were engaged in some experiment that might save or lose a life, like a research worker from a college of the troll kingdom. We applauded the devotion of these dancers, but they brought us no joy, no lightening of the spirit. Unlike the ventriloquist—the only performer who shall be given his name, which was Wences—a whimsical entertainer, essentially un-American, of great talent, who brought me much joy. He began by having a rapid and rather fierce exchange of talk with a head in a box. This head in the box had a dark-bearded aquiline face, and was obviously a severe and pedantic type, reminding me strongly of some of our fashionable professors of literary criticism, who not only talk in the same manner but also seem to be merely heads in boxes. Having tried to satisfy, not too successfully, the querulous demands of this boxed head, Wences then painted a boy's face on the side of his closed fist, clapped a tiny wig on it, attached a body to it, and immediately gave the creature a life of its own, so that I still feel I really encountered an impudent small boy in the Music Hall at Houston. Indeed, I felt he had more individuality, zest and sparkle than many so-called real people I met that night. It was quite a shock when he disintegrated into a dummy body, a wig, a painted fist. Bravo, Wences! If only a constant stream of such humorous magic found its way through Channel 13!

Between these stage items the more modest programme material from the studio occupied the screens. The most important figures who appeared were well-known TV entertainers in New York or Hollywood whose weekly programmes had been booked by this new channel. I have no doubt that promptly at 8 p.m. every Tuesday or 9 p.m. every Friday these fellows could be witty, droll, satirical, charming, exquisitely pathetic, but in these advance talks to their new audience down Houston way, they were the dullest dogs who ever reached a TV studio. One after another of them stared at us with gloomy earnestness, and, without one gleam of wit, without even a glimpse of a clown's grin, said hollowly that he wanted to let us folks know that it was just great to be on KTRK-TV, Channel 13, and that we were all going to have fun, folks. It was impossible to imagine what kind of fun. The commentators and announcers who followed these personages were shown to us in twos and threes, and as each was

telling the other men what those other men obviously
knew already, the dialogue had an air of unreality which
one always found in the opening scenes of old plays,
in which two servants told each other that the master
and mistress had been away. Something different was
achieved by three oldish newspapermen, whose television functions I cannot recall, for there seemed to be
dark menace in their looks and sparse talk, as if the
three Fates had changed sex. The only sprightly relief
from all this hollowness and gloom came from an arch
woman who had been engaged to amuse the weeny
kiddies in the mornings. Perhaps mistaking the time by
twelve hours, and certainly mistaking her audience,
she talked to us as if we were all weeny kiddies just longing to hear some winsome chummy chat. Deprived of
tobacco, beginning to feel some need of alcohol, we
coarse old males regarded this nodding dimpling image
stonily, our thoughts far removed from any vision of
happy weeny kiddies pointing fat fingers at their television screens.

By this time the orchestra had vanished from the pit,
only to reappear, much enlarged, on the stage as the
Houston Symphony Orchestra. There was a little more
singing, an all too brief orchestral piece, and then, as a
more solemn strain rose from the ninety instruments,
the focussed lights seemed to brighten, the television
cameras appeared to be making a final effort, and it was
obvious we were now approaching the supreme climax
of the eventful evening. It was then I noticed that the
row of seats next but one to ours was empty. All the
stockholders, the white-carnation-men, had crept out.
Who or what had called them away? While I was still

wondering, the music, though still solemn and majestical, sank to an expectant murmur of strings, and into the glaring white vacancy downstage walked a man in evening clothes wearing a white carnation. It was, he told us as we held our breath, his duty and privilege now, as Chairman, to introduce to us one by one his colleagues the directors and stockholders of Channel 13, KTRK-TV. As he named them, like Owen Glendower calling spirits from the vasty deep, so one by one, without a white carnation missing, they came on, shook him by the hand, stood by his side, until at last there was a line of middle-aged men in evening clothes, white carnationed, stretching across the stage. I had now a wild hope that perhaps some magnificent stockholding chorus had been written for them, with the basses proclaiming their belief in service while the tenors cried for respectable dividends; but no such delectable finale was achieved; they merely stood there, frowning or grinning at us according to their varieties of temperament, natty symbols of the power behind these scenes that had set in motion all the frenzied activity we had seen, and had brought us all this 'glittering talent'. Not forgetting—and now I quote again the press report I read later—Supervisor Tom Morehead, with Phil Lampkin as musical director, and Frank Fisher and Bill Wagner, and Alfred Urbach directing the choral group, Hallie R. Pritchard and Earl Ehret, KTRK-TV art director, doing the sets. The list ends simply: 'And Jack Gas.' It does not tell us what Mr. Jack Gas did, but my guess is that he was kept pretty busy that night and will be hard at work many a night for KTRK-TV, Channel 13, now securely launched into the wondering upper air, the hypnotised world, of mass communications.

Now all was over in the Music Hall, the inaugural programme of Channel 13 having come to an end. But there was still the party. As the *Houston Chronicle* told its readers later: 'Following the show, stockholders, stars, and distinguished visitors were guests at a reception held at a reception buffet at the Rice Hotel Crystal Ballroom.' Quite true; but like many events reported by a favourable press, it could not quite live up even to this brief account of it. A reception held in a Crystal Ballroom suggests Cinderella, the Prince, perhaps some memorable glass slipper business. I hope I shall not seem ungrateful for some pleasant hospitality if I declare that this romantic atmosphere was entirely missing from the actual occasion. We were just some people drinking over-iced Scotches in a room too large for us. Certainly the stockholders, or most of them, were there, but to see them merely scattered about, a white carnation here, another there, was an anticlimax after their parade on the stage. Most of the stars were there, the ladies looking prettier than ever; but I could not discover that jovial magician Wences, whose talking head in a box might have made some severe but not altogether unjust comments on the party. True, the fried shrimps, for which I have a passion, were delicious; but I ate too many of them. This was not entirely greed, for sometimes I returned to the fried shrimp table in the hope of escaping a fellow guest, who had attached himself to me. He was not unlike the head in the box— a cousin, perhaps—and had an air of keen severity about him; his profile was so thin and sharp that he looked like a six-foot paperknife. He was a born party-wrecker, a man who would not stop talking but would not talk like a human being. Fastening a large bony hand on my forearm, staring at me with a terrible intensity, he went on and on, very deliberately and without mercy, in the sort of language that official reports are written in: 'I want you—to understand—Mr.—er—Priestley—that there are—various overall contributing factors—to the immediate situation—which negative complete finalisation——' I would go for more shrimps, another Scotch, but he came along too, never releasing me: I felt I had been put under arrest by a memorandum. Then at last I saw my friends looking my way, and signalled for instant help. We thanked a stockholder or two and took our leave of Channel 13.

In the equally large room next door another reception was being held. As I lingered a moment outside the wide doorway I was sorry this had not been my party. A lot of middle-aged men were weaving around and shouting in there, and each of them was wearing a fez. This was not the plain red fez of the Shriners, who had once startled me in an Arizona hotel by their sudden arrival, as if the Old Turks had taken over the state. No, so far as I could distinguish it, this was a dark blue fez, lavishly embroidered with strange lettering or designs in silver or gold, a fez fit for the ivory courts of Mogul emperors. Yet these revellers were no dark figures from the East; they were inflamed drycleaners and dithyrambic dentists. I was staring through that doorway at the Mystic Order of Veiled Prophets, in full and uproarious conclave, as I read next day, because the Grand Master of the Order was paying an official visit to the local Grotto, whose Grand Monarch, Mr. Jack B. Schwartz, was entertaining him. As I allowed myself to be dragged away, I wondered wistfully if Wences and his talking head in the box were in there, surrounded by Veiled Prophets; I almost heard that talking head, in its severe pedantic style, catechising the Grand Master and the Grand Monarch. Plagued by such fancies, and feeling by this time rather dazed, I followed my friends into the tumultuous razzle-dazzle of the street, rode with them past miles of neon signs and flashing advertisements, arrived outside my hotel, an illuminated cliff against the wide night of stars, and said my *thank yous* and *good-nights*, and finally reached my high and lonely bed. Here the fried shrimps and iced Scotch—as that monster at the party would have said, probably did say—failed to achieve any symbiotic relation and declined full co-operation with my metabolism, so that I tossed around for hours, either remembering what I had seen and heard during the evening or trying to grasp some flickering dream in which black-cat girls mewed at Veiled Prophets and scores of men with enormous hands signalled to weeny-kiddy ladies and the head in the box drilled a vast parade of stockholders in full evening dress. Next morning, making some notes, I had to be very careful not to confuse such dream phantasmagoria with the actual events I was determined to report as faithfully as I knew how. And this, believe me, I have done, inventing nothing. Some things I may have missed, others I may have forgotten. What is certain is that on Saturday, the 20th of November, 1954, there occurred in the city of Houston the inauguration of Channel 13, KTRK-TV, and I was there.

15

Alley Theatre,
Houston
·
J. B. P. TO J. H.

... Last night I went to the Alley Theatre, on the invitation of the charming woman who directs it. This too is a theatre-in-the-round, like the one at Dallas and not very much bigger. I am certain these theatres are too small. Actors and audience are too close and confused: they should be more obviously separated. But last night I didn't find myself regretting our usual picture-frame stage and its sets. If there was not any clear gain artistically (the cut in costs is clear enough), neither was there much loss. I still believe that London should have one professional playhouse of this kind—there is an amateur company already working on these lines— if only for the sake of the experiment and its economical production and running costs; but I can't pretend these theatres in Houston and Dallas have kindled any fresh fires in my mind. Last night the acting, for a stock company, was fairly good, and the production adequate. The play, *Picnic,* had been a Broadway success, receiving both the Pulitzer Prize and the Drama Critics' Circle Award. I can't imagine why. No doubt the New York production was very different from the one I saw last night, but a solidly good play does not depend upon being jazzed and tarted up by a brilliant director and some dazzling performers: it ought to be good anywhere. If *Picnic* is worth a couple of prize awards, then I am rapidly forgetting all I ever knew. It is about an amoral young vagabond bursting into a circle of drearily conventional people in a small Mid-Western town. After the first quarter of an hour I could have told you almost everything the characters would say and do. This is, of course, if the playwright dealt in dramatic clichés—and he did. Not one character ever gave me one moment's surprise. All right, they were drearily conventional people, but even such people are capable of surprising us, and it is then that the playwright should invite us to take a look at them. But this man wasn't tedious because he was imitating life too closely but because he had concocted a play out of other plays. It is all Theatre out of Theatre out of Theatre, with no new life coming in anywhere. This makes everybody, critics and all, feel comfortable. It also gives the Drama a further dose of pernicious anæmia just at the time when it should be lively and challenging. . . .

Fun and
Fantasy
·

J. B. P. TO J. H.

. . . The Allied Arts Costume Ball was a lot of fun, far better than anything we could do away from the Chelsea Arts. Hundreds of costumes, some of them very ambitious. The prize-winners in the 'best group' category came from the Technical Institute: there were seven or eight of them all linked together, dressed in gauzy black stuff with their heads and faces covered, and showing appropriate symbols; it was fancy dress of the atomic age, for they represented 'Chain Reaction'. I was happier when they were out of sight. Handsome wenches abounded, dressed as anything from poodles to can-can girls. Thousands of balloons floating about, champagne popping, a fine noisy band, everything as it ought to be on these occasions. I was at a table with pleasant young middle-aged professional people, not in costume, and as most of the men seemed disinclined to dance, I took one after another of their neglected ladies on the floor, dutifully but enjoying myself too. Because most of these people must have had some interest in the arts, they knew how to make the most of a party of this kind and were really gay, bringing more zest and less self-consciousness than we English would do. Probably the sun helps, likewise the lashings of money to spend. Also, the feeling you are doing it bigger and better all the time. This, I thought, was Houston at its best.

Two press items you may have missed. First, the

meal that Vice-President Nixon ordered in his hotel at Seattle. (Because of some mysterious warning, it had to be examined for poison.) It was entirely his own choice: tomato soup, a Swiss cheese sandwich, strawberry ice-cream and tea. A man who can order a meal like that ought to be charged with attempting to poison himself.

Secondly, a fantastic incident vouched for by George Jessel, a Hollywood producer, late of the theatre, and famous now as a master of ceremonies. I quote the story as it appeared. 'He signed a 13-week TV contract. The sponsor, a new beer company, deposited all the money in advance, then went bankrupt. Although no beer was ever brewed, Jessel did the 13 telecasts. And each week he quarrelled with the ad agency about the commercials for the non-existent product. At the first show the agency wanted a longer commercial. Then, instead of "Go to your nearest grocery store and buy this beer", the agency wanted to change "Go" to "Hurry"—although there was no beer to sell. On the fifth programme the agency suggested a bargain deal, 3-for-25 cents instead of 10 cents a bottle, although there was none for sale. And for the sixth show the agency submitted a commercial offering a bonus for bottle-tops—of the beer which had never come into existence.' Now match that, for elaborate imbecility, anywhere down all the centuries you are exploring. . . .

Jazz Concert

J. B. P. TO J. H.

... After dinner on Sunday I went to the Music Hall, a new and enormous auditorium, to hear a jazz concert, the second of two given there that evening. The place seemed to be pretty well filled. All the seats across the aisle from where I was sitting were occupied by youngish coloured people, gaudily dressed; some of the young women, brilliant as parakeets, were very striking and handsome. I hoped for scenes of wild enthusiasm, youngsters dancing down the aisles, coloured folk almost drummed out of their senses; but except for an occasional yell at some climax, this might have been a symphony concert devoted to the works of Brahms. It wasn't called a concert, by the way, but *Stanley Kenton's Second Festival of Modern American Jazz*. This must have been Mr. Kenton's idea. He was equally portentous as a master of ceremonies—a tall, thin, greyish, professorial sort of man with a quiet and rather pedantic manner, about to announce, you would think, the performance of some recently discovered eighteenth-century fugues. His 'combo', as the local press called it, was very different. It had an unusually large brass section which played *fortissimo*, standing up most of the time, and nearly blowing us out of our seats. I can just understand, even though I can't much enjoy, the jazz that takes a simple tune, playing it

212

straight first, and then improvises wilder and wilder variations on it. But this band never played the tune at all—that is, assuming there ever was one. Maestro Kenton—and this suits him better than 'Stan', which is what the local paper called him—would look as if he were about to lecture on T. S. Eliot, clear his throat in a donnish way, tell us that the next number would be 'Grey Mood In The Negative' or something of the sort, and then signal to his boys to boom and blast the hell out of us. Never once did I detect two bars of melody. Yet there must have been something in that cacophonous din which pleased the audience. They didn't dance down the aisles—there was nothing any-how to dance to—but they listened in a kind of rapture and broke out into applause when the trumpets and trombones were almost smoking hot. Well out of my own depth now I had better call on the local critic to describe the rest of the concert. 'There was Candido, the bongo king (and a Kenton ex.),' he writes. 'Another Kenton graduate, Shorty Rogers, was on hand with his Giants. Good drummers abounded. For instance, with Rogers was a third Kenton ex., Shelly Manne, who seems to have now gone in for Latin explorations using one hand and a wire brush. And with Charlie Ventura's combo was drummer Sonny Igoe, who used to stam-pede Woody Herman's herd. Igoe gave a tremendous beat to tenor man Ventura's rollicking group. The Ventura unit in general had an earthly touch that con-trasted nicely with the austere Kentonians. . . .' All this, either to read about or to hear, seems to me nearly as remote and exotic as classical Chinese Drama. Is there a new art form somewhere here or is the Western

HUNT LIBRARY
CARNEGIE-MELLON UNIVERSITY

mind breaking down? I don't know. In fact, as I realised on Sunday night, I know less and less about more and more. . . .

Indian Crafts

J. H. TO J. B. P.

. . . I have been buying some odds and ends of things—an embroidered cambric shirt from Mexico, some reproductions of Indian paintings, a pair of Zuni ear-rings and even a pot or two. All of which will help to swell our luggage in the way you most dislike. I can't help it, like all other tourists I find the Santa Fé shops that sell this kind of stuff irresistible. I'd like to buy more silver and turquoise pieces if I had the dollars, and a really noble antique Pueblo jar if I didn't think you might go out of your mind at the sight of the packing-case. (I think it must be the nomadic streak in your nature which gives you such an abhorrence of baggage; it's well known that nomads never take to pottery.) There are a great many of these shops, and I believe their turnover in the summer is enormous. They range from dreadful emporiums selling bogus 'Western' things, counterfeit chased leather cowboy boots, belts and so forth, as well as Indian jewellery straight from the factory and mass-produced moccasins, to a few stocking only the finest antique Spanish and Indian specimens. In between are a number of small shops selling genuine Indian craft products, including the famous Thunderbird Shop in the plaza specialising in first-class silver and jewellery. As well as these city shops, there are a great many trading posts along the highways where they run through reservations; the Indians bring their handiwork in and very often trade

it for goods. Sometimes they pawn their own ornaments at the post—especially, I fancy, the reckless
Navaho who are much given to drink and gambling.
Most of the Santa Fé shops depend on Indians from the
reservations for their goods, but a few employ them on
the premises—the Thunderbird Shop, for instance, has
quite a large workshop at the back. (The other day
when I was in there, Miss M. who runs the shop was
speaking, fairly severely, to a very sheepish-looking
Indian—a Navaho. He was one of her craftsmen who
had just staggered in after a week's blind—the last
of many. She told me that the only way he could
stop drinking for any length of time was to go back
to his own people and be treated by their medicine
man.)

The history of these Indian crafts now enjoying such
a boom is really very interesting. One tends to think of
them as ancient, whereas in their present forms they are
quite recent. After all, there was no wool for Navaho
rugs, no silver for Navaho and Pueblo jewellery before
the Spaniards—just as there were no horses for the
Plains Indians to live in the saddles of—in the best
filmic manner. It is very odd, when one comes to think
of it, the number of supposedly dyed-in-the-wool
national specialities which are really imports—our own
tea, Irish potatoes, and a good many more. In fact the
Indian use of silver and wool isn't nearly as old as the
Spanish Conquest. Navaho rugs and blankets were
noted by the eighteenth century (they probably learnt
weaving from the Pueblos, who of course had practised
it since prehistoric times) but the earliest specimen preserved is already nineteenth century. As for metal

work, the Navaho only seem to have developed it in the infamous days of their Captivity at Fort Sumner in the 1860s, starting there with copper and brass and going on to silver after they were allowed to return home. The Pueblo learnt silver-smithing from them, but before long developed their own styles; the Zuni, living just across the border into Arizona, are by far the best Pueblo jewellers today. But this is where ancient influences come in. While the Navaho mostly imitate Spanish Mexican silver, using a lot of die stamps and chasing and not caring too much about stone inlays, the Pueblos have adapted their prehistoric skill at turquoise and shell inlay to their modern silver work. And of course it isn't only a matter of techniques, they have also adapted their own designs and something elusive in style and feeling which has always been their own. I find it rather moving to think how the Indians of Mesa Verde who made such dangerous journeys to the Turquoise Mountains and spent so much of their slow, prehistoric time on mastering inlay work—all long before the Old World had discovered the New— should have been preparing the way for their descendants to retrieve their fortunes by this trade with the 'Whites'.

Potting is rather a different matter. There is something like full continuity with prehistoric times. Yet even so, the craft had sunk to a very low ebb at the beginning of this century, and there has been an astonishing revival, together with many changes, in the last thirty years. The modern designs are less strictly geometric than most of the old ones—still, there's an evident identity of inspiration running right through.

As a matter of fact, the great potter Maria Martinez at San Ildefonso pueblo, who is now known even in New York, was started on her career by some excavators who gave her a dump of unused prehistoric potting clay they'd discovered together with some patterned sherds to copy. Now she's developed a style entirely of her own (on a glossy black ware); I don't care for it much myself, but the technical perfection is truly amazing—especially as she, like all the other present-day potters, still keeps to the primitive wheelless coiling method and fires in the roughest smother kilns. Most of the pueblos produce quite good wares today, and everyone has its own distinctive style; to my great satisfaction I've learnt to distinguish most of them. One can look out for special designs, such as a fantastic crested bird peculiar to Zia, a formalised parrot to Acoma and the Zuni rosette, but one ought to be able to recognise more general differences of feeling. How I love this uniqueness of all true creations of the human imagination! This sounds very phoney, I know, but I've felt it since I was a child—and it made me take to archæology.

What is really interesting in the present situation is the way all tourists respond to these Indian creations. I suppose it's true to say that a great many of the people living here have come to seek a life where this response to true quality instead of commercial value exists, and there's no doubt at all that as soon as tourists see it they respond too. Perhaps I ought to qualify a little, for a great mass of tourists allow themselves to be fobbed off with terrible rubbish, and haven't got beyond the souvenir mentality. Still, even they have an inkling, and there are very many who quickly understand the real thing. Hence all these shops, good ones, where I have fallen along with the rest. . . .

Politics in Houston

J. B. P. TO J. H.

. . . This morning the friend of a man I had met in Dallas called to take me to his house for lunch; an oddish but attractive chap, who had once been some sort of chapel parson and had given it up, I gathered, to start some mysterious religious enterprise, about which he didn't want to talk. We lunched under the trees in his garden —it has been a dazzling warm day—on a wonderful shrimp dish cooked indoors by his wife (small, handsome, smiling, silent), and then enormous steaks grilled outdoors by our host. Several other men there, odd types, probably colleagues in the enterprise. They all drank a lot of whisky-on-the-rocks, chiefly while we were waiting for the food, and what with that, empty stomachs, the warm sunshine, the glitter and shade under the trees, one or two of them were soon very flushed and talkative. One was aggressively Southern, as if the Civil War had only just ended, and in an angry drawl—this takes some doing but he did it—produced some astonishing ideas, half-glaring, half-squinting at us with little bloodshot eyes. He defended the duel; indeed, wanted to restore it; the only way a gentleman could protect his honour, etc., etc., waving away my objection that the best revolver shot or swordsman might soon be left with most honour. He also announced, in all seriousness, that the frequent mockery and burlesques of the old Southern chivalry were all deliberately inspired by the Communists. I reminded him that there had been plenty of fun poked at Southern chivalry, by Mark Twain and other humorists, long before Communism set up any propaganda bureaus. He was not convinced. He was the first man I had met who really talked as those newspaper correspondents I had read seemed to think. He saw Reds everywhere, Red plots in everything. He had unmasked some of them himself, he claimed. He was really a bit dotty. If the steaks had been spoilt, he might easily have blamed Moscow or Peking. As it was, he rather spoilt my otherwise excellent lunch. Not because he was quarrelsome, too loud, too violent—his manners were civil enough—but because there was something frightening in his political dottiness, his fanaticism, his montrous unreason, his refusal to question any evidence that supported his case, his permanent state of bloodshot anger. A thousand like him, all fiery with bourbon, would be ready to lynch anybody merely on suspicion. And among a lot of *Admass* people, no longer really interested in politics, merely anxious for complete security without reference to ideas, a man so passionately single-minded, so forceful and fluent, so ready to appeal to prejudice and to the violence that lurks behind the *Admass* sense of frustration, could soon stampede crowds into lunatic action. And a man with the same temperament but on a much bigger scale, with both more charm and more ambition, a platform and radio spellbinder, could soon enlist men like this to recruit for his Party; and if this leader were a showman too (for *Admass* loves a show), and knew how to entice millions out of the oil tycoons to dress the big parades and buy time on the air, God only knows what kind of a crackpot but dangerous thing could soon be let loose in these parts. Something angry and bitter in a lot of the women would respond too. Nor would I like to say how far it might spread. I don't believe in *Admass* as a bulwark of political democracy. Such democratic demands as it has can be paid off in cultural democracy.

Los Alamos

·

J. H. TO J. B. P.

. . . I have been to Los Alamos, cradle of the first atomic bomb. Unfortunately it wasn't nearly so horrible as I'd expected—nor, on the other hand, nearly so fine as it might be. It's only about thirty-five miles from Santa Fé, and I was driven out by the nice New England poet and his wife, who were both quite as suspicious of the place as I could be. For most of the way the road is the same one I followed going to the Bandalier Monument, for the prehistoric and atomic towns are near neighbours up in the foothills of the Jemez mountains; as we passed the colossal dark drum of the Black Mesa I wished Los Alamos had been built on its summit, then we'd have the devil's stronghold without disguise. Far healthier, I'm inclined to think, than dressing the place up in an outer garment of sweetness and light, all pastel shades and golfing greens. It makes me think of *The Loved One* and calling the undertaker's a Home of Rest. No doubt about my prejudiced mind, you'll notice.

We'd armed ourselves with the necessary visitors' passes and weren't long delayed at the guard post which admits one through the outer barbed wire fence. It's only fair (my prejudice has limits) to note at this point that there has been a move to make the residential quarters into an open town, but there's opposition to it even among the inhabitants—some of whom like to feel they live in a place that puts barbed wire and

223

holstered guards between them and possible undesirables. So Los Alamos remains uniquely exclusive. Nowadays employees can, if they like, live outside, and a good many do in fact commute from Espanola and other near-by towns. So 'The Hill' is very unlike the hidden eyrie of war-time, when it was a mystery only to be addressed as P.O. Box 1663.

I'd been told that the peculiar horror of the town (there are about 15,000 inhabitants of whom some 3,000 are employees of the Laboratory) was that everyone had to live in houses automatically assigned to them according to their salary and status; also that in everything there was rigid control by the Atomic Energy Commission. All this was very smoothly denied by their chief administrative officer when he received us in his office and gave us a propaganda talk. He spoke of the Town Council of freely elected citizens, the fact that the town was now self-supporting so far as running expenses were concerned, and in general suggested that Los Alamos was very nearly an ordinary American town except that the AEC having invested a fortune there was bound to keep a paternal eye upon it. He did admit, however, that like every other place, they had some chronically non-co-operative neurotics who didn't always appreciate what was done for them.

Soon afterwards we met a scientist's wife who was, I suspect, one of these nonconformists. She declared the very administrative officer who had been haranguing us on the freedom of the town was its petty tyrant, that she couldn't paint her door a different colour or add a veranda without going to him cap-in-hand and very likely being refused. The greatest hardship of all was that although the strict house-by-grade system was slightly mitigated by allowances for seniority and also a modicum of free choice as to type and position, the number of rooms allowed was in a cast-iron ratio with the number of family. No wonder, she said, that 'grandmothering' had become a regular practice—a device by which an elderly parent lived with the couple just long enough to qualify them for an extra room. I suppose the truth is somewhere between the two viewpoints; it is very easy to conform and some of the restrictions may be good from the point of view of amenity. Yet the tyranny is there however benignly paternal, and is enough to make some spirits feel they live in a vast institution.

The personnel officer drove us round the town, and on the whole it is very pleasant-looking—and of course wonderfully hygienic. To begin with the natural setting is marvellous; one is up among the Jemez pine forests, the various residential areas are on mesas divided by dramatic, tree-filled canyons, and there are noble views across the desert to the Sangre de Christos. Also there are no advertisements—you can't imagine what a rest that is to the eye and mind. Schools, hospitals, library, auditorium and so forth all splendid and of course correctly sited; the little shopping centre quite decent though none of the shops had the slightest distinction —as might have been hoped for in a town run for men of science. The houses, I think, are where the chance has been missed. There is quite a wide range from blocks of dormitory rooms and 'Efficiency Apartments' up to four-bedroomed houses, but on the whole they're monotonous and impersonal. Most of the better detached houses are flat-roofed bungalows painted various pastel shades; not at all bad, but one would like to see some real urban architecture in place of rows and rows of 'units'. I found that one wife hated her house, and I didn't blame her, for apart from the fact that she felt their life demanded another room, the whole place had a flimsy impermanent look inside which must have given her the feeling of perpetual camping.—Oh, one thing amused me very much. Although the proper houses (as apart from the war-time shanties, which are mostly down by now) have only been going up since 1945, there is already a feeling for the good old times in building—with reason, too, for of recent years there have been economies which have resulted in further skimping.

I made our guide drive us along the edge of what are called the 'Tech Areas'; still higher barbed wire fences and a shapeless crowd of laboratory buildings. Of course no visitor is allowed in, and the staff themselves have to produce passes at every turn. I suppose the University of California, who manage the place under contract for the AEC, try to keep the atmosphere in the 'lab' as liberal as possible. But how can they succeed? As the brochure says their 'primary responsibility is the development of new and better military applications of atomic energy'. I respond to the word *better*.

After the visit I find myself wondering about two things. The first is, do all, no, a great many, of the people who live in this city, which has a destructive purpose at its very heart, suffer from it, feeling guilty, corrupted, or at least uneasy? Hiroshima and Nagasaki came directly out of these lovely mesas. The second thing is this. Setting aside all questions of the Laboratory and its purposes, does Los Alamos represent more or less what socialism would achieve if it had its head, plenty of money and a clean slate? I can't help fearing it may: the be-done-good-to-or-else paternalism, the standardisation and model planning, the virtuousness of everything that leads only to the ghastly feeling of being institutionalised for life. . . .

Tribe and
Mass
·
J. H. TO J. B. P.

. . . From our two points of vantage you and I are able to see how one of the largest wheels in history has turned full circle. Not quite this, though, for the cycle hasn't come back to the same place—but I'll explain what I mean and you must let me know whether you agree. The Pueblo Indians here represent the survival, astonishingly little corrupted, of a traditional and tribal society —more or less of the kind that we can assume to have been prevalent throughout the Old World in the early stages of agriculture. It is a stage before the individual has emerged into full independence; he is still merged in the tribal society—not from either conscious choice or weakness, but because that is the state into which he is born. Life has not gone beyond that. It would be an obvious exaggeration to say that his thoughts and actions conform with those of his fellows and his ancestors as one bird conforms to a wheeling flock— but it points in the right direction.

You, on the other hand, are commanding a particularly good view of modern man returning to a point where the individual gladly allows himself to be swamped, where he is happiest living exactly like his fellows and accepting their judgments. In this society just as among the Pueblos, the exceptional, difficult individual is looked at with disapproval and must generally submit to being rubbed smooth, pulled down

—or thrown out. But of course there are enormous differences between the two societies, caused mainly, I think, by the hundred-times increase in the number of human beings. This increase has meant that the vast new society is bound together not from within by personal knowledge and spreading talk but from without by mass communications. These different forms of cohesion produce two very different kinds of conformity. I distinguish them in my own mind by comparing one to a plant, organic, indivisible, the other to a crystal, held together by mysterious magnetic forces but composed of countless separate and identical particles—the lonely crowd. There is another essential difference: the primitive is not only merged in his tribe but also in nature, being linked by a thousand hallowed traditions with a numinous natural world. The modern is completely cut off from that world and his thoughts and actions are swayed not by its natural rhythms but by moods and fashion surging to and fro through the human mind, starting one seldom knows where and often ending in great breakers of irrationality utterly remote from their starting point.

In short, are we watching society turning from a point where the individual hasn't yet tried to one where he has failed? It seems to me that if the intermediate stage, the individual humanism which we still try to serve, is to control the next revolution of the wheel we have got to see that the acceptance of the irrational is a part of reason—which is to say that reason must honour what is still beyond its grasp. These Indians live by an intuitive psychological wisdom which we have lost. We, with all the handicaps of our greater consciousness, have got to try to incorporate psychic factors fully and generously into the life of the mind—hitherto much too narrowly defined by Western man. Or is this idle talk ... is the swing of *Admass* on the wheel too strong for any check?

16

The Shalako,
November 27th
1954
Now we have arrived, it is hellish. Surely nothing is more hellish than dust, cutting, choking, all-permeating dust? I thought nothing could be worse than the hotel car-park at Gallup where I had to grope between motors blinded and stung; but it is worse here at Zuni. Long tongues lift up from the dry roads and alleys, then loosen into grey clouds twenty feet high; those dark holes with flames licking out looking like little mouths of hell must be ovens, the plump, comely ovens I usually love so well. This is going to be a most horrible night, perhaps unendurable. So many cars everywhere, too, wheeling round, backing, trying to find parking places, dashing through the village; all of them raising more dust, themselves grey with it. Navaho in most of them, but a few native Zuni and a few whites. So this is the great day of the Shalako, the wonderful, unspoiled Shalako ceremony.

Round on the south side of the river it is quieter but more bleak. There are a few houses here, then a bare rough field leading down to the river with the main part of the village climbing up a low hill beyond. It is a large, squalid-looking village, mostly loose masonry in place of the trim adobe of the Rio Grande pueblos. And there seem to be a number of alien buildings sticking up among the low Indian houses. Chapels, schools? The whole cheerless scene half hidden by dust. What—those queer-looking figures fumbling about down by the river are the Katchinas, the gods themselves just arrived from White Rock? This is the worst of all; they look like nothing but a miserable huddle of little men fighting against the dust. Now some women (shielding their faces against the dust clouds) say I mustn't go across the field to approach them. It is for Indians only; it is where the sacred races will be held the next morning. Well and good, the Katchinas don't look worth following anyway.

The sun is dropping fast now, but even the sun looks grey and weary in this miasma. Could it be that with sunset the wind might drop and the dust with it? It is a hope, perhaps even now it is a little better; anyway, as we're here, we'd better park the car with the rest and go to see what we can of the Katchinas and their prayer-stick planting. At the foot of the main village a crowd has gathered; I can hear a hollow rattling—and now something really a little eerie, a call like a coyote's. The Katchinas are in there at the heart of the crowd where I can see patches of whiteness and bright colours. Again the coyote call. Now I'm caught up well to the front of the crowd as it moves off along a narrow alley; I believe the gods are only a few yards ahead of me. Now the congestion is eased for we've reached a square enclosed by houses—but quite small, not like a plaza. Small and intimate. Crowds of Zunis standing on the roofs, and relatively few of us here in the square finding places round the walls. We settle down like leaves after a gust—I on a projecting step.

The Katchinas! I have been wrong; they are superb and have a look quite superhuman. There are six of these figures, but only four are dancing; the other two, holding bound switches of yucca leaves, walk or skip about the square. The dance itself centres on a little hole dug in the earth of the square and with a stone slab lining one side of it; I think already painted and befeathered prayer-sticks have been dropped in the hole, and the dance is to bless them before they are buried. Again and again the two pairs of masked gods approach the prayer-hole, facing one another in line, raising their feet, holding them there for an instant, then bringing them down in unison; hardly a stamp, but a powerful, heavy planting of the foot. I am very much aware of the supple leather meeting with the dusty, trodden earth, yet the massive white bodies, the great masked heads, are little moved by the heavy stepping, remaining all but still above it. Each downward drive of the feet is marked by a clank of bones. Now again as they reach the hole, that weird cry I heard before; *Hu tu tu* I know it is written, but to my ear it sounds like a ghost coyote in the hollow of a moonlit night. The dancers wheel away, then renew the approach; something is being softly driven home, softly but powerfully reiterated to the earth by the moccasined feet.

This won't do. The general impression is all very well, but I need the particular. After all I am a Westerner, a conscience-blighted Westerner, and as such must observe. Clearly these six impersonations of divinity are in two pairs. The wandering, errant pair, hovering ready to whip us all if anything goes wrong with the rites and bad luck has to be driven out; they must be the Sal'imobiya or War Brothers. They have dome-shaped masks set in a colossal black ruff of raven feathers through which project cylindrical beaks; one of the masks is yellow for the north, the other blue for the south; below the raven ruff, bare torsos are painted to match the masks and crossed by ornamental bandoliers; the white skirts have patterned borders, one with a butterfly design, one with a Zuni rosette. The War Brothers hold a pointed yucca switch in each hand, and in one hand carry also a bundle of dry shoulder bones. Probably deers' scapulae. In spite of the ruff, these bird-headed figures look slender, agile, but the two dancing pairs are heavy, and soft like their steps. The outermost pair have cylindrical masks, white, with circular black eyes and mouth; across the flat top of each lies a wand, feather tufted at both ends, and at the base they rest on a neat black and white roll—a close-trimmed boa of feathers. These two Katchinas wear necklaces, bandoliers, full white kilts, and they carry scapula bundles (painted black and white) as well as antlers. I am told that the feathered wands poised on their heads symbolise the trees under which the deer are found; these are Yamuhakto divinities and concerned with hunting. It is the leading pair who give the dance its weight, its power, its majesty. Long Horn (Sayatasha) and his 'son' Hututu. Both are huge, white, and soft—yet with great force in them. Their softness makes me think of the pussmoth; but, no, they are more like barn

234

owls, or the great snowy owl, with its deep, white plumage and implacable eyes.

Long Horn and Hututu are both wearing white shirts of coarse, handwoven cotton, with full wing-like sleeves, white buckskin kilts and leggings; round their waists two of the finest of those white and bro-caded rain sashes which the Zuni weave so well. Both masks are dead white, eyes and mouths appearing as straight black lines—no more than this, yet they have a strange intensity of expression; the lower edge is finished with black and white feather rolls like those of the Yamuhakto. Hututu's mask extends sideways into two immense ears, yet they don't look so much like ears as a widening of the face, adding to it an extra suggestion of calmness and weight. Long Horn has one similar ear, but from the right side of the mask face there projects his huge single horn, turquoise coloured and curving upwards to a point. Both these divinities carry black and white shoulder-blade bundles in one hand, feathers (probably prayer-sticks) and bows in the other.

Now the four Katchinas are approaching the prayer-hole again; down and down and down tread their feet, deftly, softly, powerfully; at each tread a jerk of the wrists makes the scapulae clap together. Hututu and Long Horn are face to face over the hole. Two inscru-table countenances confronted; two figures of white, black and turquoise. The cry again, but this time more guttural and fierce; probably this is the last movement. Is it really only Hututu who cries? The weird note seems to come from all sides, I suppose because it curves round and round inside the thin wooden cylinder of the mask. I think they are dropping more prayer-sticks and sprinkling meal. Yes, it is over, the six Katchinas are in line and making for a lane leading from the upper corner of the square. Two young Zunis, legs seeming very long and slender beneath black, cloak-like blankets, step forward to throw earth back into the hole and tread it down. I think they must be priests, perhaps priests of one of the minor orders. As I move forward with the small crowd (Indians are springing away over the roofs) I take care to pass the sealed prayer-hole. Among the white scatter of corn-meal I can see blue specks; stooping, I see they are tiny chips of turquoise.

That was really a wonderful scene—I was caught up in it, far more than by the dance at Santo Domingo. I hardly ever thought of them as men, only when I made an intellectual effort; the rest of the time, willynilly, I saw them simply as Katchinas and was caught up in their divine purpose. Yes, it was wonderful. But, good heavens, half an hour ago I was full of disgust and desperation! I look up. The little square is roofed with a clear, pale evening sky; it looks ringing-hard, like a porcelain dish. No more wind, no more dust. During that ritual the horror passed without my noticing it.

The gods have several more consecrations to make; altogether they visit six prayer-holes covering the whole anatomy of the village. Each year these shrines are in the same spots and have nothing to do with the blessing of the new houses. That is one of the chief acts in this religious drama, but it will come later. I follow the crowd, but now rather carelessly, looking at one detail or another, or half closing my eyes and listening. Here, unexpectedly, is something I've missed at the other shrines. A line of Zunis, men and women of all ages, is waiting for the procession of gods on their route to the next prayer-hole. They are motionless, frozen with intent. Now as the Katchinas pass them they are raising their arms. I can see little white clouds —they are sprinkling corn-meal on to the masked figures. Closer now, I can see one girl alight with serious faith, reaching to dust her meal among the raven feathers of the War Brother for the North. How familiar it is, the feeling of these Indians! I have known it often in southern Europe; in Sicily on Palm Sunday. The faithful waiting for the passage of *mana*, reverencing it, contributing to it with muttered prayers, with corn-meal. These men and women are probably house-holders from the neighbourhood of the shrine, come to honour and strengthen the Katchinas before their dance of consecration.

This is the gods' chosen house; the house where they will be entertained during the night ahead. Soon their procession will make its way here from the sixth and last prayer-hole. Two solidly handsome Navaho women are sitting near the front steps, one in a flowing crimson dress, the other in a brilliant green one, and both with bright blankets over their heads. The full, flounced and gathered skirts fall round them with a fine amplitude. Navaho women were led (or forced, I don't know how it came about) to adopt these dresses during the time of the punitive detention of their tribe at Fort Sumner. At the time the tight bodices and voluminous skirts represented everything that was most tamingly puritanical. Now rendered in proud colours and worn

237

by these women, free nomads once more, they suggest the great Cretan love goddess rather than the Daughters of the Revolution. Among other Navahos hanging about the house there are some American visitors, mostly anthropologists, I think, or people concerned with the work of the Indian Association. They have a bulky look: huge furry boots, fur coats, duffle coats, windcheaters, knotted scarves, gauntlets, fur-lined caps, earpads, all the rather over-elaborate dressing up whites like to do when going a little off the beaten track. Interesting to compare the curiosity and interest in these western faces with the faithful look of the corn-sprinklers. A fluffy puppy is lying under the lowest step of the gods' house and now two rather draggled-looking ducks have appeared from somewhere and are waddling across the path. This may be Shalako night, but here is a village still full of all kinds of ordinary life.

The procession is advancing up the slope towards us, drawing its train of followers along alleyways and roof. If a higher being were examining this village through a microscope, what physical force would he suppose to be drawing these little creatures here and there over the crowded cells of their colony, making them swarm over and round these concretions of mud and stone? There is a crowd now all round me and I get only glimpses of the gods. They have stopped at the steps to plant prayer-sticks behind the threshold. The puppy is still there; I wonder what impression he gets of the masked beings who are roofing him over? Now they seem to be entering; I think they will walk up the path of corn-meal which leads (as I saw through the window)

from the door to the small altar set out on the floor at
the end of the room, and put seeds and other gifts into
the bowls and baskets ranged before it. Yes, but there
is Long Horn outside once more passing round to the
flank of the house. He's emerging above the crowd,
now; I can see his white and black countenance above
the massed brown faces below. He's mounting slowly,
step by step, up a ladder; he's on the roof; colour shed in
the alley, he's become a monumental silhouette, the
massive head, the great horn lording it against the
evening sky. But he has to bend in a humble and mortal
posture to climb down through the trap-door. Once
inside, I believe he will be placing prayer-sticks in a
shrine attached to the ceiling. Long Horn's house-
blessing is one of the few texts I know:

> *Then my father's rain-filled room*
> *I rooted at the north*
> *I rooted at the west*
> *I rooted at the south*
> *I rooted at the east*
> *I rooted above*
> *Then in the middle of my father's roof,*
> *With two plumed wands joined together,*
> *I consecrated his roof.*
> *This is well;*
> *In order that my father's offspring may increase*
> *I consecrated the centre of his roof*
> *Then also the centre of my father's floor;*
> *With seeds of all kinds*
> *I consecrated the centre of his floor.*
> *This is well.*

239

In order that my father's fourth room
May be bursting with corn,
That even in his doorway
The shelled corn may be scattered before the door,
The beans may be scattered before the door,
That his house may be filled with little boys,
And little girls,
And people grown to maturity;
That in his house
Children may jostle one another in the doorway,
In order that it may be thus,
I have consecrated the rain-filled room
Of my daylight father,
My daylight mother.

Most of the Zunis seem either to have gone into the gods' house or left this corner, but a few of us whites and a number of Navaho are hanging about outside, or trying to peer in through door and windows. It is not a nice spectacle, though the two Navaho women are still sitting there, lending us a little dignity. All the same, I'm going to edge up to this side window myself; I'm always just as bad as everyone else, I notice, only a little slower in making up my mind to it. I can hear a droning of voices through the glass. Along one side of the room two lines of Indians are sitting on benches facing one another and smoking. But those with their backs to the wall are the gods with their masks removed. Both lines, in alternation so far as I can judge, are reciting in a humming monotone. Evidently this is the litany I have heard of, when the householder hosts question the gods about their past history, their present

240

journey and its purposes; it has to be word perfect, and I'm warned it goes on for hours. Here is logos, the power of the word. I marvel how they can memorise so many thousands of lines. The Katchina impersonators are chosen only for the one year, yet they have learnt their litany; English parsons, I've noticed, always have to read marriage and funeral services: the one seems to me as surprising as the other. At the innermost end of the bench I can see a solitary figure, smallish, and taking no part in the litany. I'll work along to the next window for a closer view. It is a boy, blackened all over, then spotted with brilliant colours. Tipped on the back of his head is something that looks like a large and deep bowler hat, also brilliantly spotted. Who is he?—I ask. Pityingly, the anthropologist tells me it is Shulawitsi, the little Fire God. He crossed the river with his lighted torch ahead of the rest of the Katchinas, so I missed him. Probably at that time, masked and inspired, he showed his divinity, but now the face is that of a weary boy, and his toes turn in pathetically below the bench.

Someone is speaking loudly behind me. More than speaking, making a speech. It is a very small and unusually sallow Indian. He is talking eloquently and there is an appealing look in his yellow, wrinkled face. But he speaks in Zuni. How uneasy we all look, sheepish before his unintelligible oratory! Now an American is going to say something; he has a crew-cut and a very earnest Teutonic face; he is nearly twice as tall as the little Zuni. He translates; the Zuni has told us that he and his people would be glad if we would go away. This part of the ceremony is holy and secret. After the

Shalako have come then it will be quite different, then they will be glad to see us for the Shalako dances are for everyone. A visit to the café and trading post near the track into the village seems the best way to restore both warmth and self-respect.

From cold, clear evening light into warmth and shadows. The trading post is high and dimly lit, and full of things and people. Not at all like a city store, though, for here goods are not being displayed, made enticing, they are simply for sale (or exchange) and so must be laid, stood or hung somewhere. Extraordinary numbers of things seem to be hung; the high dim spaces are heavy with hanging curtains of dresses, of linen trousers, of ropes and spades. It is unlike a store, too, because most of the people in here with me are Navaho, and most are here for social and not commercial purposes. Those few who have trade in view are probably quite as keen to sell as to buy. They want to barter.

It is a twilit world, full of dark faces and black, glinting eyes. Yet there is a strong, homely smell of miscellaneous goods. The Navaho men are nearly all wearing jeans fitting tightly to their fine slender legs, and large sombreros with brims curling up at each side. They must spend hours making them so fantastically curly. It is one sign of their dashing ways, their individuality. Remarkable that these nomads should remain so utterly unlike the Pueblos after being their neighbours (even if wandering and hostile neighbours) for so many centuries. They were the last tribe to keep up raiding and fighting. Hence the Fort Sumner captivity. This lot have come in from their lonely hogans, the little round wooden huts with a corral or two for horses, which we saw widely scattered in the pine scrub and desert round Zuni. Or some perhaps from further off, from the main Navaho Reservation. So of course there are meetings and greetings; the Shalako is a great social occasion which their tribe has attended beyond memory. A tall Navaho woman is approaching the grocery counter where the manager is serving; she has a little girl following behind her with a big bundle of sheep-skins. The woman looks indifferent, even a little haughty, but the child shows her eagerness and anxiety. Perhaps she has been promised some much desired thing if they get a good bargain. The short arms reaching round wool and hide, the small brown face with eager eyes beneath the black fringe—a high electric bulb above the manager's head lights her wordless appeal. They say the traders are good to their Indian customers, and I hope this one will be. All three disappear somewhere behind the counter.

Their going makes me notice something; there is a passage leading to a far room where the lighting is much brighter. Yes, it is an altogether different kind of shop, but still a very attractive one. It is well-lit and relatively empty with a settee and comfortable chairs for customers. All round are show-cases displaying Indian craftwork, the great bulk of it fine Zuni jewellery. One case contains nothing but magnificent turquoise and silver necklaces. Very expensive these, but the workmanship is exquisite and the designs good. On wall shelves are some antiques (the manager's private collection) including little carved stone animal fetishes. The Zuni have always been noted for these, that is why I'm turning over a basket of modern ones. I pick out a frog, cut in a deep blue copper mineral of some kind. It is essential frog, much the best piece in the basket and I shall buy it. As if by magic the carver is produced— a little man rather like the Zuni who had asked us to leave the gods in peace. But this one speaks fair American. I ask him how long it took to make the frog, and he shoots back 'An hour'. He notices my disappointment. His voice and manner change. 'But what did you want to know for?' he asks, seeing he has said the wrong thing. We stare at one another, he realising I had wanted him to say it had taken days to carve the frog, I realising that in saying an hour he had lied in a wish to suggest skill and prowess. Slowly, we both grin. This is the closest contact I have made with an Indian.

What a transformation! When I step outside once more, Zuni is radiantly lovely. The west and south are still burning with the afterglow, and against it, copper-coloured sunset clouds are winging their way towards me like a line of delicately feathered egrets. The flat top of the sacred Corn Mountain is jet-black against the horizon. Higher up, the glow gives way to a faint, ethereal green, and there above the pueblo hangs a crescent moon, the old moon a pearly bubble within its arms. Even the village itself is transformed. Its flat roofs climb the hill in sharp black steps; chimney-pots send up their fountains of sparks and now the delicious smell of pinyon smoke defeats the reek of automobiles. If only the Zuni would ban cars on Shalako night. Wandering through the lanes I think how even more enchanting and mysterious it must have been only a decade or two ago when the Navaho came not in trucks and automobiles but on horseback or by wagonette. (One still sees these narrow, painted carts on the Reservation, but there is none in Zuni tonight.) Then it must have been wonderfully hushed and dark. Tethered by the corrals, horses would have stamped, snorted and shaken their ears, but it would have been very still, with occasional groups of priests slipping through the lanes, and the secret migrations of Katchinas.

I pause for a moment in the little square where I saw the dance of the gods; the small curtained windows show some light, but far less brilliant than that of the young hanging moon. Then I slip down to join the crowd waiting for the coming of the Shalako. I find a place commanding a clear view down the rough little lane leading up from the sacred bridge. There aren't too many people, but Navaho will keep driving their trucks to and fro in front of us. Down there towards the river it is quite dark; I can see nothing beyond the rough wooden bars of the corrals at the top of the lane. We wait and wait. Evidently I have come much too early, but I like the atmosphere of expectation and soft talk. In front of me a Navaho family has just recognised some Americans they had known years ago; a whispered conversation about babies and children goes on between them. More and more members of the family saunter up and are introduced. The moon is dropping fast into the west. I make up my mind that the Shalako will come with moonset. Down, down it slides; with steady concentration I can see it move. Now it is caught up in the branches of a tree. I believe I am right. There are sounds coming from the darkness down there. Strange noises—a slightly resonant tapping or clapping. Then, owl cries. Also I can distinguish some pale shapes, seemingly faintly luminous against the black gulf beyond. More owl cries; they flit about like the light of a Will o' the Wisp. The moon is half buried in the desert, its one curving arm recalls Sayatasha's horn, transmuted from turquoise to pale copper. It dwindles to a point of light; is gone. Nothing happens. My fancy was only my fancy. Still, there is something magic now in this silent wait. The calling and tapping become more insistent and the pale shapes are taller; above each tall white column there appears to float a white arc or fan. Chanting, sudden as a skirl of bagpipes. The Shalako are coming at last. Up the slope towards us out of the pool of darkness come six gigantic figures, twelve feet high and eagle-feather crowned. The tapping has come from their beaks, which now sound rhythmically with the chanting; each Shalako is attended by a man dressed in black tunic and white cap with bells jingling on his legs. That is all I can see. They are reared right above me now, the white giants with the clapping beaks; the little crowd is swinging out of their way as four of them climb towards the heart of the village and the other pair turn parallel to the river. The Shalako keep up a little tripping step which makes them appear to skim the ground. Black-cloaked priests hover round them, and the chanters, following in a group, have also the air of priests. The stir of this passing has been tremendous and we all feel lost, unfocused. I follow in the wake of the riverside Shalako, follow weakly, seeing the high feathered heads swaying above the house-tops in front of me. They are turning left to cross the modern bridge, heading for the one Shalako house which this year is south of the river. I cross the bridge, then stand leaning against its last rails where I can watch the knot of Indians gathered round the door, hemming in the giant masks. There is much coming and going of the men in white caps and the priests, and I can see women moving to receive them inside the house. This is one of the new or refurbished houses which is to be blessed this Shalako night, and doubtless the women are its owners. I go down and push boldly through the door; the light at first is quite blinding; by good luck the young man who is in charge of this room leads me to a seat at the inner end. The Zunis certainly don't fear the influence of electric light. Powerful naked bulbs hang from the roof. I would have preferred it when there were only lanterns or (before that) firelight. Still, the colours are certainly terrific. The walls of this forty foot long room are completely hidden by gaudy blankets, woven Zuni sashes and other brilliantly coloured cloths. From half way along the side walls two stags' heads stare across at one another; they are mounted and glass-eyed in quite the baronial style, but round their furry necks hang row after row of turquoise necklaces. I am lucky to have got this seat, for at the end of the room round the door there is quite a huddle of Americans, squeezing themselves discreetly into corners; also some Navaho men. Several rows of women, both Navaho and Zuni, are sitting on stools and benches in the body of the room. They look extraordinarily blank and placid. Across the room from me I can see the feathers on the Shalako masks peeping out from behind priests' blankets hung as a curtain at the end of the room. In front of it another litany is evidently beginning—but a litany I am allowed to witness? Four of the page-like young men are taking part, questioned by male members of the household. Now I realise that these men are the Shalako Impersonators and their Assistants. I shall consider them all as Impersonators, for I can't distinguish between them. In their black satin tunics, shapely white leather caps worn above a red circlet stitched with silver discs they really do look exactly like a Hollywood designer's idea of a medieval page. Ribbons, too, hung round the neck. The costume seems to me entirely un-Indian. Surely there is some Spanish influence here? One of the Impersonators is marvellously good-looking. Quite the most handsome Pueblo I've seen. Tall, with a slightly aquiline nose instead of the usual flattish one; large eyes with thick eyelashes, and a wonderful glowing red-brown complexion—he really is a redskin. Most of the time the Impersonators sit with their heads held a little back and their eyes closed. To and fro between them the litany drones on. Curious how religious incantations sound so much alike whatever the faith and the words. Near at hand in my corner of the room is a drum; not the painted wooden kind they make at the Cochiti pueblo, but simply a skin tied rather loosely over the neck of a large pot. There are seats round it—presumably the place for the dance band. Then beyond it at the centre back of the room, but still only about two yards from me, is the house altar, made of thin painted wood. At the back, a sort of reredos, is bright with Zuni designs and in front of it stand four conventionalised human figures, the front pair painted with the well-known coyote image which shows the heart and life-breath line on the outside of the body. Before it are the special ceremonial bowls full of seeds, a pile of meal, feathered corncobs standing like candles, and a line of meal (now disturbed by all our comings and goings) leading to the door; above the altar, swinging gently in the hot air like a mobile, hangs a wooden cross with a bird above it, very much in the form of a wind-vane, and representing, I suppose, the four cardinal points of which the Pueblos are so conscious (though often adding nadir and zenith). How right it seems that a people knowing only their own place should still always live with this awareness of the whole world stretching out round them. . . .

What is this hard curving thing suspended just above my face? A steering wheel. Heavens, what time is it? I turn on the car lights. One in the morning. What was meant for a nap has lasted four hours. That soup and whisky were too effective. The dancing will have been going on since midnight. I take another peg of whisky, uncramp myself and set out across the river once more. I shall be faithful to my chosen Shalako house though there are several others in the village. No chance of getting back into the dancing room this time, but there is an annex at the side, with wide glass windows looking into the main room—it seems a very odd plan, and I can't imagine what its use is in domestic life. Now it is just what is wanted, offering a fine commanding view of the dancing: rings of seats are drawn up round the windows and they are occupied by women and children of the household, all well dressed and loaded with silver and turquoise. Here at the back the Navaho already show some signs of having drunk more spirit than I have. I can see tantalising fragments of masked figures through the windows and above the rows of glossy black heads. There is a door between the windows where the same major-domo who showed me to my seat before is controlling exits and entrances. I must bide my time; slowly percolate. I percolate, and at last, when two young American students who have been standing behind the major-domo decide they have had enough I take their place and find myself with a clear view and no more than two steps from the dancing space which is a narrow strip along this near side of the room. What a spectacle! Against the background of brilliant hangings and equally brilliantly dressed Indians packing every inch beyond the dancing strip, the two Shalako are sweeping up and down the length of the room, their feathered crests almost brushing the rafters twelve feet above the floor. And capering round them the strangest-looking monsters imaginable. At last I am looking at the Koyemshi, the Mudheads, the famous Zuni clowns. The Shalako all grace and grandeur, the Koyemshi ugly, clumsy, just emerged from the earth; the Shalako, those slender white giants sweeping to and fro, seem like beings from a loftier world, the half-naked clay-plastered Koyemshi might belong to a lower one; the Shalako are all lordliness, the Koyemshi the very spirit of mockery. Yet both are divine, the Koyemshi perhaps even more potently than the Shalako.

In the far corner the band is now hard at it; seven or eight men, rather old men for the most part, are chanting, beating the rhythm with rattles and the pot-drum— played with a ring-headed drumstick. They are members of the Curing Society in attendance on this house.

They smoke, drink Coke and go out from time to time to relieve themselves, but they will keep up the chant and the drumming all night long without slackening; always ready to achieve a climax when the dance demands it. They fill the crowded room with sound and rhythm—chant, beat, colour, movement—the charge is terrific, yet still the Zunis keep the true Pueblo moderation. There is no savage abandon, no Dionysiac ecstasy. The nearest approach to it is shown by the Shalako Impersonators who, when they are not impersonating, dance before the Shalako with a wrapt expression, a yucca-leaf sceptre grasped in either hand, sweating profusely as hour after hour they keep up their high-stepping tread.

Even in this glare, robbed of the mystery of flickering light and shadow which should have been theirs, the Shalako have a weird beauty. Behind the fans of twenty-four black and white eagle feathers spout circular plumes of red parrot feathers. The top of the masks are crowned with black buffalo fur, from which a pair of small turquoise-painted horns curl upwards; the faces are white, the eyes small but prominent, on one the black pupils look straight forward, on the other they are looking down; the long beaks are turquoise above, black below, and, when opened to clap the rhythm or tweak a clown, show a scarlet lining. Full raven-feather ruffs separate these horned bird faces from the tall conical bodies which are clad in turquoise blue collars and white handwoven cotton shirts falling over immensely full conical skirts. The skirts are bright with woven tapestry designs; on one of them the patterns represent storm clouds and rain, on the other golden

251

rayed sunflowers. Down the back of each gigantic figure falls a yard or more of human hair with a cotton thread down the centre supporting a line of four exquisitely fluffy white feathers—cloud symbols shown against the falling rain of hair. As the whole towering cone of the body is rigid, when the Shalako makes one of its gliding runs down the room, it leans slightly forward with a curiously graceful effect reminding me of a swan when it surges forward over the water.

The costume of the Koyemshi has genius. I judge them the finest clown figures in the world. To begin with, the men chosen (and it is a high honour) are often thickset; one of this pair is even corpulent, though muscular. Their bodies are smoothly covered with ruddy desert clay from the sacred lake beyond the Corn Mountains; so too are their masks. These are round, giving a bullet-headed effect, with four knobs projecting comically from sides, back and top; in addition one of these Mudheads has tiny feathered horns. The faces are of something elemental, idiotic almost, yet magnificently grotesque. The features are raised from the face as though made of fat rolls of clay; the eyes are shown as rings, the nose is a blob, the mouths vary, some being oval as though yawning, some drawn out sideways in a fearful thick-lipped grin, some with the immense upper lip of ape or idiot. The whole, body and limbs, the head and all its features, are of the same ruddled complexion, and the clothing consists of no more than a black cotton loin cloth or a black tunic left open on one shoulder. All, however, wear the entire skin of a deer slung round them, the body making a vast pouch, but the head stuffed in a lifelike fashion, with huge, pathetic ears just dragging on the floor. The Koyemshi in action never stands upright but moves from one grotesquely angular pose to another, knees and elbows bent, head sideways or waggling.

So, within a yard of my eyes the Shalako dance with their Impersonators or come sweeping down to sport with the clowns. I can see the coarse clay limbs dodging between the great white tapestry skirts; as the Koyemshi mock the giant Katchinas, then kneel and grovel before them begging for mercy with a caricature of fear and abasement. To the rhythm of the band the Shalako stoop and snap at them; when the fun grows most furious and the crowd laughs in great bursts they may even seize a knob on the Koyemshi's head in their scarlet-lined bills. Then at last, leaving the clowns rolling abjectly or on their knees, they will sail away, fleeting up and down the room seeming almost to take wing in contrast with the grovelling red bodies on the floor beneath them.

Hour after hour I watch, riding time lightly on the rhythm of chant and dance. In the glaring light, the faces before me tend to turn into patterns made up of women's faces framed in blankets and men's bound with coloured head cloths. One woman stands out from the rest; she is large and wears a shiny silk dress under her blanket; she is nursing a huge brown baby horribly clothed in Western baby things, even down to white patent-leather bootees. The baby stares at the dance as though hypnotised, but every now and then the woman pulls a breast through the neck of her shiny dress and suckles it—I am sure abundantly. As the small hours pass, some of the little girls and boys who have been watching spellbound through the windows beside me creep off to bed. Generally the crowd is quietly intent, solemn, but breaking into laughter at the height of the clown play. Occasionally a Koyemshi will go up to a woman and make fun of her, gibbering and gesticulating in her face; his victim, evidently, has to take no notice, not a smile nor a protest. To touch a Mudhead may cause sexual madness. Tonight I have only heard them uttering grunts or short guttural cries, but I know that at other times—when they go from house to house and during the later days of the Shalako festival—they pour out bawdy jokes and personal abuse. There is one moment when after much of this bawdry the woman householder throws her slops over the Mudhead who laughs with delight. I do not understand what the Koyemshi are. I have been told they are the first ancestors, that they are fertility gods or representatives of the animal in man. Certainly they are full of power and are divine Katchinas just as much as the other masked gods. Perhaps it is best to see them as embodying the eternal clown, but the clown without that sadness which is the gift of civilisation.

Every hour or so the Shalako Impersonators change places, while priests hold up their black blankets as a screen—maintaining the ritual pretence that women and children do not know that it is their men who are acting the part of gods. These, I find, are the only times when I think of a man within the giant's mask holding a pole and looking out through the little triangular space between shirt and skirt. Generally as I watch I accept them as being simply Shalako—

just as I did with Long Horn and the other Katchinas. I am glad to have had this experience, to know how even for a Westerner it is natural to suspend disbelief in the face of these great imaginative creations. So through the small hours the audience continue to sit absorbed, the chanters and drummers renew their energy, Shalako skip and run, the Impersonators maintain their high-stepping, the Mudheads their antics. About five o'clock the two War Brothers arrive and join in. So energy is generated and expressed in this and all the other Shalako houses, so it flows out through the whole land and the coming year.

Outside, how lovely it is! As the dazzle of the dancing room fades from my eyes, I see Lucifer, the Morning Star, hanging in a peacock sky above the dark bulk of the Corn Mountains. Motor-cars are stilled at last, and the grey dawn village belongs to the knots of people who wander about its lanes, to the dogs and waking cocks. Between the light of the crescent moon and the light of the Morning Star I have known Shalako night, have gone out to it, and been—as by all living experience—a little changed. I shall not stay to see the sacred races by the river, nor even to see Long Horn climb on a roof at dawn to untie the last of the forty-nine knots in the ritual tally cord which have marked the days leading to this one. He will be climbing his ladder any minute now, for already the peacock-blue is bleaching above the eastern mesas. But I want to leave Zuni while moon and star still chime in my mind, holding taut between them the bright pattern of this night.

Such was my experience of the Shalako ceremony on

November 27th in the year 1954. I have thought it best to tell what I saw and felt without attempting to explain the meaning of this most complicated religious festival. Indeed, it is impossible fully to explain it; the Shalako is so many-sided, so crowded with detail, that perhaps even the Zuni can hardly comprehend it all at once. They have built it up through the millennia, and here, in all its richness of expression, it continues. It is All Hallows night and the night of the blessing of new houses and of village shrines. It is a night seeking for fertility, in Long Horn's words: *In order that my father's fourth room may be bursting with corn . . . and that this house may be filled with little boys, and little girls, and people grown to maturity.* Neither is good hunting forgotten, nor health. Perhaps it is best to say that the Shalako is to secure universal well-being—well-being that spreads out to the four quarters of the earth from Zuni, its most sacred centre. It should only be understood that this festival is no more than the great climax of a ritual year of preparation. All the priestly orders, the curing societies, the men chosen at the last winter solstice as Katchina impersonators, have fulfilled the exacting parts laid down for them through the whole course of the year. Prayers, continence, the memorising of the steps of dances and the words of long litanies, hard labour on the new houses, all have been duly undertaken. Every feathered prayer-stick out of hundreds planted has been bound and painted with the right words and actions. Everything has been rightly and knowingly done, and so there is good hope for the coming year. And of one thing I am sure: so long as the Zuni and the other Pueblos maintain these observances, so long as they can see their years and lives in these sacred terms, they will keep their souls and remain a living people.

Perfection

J. B. P. TO J. H.

... Every time I go from downtown Houston out to the Shamrock Hotel, I read my favourite notice: *Turn Right On Next Block For Perfection.* I believe it has something to do with oiling or cleaning cars, but that doesn't matter. Half the people in these cities are turning, or about to turn, on next block for perfection. There it is, they believe, just round the corner. Not something a little better, nor much better, than what they already have or are—but *Perfection.* So one wall out of every four in the bookstores is filled with volumes explaining how to turn right on next block and the perfection you will find there. Exercises, from Muller to Yogi; every possible variety of diet; Gracious Living and Finer Things; armour-piercing salesmanship; Personal Magnetism; Daily Rejoicing; Mystic Secrets from Tibet: take your choice, remembering that Perfection itself is close at hand. Probably the parents of the people who buy these books came here from Europe believing they would find Eldorado, the Fountain of Youth, the philosopher's stone. This generation is continuing the quest. Somewhere, somehow, perfection is to be found. This belief is one of the keys to the character and behaviour of the American people. It explains much of their optimism, the moods in which they feel that one vast generous gesture from them will put the world right; also their sudden and dangerous anger when they discover that

258

perfection is not there round the next block; their bewildering alternations of naïve hopefulness and cynicism. Moreover, we can see signs of this character and behaviour elsewhere. The urban industrial people in other countries are coming more and more under American influence. In *Admass*, wherever it may be, you are always being told to turn right on next block for perfection. It is good *Admassian* dogma that just round the corner everything is wonderful. And *Propmass*, the Red version of our society, takes the same line, even if it does not ask you to turn right but orders you—and wipe that counter-revolutionary grin off your face, Comrade—to keep left. And the end product of all this, I suspect, will be explosive mountains of frustration, Krakatoas by the gross. If the patient virtues have withered away, after so much discouragement, and it is finally discovered that magic can't be laid on—then to hell with it all! . . .

17

Night Reverie   When I was younger I liked to
                travel alone, especially on long
   at the   journeys that were not holidays
 Shamrock   (at least so I told myself) but had
                some connection with work. My
reasons were various. I didn't want to accept, as one
has to accept the weather, the moods and whims of
travelling companions; I did everything quickly myself,
and hated hanging about waiting for other people,
particularly men, who always seemed so idiotically
slow changing their clothes, packing or unpacking.
(The time some men take over these routine chores still
astonishes me. Women are different—not slow but
existing in another set of time values.) Then there was
always the chance—though God knows the odds were
against it—of meeting at last somewhere far away that
strange beautiful woman, not Greta Garbo but her
sister perhaps, whose image, which is that of their
own *anima*, haunts all young men about to travel.
Hopeless, I felt, to move towards that encounter as
one of a guffawing group. Finally, I believed that the
solitary traveller sees and remembers more, is more
sharply aware of new experience, than a man who is

enjoying other people's company along the way. This I still believe, and if it should be strictly necessary I will act on that belief. But at some sacrifice. At sixty I no longer look forward to travelling alone. I have met that woman, and know now who she is, when I can return to her. I can make more allowance for other people's moods and whims and am less impatient if I am kept waiting. On the other hand, though I am not afraid of solitude, which is the writer's natural element, now that I am older I dislike more and more the peculiar isolation of the solitary traveller, that homeless and lost feeling which can strike all the harder when one is continually surrounded by people. These people may be wonderfully friendly, kind, hospitable, but they are strangers with whom nothing can be taken for granted, to whom so much has always to be explained. Even the barest acknowledgment of their hospitality and helpfulness, especially in a society fizzing with vitality, demands nervous energy; and constant travelling and sightseeing have already depleted your stock of it. Then suddenly the smallest visiting card becomes a burden; the blue sky turns black.

You feel tired and you have nobody to be tired with. If a fit of depression follows, you cannot talk your way out of it, nor be talked out of it, because you are either alone or with people who quite reasonably expect you to entertain or enjoy being entertained. You are not too exhausted to think and to feel, have not reached a blank numbness, but your thoughts go rattling round like cheap motor-cycles, your feelings arrive like mysterious fogs; and like the insomniac you have enough energy to maintain this gloomy rout but not enough to control it. Not that everything is false; the truth may arrive at such times, perhaps a truth you have not been willing to accept before; but having no scale against which to examine it, you cannot estimate its importance; your sense of proportion has gone; you lose yourself among mountains that may be molehills in the next cheerful daylight. And undoubtedly I was groping about in some such mood, regretting this lonely travel, all the more lonely because it had been packed and noisy with people and social occasions, when I returned to my room at the Shamrock Hotel, Houston, that late afternoon, to write a letter or two and make a few notes. Comparatively and on a molehill-and-daylight level, there was nothing wrong with Houston and its Shamrock. I would rather visit Houston than a large number of cities I know, cities in which I could never have found such friendly hospitality, such a quick desire to help and to please a visitor. Again, from the point of view of the ordinary sensible traveller, not indulging himself in a mood, the Shamrock is a very fine hotel indeed, with admirable rooms, food and service, not unreasonably expensive, deserving a high place on any tourist agency's list. But by the time I had returned to it, that afternoon, I had dropped out of the tourist agency world, whose inhabitants are assumed to be keen, eager, untiring in their pursuit of new business and pleasure; I was where the most artfully written and illustrated travel booklet ever planned could never mean anything. And all this must be remembered throughout what follows, grasped at, twisted round the finger until it bites into the flesh, like the silk thread in the dark mazes of the labyrinth.

I saw almost at once that the unknown insect, about two inches long, was still attached to, though not noticeably flattened against, the fine wire mesh outside my window, just as it had been at breakfast-time. The screen hid nothing of the view. It was a wide view; the window was large and my room high up. It looked towards the centre of the city, at least four miles away. The sun was setting in some invisible quarter; all I could see was the reddening haze that was the sky, the burning plain below. The skyscrapers looked quite different from their prototypes in New York, the only city I know where they seem natural and inevitable, growing out of the Manhattan rock, stalagmites massed and shaped and windowed into towers. Here in Texas, widely separated in illimitable room, they do not seem like any kind of urban building it is possible to imagine; they have nothing remotely to do with banking, insurance, oil and wheat, or indeed with our age at all; and as I stared at them now, their bulk increasing in the sunset air, in the haze in which the distant streets dwindled and then vanished, they looked like inexplicable and monstrous monoliths, the ruins of some age of pious giants, melancholy relics of a worship utterly meaningless to our day. This may be considered nothing more than a mere fancy, to be enjoyed by the mind that entertained it; but I can remember here and now, at home and months afterwards, the depth of feeling, infinitely forlorn, that accompanied it. Below me, between the hotel grounds and the highways into the city, two main roads crossed, and along them the cars went in a continuous stream. It was not quite a liquid flow, though the light was going fast now; the individual

263

cars were still vaguely distinguishable; they suggested an unending scurry and swarming of greyish-greenish shelly insects. There were no people, no houses, in the scene; only the fiery sky, the plain that had burnt out and was sinking into darkness, the strange monoliths, the insects running on their unimaginable mass errands. Out of my tower I seemed to stare, homeless for ever, at the wrong planet.

It is at these times, when the innermost feeling and the outward prospect conspire together against heart and mind, that solitary women, we are told, out of the foolishness and weakness that are wisdom, have a quiet little cry about nothing in particular; after which, feeling better, their chemistry tidied up, they attend briskly to their persons or their apparel, arming themselves against any further challenges that life may fling at them. What I did was to switch on the light above my typewriter, then stay with my easy tasks until I had finished what was to be done. But I was still feeling hollow and forlorn when I took a whisky-on-the-rocks and a pipe back to the window. Not a glimmer of daylight lingered. Opposite, clear against the velvet darkness, was the giant new insurance building, with innumerable little lighted windows, and a green outline, high up, of the Rock of Gibraltar, and *Prudential* in red fire. There seemed to be miles of coloured neon signs, very clear and bright. The cars, as many as ever on the roads that crossed, were now insects with luminous eyes. Seeing them reminded me of the insect attached to the wire screen: it was still there, I discovered, but had no luminous eyes; probably it was dead. Or it might seem dead to me but still seem desperately alive to itself. Just as there might be beings to whom I would appear to be either dead or a rather cheap sort of mechanism. Ignoring the insect, which indeed was easier to ignore than to see, I stared out of the window again, drinking the iced neat whisky. There are few more insidious and potent drinks; it slides over the tongue like something merely cool and refreshing, so that you don't feel obliged to sip it, and only later begins to glow and burn. And as usual this whisky did not change my mood but heightened and broadened it and gave it a more luxurious air, moving my hollowness and forlornness from a small back bedroom to a de luxe suite. The night view now had a certain magnificence. Against the indigo velvet, like an immense jewel-case, were roads that were rippling rivers of light, and all the coloured fires of commerce, restaurant and bar signs like scattered rubies and emeralds; vistas of remote and illegible advertisements blazed like Ali Baba's cave; the dim towers were gold-dusted with lighted windows; and behind and above the beacons and searchlights and mysterious flashings, as if a giant had lost something in the dark, the reflection of the city's illuminations in the upper air brought a wide flush to the sky, hanging in the night a vast pale rose.

If men of other ages could have looked through my eyes for a moment, I thought, how they would have cried out in amazement, wonder and joy, to see a city, after the sun had gone down, blazing like a garden at noon. Knowing no more than this one glimpse told them, what questions they would have asked? What people were these who could release such fountains of coloured fire? What sacred place was this,

wearing such a robe? Who were the gods whose worship here defied and defeated the dark old night? What
last secrets had been revealed to the priesthood guard-
ing this glowing shrine? Whose were the hymns of
joy being chanted in these glittering towers? What
majestic king, already half divine, had summoned this
army of lighted chariots? Was this another and greater
Golden Age? Like hell, Mac! Definitely not, old boy!
The answer is in the negative, declared an official spokes-
man of the mid-Twentieth Century. If you must know,
our favourite name for it is the Age of Anxiety.

I had been standing at that window long enough,
holding an empty glass, composing lush rhetorical
questions and then repeating them with angry irony
in the little town hall of my mind. (The time I waste on
that platform in there, shouting at the empty seats!) I
filled the glass, lit a pipe, then took some odds and ends
of papers from the desk, in the vague hope that I might
do something useful with them, and sprawled on the
wide divan that would be transformed later into a bed.
All right, it was a fake, a cheat, a stupendous waste of
power and material out of which art and worship might
have been created, to show us a way out of the trap.
What trap? Well, anything—breakfast food. You
bought and ate some breakfast food; it gave you, let us
hope, the energy necessary for the morning's work,
which in turn brought you some money to spend when
you went out at night. And what did you see then, so
magnificently resplendent against the dark, reducing
the meaningless stars to the dimmest insignificance,
written in fire and glory? Why, the breakfast food. Or
the name of the car you had bought to take you to work

to earn some money to spend when you went out at night to be dazzled by the name of the car. But perhaps, I thought, the continuous performance in the movie theatres was a better symbol of our time and *Admass* life. In those theatres you are always hearing yourself or your companion or the people in the next seats muttering that this was where they came in. And suppose you keep on discovering that this was where you came in but there are no longer any lighted signs indicating the exits, and indeed no exits for you at all? No, brother, don't kid yourself, you don't remember another kind of life outside, something different from shadows on a screen and mechanical voices. Don't ask too much, sister, be reasonable: just settle down and see the programme through again. But pass the word along that those fellows in front say they can bust up the whole show, blow us out like a light. How about it, folks?

Let's stop this beefing. Here we are in the Shamrock. I have all the dope here in these papers. Listen. It was built by multimillionaire oilman Glenn McCarthy, whose portrait, not a bad job, is hanging in the Lobby by the elevators, where you can't miss it, and where it looks angrier every time you pass that way. But then he had to get out and leave it to Equitable Insurance, which finally handed over to hotelman Conrad Hilton, who, I'd say, was making a go of it. Took about three years to build, cost about $21,000,000. Want some more figures? Here they are. 7,950,000 *cubic feet. Materials used consist of equivalent of* 690 *rail carloads of sand and gravel,* 190 *carloads of cement,* 4,200,000 *pounds of reinforcing rods,* 100 *carloads of bricks,* 140 *carloads of tile,* 125 *carloads of mortar.* Something ought to come out of all that. And never mind about going back to that window, just listen to this. *More than an acre of glass in aluminium windows.* Yes, that was some of it you've been staring and glaring through, making yourself miserable. And for what? If you haven't a date or have ducked one and don't know what to do with yourself (and that's all about it amounts to, if you ask me, all this beefing and bellyaching), you needn't stay up here, you can always go down to the Lobby. . . . *The walls are panelled in Honduras mahogany. All the wood in the panels is from the same tree, so the grain and burl match perfectly, bleached and finished in a light nut colour—22,000 feet of wood from this one tree.* You could sit down there with the same tree all round you. Now Art's been mentioned, hasn't it? Okay, Art then—listen. *This room clearly embodies the International Modern theme, taking the best features of every period, every century, every style, combining them with new ideas to evolve a new décor that will never be dated, embodying the artistic achievements of all ages and all cultures, no one of which was adequate by itself* . . . How do you mean— Hashadmass? Never heard of it. Let me finish. *In the Lobby are found modified examples of Empire, Regency, French, Grecian, Chinese and Modern—all blended into a new feeling—International Modern.* You wanted a new feeling, didn't you? Well, go down and take some International Modern. Or look at some of the Private Dining Rooms—the Ming, the Venetian, the Normandy, the Castillian—all right here. We got Art, bags of it.

A lot of other things too. Now take this room we're in. It's a *Doublette (Efficiency Apartment), larger than a bedroom but a one-room unit with kitchen facilities, and so named because it serves a double purpose—a sitting-room in the daytime and a bedroom at night.* Of course if you sneak back here just between daytime and night, the way you did, you could easily start taking everything the wrong way. Otherwise, instead of staring out of the window, giving yourself a bad time, you could have done something with the air conditioning. *It is individually air conditioned, controlled by the patron.* Patron, see? And a fine patron you are! What about the air in this room? You don't know, do you? As far as you're concerned, it's just air. And that's all you know. *Air is dried in the basement and delivered through high pressure ducts.* Yes, dried and delivered for you to sneer and grumble with, a waste of high pressure ducts. Do you want to know about the refrigerant? I thought not. But you're living in this day and age and it's time you did know. *The refrigerant is trichloromonofluoromethane, odourless, non-irritating, non-inflammable, non-toxic, and non-explosive, has the highest classification for any refrigerant approved by the Underwriters Laboratory.* Never give 'em a thought, those boys in the Underwriters Lab, do you? And there they are, sampling, testing, rejecting, approving, all for you. No, listen. *Carrier Centrifugal Refrigeration Machines are used, the first to utilise a safe, low-pressure refrigerant.* All right, don't listen, stay ignorant. But my guess is that some people, some of these scientists and engineers who've been working to keep you happy, would tell you it ought to be possible to have a nice time just breathing this air. How do you mean—trichloro-what's-it perhaps doesn't suit you? How can it be *too* odourless, non-irritating, non-inflammable? Of course you don't need a touch of what it's *non* of.

269   K*

They know, don't they? Just breathe, and enjoy it.

Turn on the radio then. Never mind about the same voices telling you to buy something you don't want. What if they are too smooth, syrupy, false? They're paid to be like that, and you get the programme. Half a dozen, if you like. See what it says here. *Centrally distributed sound on six channels and a conduit for television. The combined power of the amplifiers serving this installation is 16,000 watts, considerably in excess of the power of most broadcasting stations.* All for free, and you haven't used any of those watts yet. All right, if you're not in the mood, you're not in the mood. No use talking to you about the Teletype room—but there is one. And here's something you *could* do with, if you want my opinion. *The Medical Department with thirteen doctors serving the clinic as consultant physicians.* I'll bet if you popped down there, third floor, explained you'd been hanging around up here, grumbling about nothing, they'd give you the right pill or powder, and in an hour you'd be downtown, having fun. And they're careful, thorough, these boys. *A department of bacteriology makes cultures of cooking utensils, foodstuffs, employees' fingernails and throats to determine presence of harmful bacteria.* You don't like a sterilised existence? You could use a few bacteria? Okay—drop dead.

One self again, I began to wonder if I needed some food. I had only to ask for Room Service, and the fabulous kitchen, described on the page I was now holding, would come to my aid. . . . *Stainless steel pressure cookers (40 lbs. per square inch) up to 150 gallon size; mixers with three speeds and bowls up to 100 quart capacity, a roll-maker that produces over 12,000 rolls an hour, a toast-*

master that turns out 250 *slices of toast per hour.* . . . (Why only 250? Perhaps some mistake here. And I am never given buttered toast with my poached eggs though every morning I ask for it. They should have installed a buttered-toast-order-receiver.) . . . *A silver-washing machine that washes, dries, and burnishes* 4,500 *pieces per hour removing all food stains.* . . . Once, 30 pieces of silver could be stained for ever; now we can remove in an hour all stains from 4,500 pieces. No, I wasn't hungry. The emptiness wasn't down there. I tried another page. Somewhere, boxed in with me and perhaps going quietly out of its mind too, was a Foreign Department (25 languages). But what do we say, what password can we give, in these languages? *Swimming-pool, fan-shaped and* 165 *feet long containing* 750,000 *gallons with sand filters and chlorination purification system.* . . . And perhaps a pint of Lethe water. Out come the purified bathers forgetting even more than they did when they went in, forgetting for ever who we are and what we might become. Next—and last. *An Hotel Sign* 235 *feet above the ground with letters* 8 *feet by* 3 *feet with power green neon tubes totalling* 14,000 *watts; and a red and green beacon for airplanes.* I had only to stay in this room a little longer and I would be a character in Science Fiction. The elevators would be operated by stainless steel electronic robots, and behind the reception desk would be creatures with two heads and eight tentacles, imported from a poorer planet.

Returning to the divan with another helping of fire and ice, I picked up a large envelope I had forgotten to open. But I did not open it at once. First, after settling down again, I had to reply to the Enemy, which at these

times apparently sends against me its light cavalry, so
many querulous objectors, invisible but clearly audible
—no mistaking their whinnying hissing voices. They
weren't madly keen, I could hear them saying, about my
reference to Science Fiction, mere whimsy and I'd done
it too often before. They were probably right, I told
them; and, taking more wind out of their sails, I added
that in these days I had to do what I could, being an
ageing scribbler bloated and pockmarked with, by, or
from, every occupational disease of our dying trade.
Nevertheless, I went on, they might do well sometime
to consider this Science Fiction and its popularity
among the younger end of the mass public. Dreams,
yes; but why these particular dreams? Horrors, certainly; but why horrors of this sort? What was going
on down there—say, in the horribly jammed trains of
New York's subway, London's Underground? Or take
the small boy who hopes to find the world of Science
Fiction in the next town. (And after all he might live
not far from Harwell or Los Alamos, where indeed I
have seen small boys.) Is he as far out in his reckoning,
as dangerously situated, as some thousands of my con-
temporaries, men of distinction most of them (they
could advertise the whisky I was drinking), weighed
down with honours, decorations, degrees, all wielders
of power or moulders of opinion? These men are either
liars and cheats or are foolish enough to imagine, and to
persuade other people to imagine, they are living in a
society that has in fact ceased to exist. Their world has
completely changed under the very noses they so often
look down. Except of course on those ceremonial,
fancy-dress occasions that are now nothing more than

shows, today's metropolitan version of the travelling fair or circus. Nearly all their addresses, lectures, speeches, solemn leading articles, are years and years out of date; they ought to be delivered or written by ghosts. Schoolboys on Speech Days are asked to prepare themselves for entry into a world that died about the time they were born. Communities assumed to be Christian are mostly composed of people who know and care as much about the Holy Trinity as pygmies in the jungle. Spiritual admonitions are addressed to men who since they were fourteen have believed themselves to be trapped animals on a revolving cinder. Inheritors of a great democratic tradition, vigilant guardians of freedom, are widely discovered among people who have already allowed themselves to be robbed of many hard-won liberties, without a murmur, and would probably swap tomorrow those that are left for a larger car or a 20-inch television set. Mobs that have been manipulated for years, badgered, bullied and hypnotised into whatever camp, party, store, type of mass amusement, has the cleverest and most unscrupulous propagandists and salesmen, are solemnly congratulated on exercising their power of free choice. Standards of value are still warmly recommended to people who would not guarantee two meals a day to any man who genuinely upholds them. All this is as close to sheer fantasy as Science Fiction. Perhaps it is closer. We have now millions of youngsters who, so far as traditional human values are concerned, especially those expressed in religion, philosophy, art, might as well have arrived here from another planet. Yes, and unless some of us— and even a tired, disgruntled author, finishing his third whisky-on-the-rocks in an hotel bedroom, need not be left out—growl and grumble and make a nuisance of ourselves, the world our great-grandchildren will know will *be* another planet. The green Earth and all its shining dreams will have vanished for ever.

At present, I said to myself, glad to be using my own jargon, we have arrived at *Admass*. I was opening the large envelope now. People of course, I continued, can live in other worlds—there are still peasants living in the Middle Ages—but the real world of today for the West, the place where the great transformations are happening, where most lives are directly affected, is *Admass*, somewhere half-way between the official ghost of the world I knew as a child and the prophetic night-mare worlds of Science Fiction. Understand *Admass*— and you understand, as they say in these parts, what's cooking. At this point, I took out of the envelope a number of press clippings. I saw at once they were all accounts of the opening of this Shamrock Hotel, and remembered then that soon after my arrival here, plagued by some recollection of a fantastic party, I had asked for these clippings. Though in no mood for clear-sighted and sober-minded social research, still feeling hollow and forlorn even if, so to speak, afloat now with the feeling, I contrived to read, and I hope to absorb and grasp the full significance of, every line of print. Indeed, I felt at the end I understood the events better than many of those who had reported them. Where these fellows went wrong was in assuming that these doings had been given their fabulous quality by some-thing equally fabulous, monstrously over-heightened to the point of wild absurdity, in Mr. McCarthy, or in

Houston, or in Texas itself. And no doubt there was an astonishing touch here and there, highlights never before on land or sea, belonging essentially to the man, the place, the regional atmosphere. Nevertheless, I read the tale differently. This occasion, I will swear, was *Admass* at work and at play. *Admass* with the lid off, I grant you. But not only are the rest of us eagerly waiting for the money, energy, time that will enable us to do some lid-removing ourselves, but also it is only when the lid is off, as it was on this occasion, that we can take a clear picture of *Admass* characteristics, standards, values: in short, see for ourselves exactly where we have now arrived. Okay, folks, stand by for the opening of the Shamrock.

The year was 1949, the day was St. Patrick's. The Shamrock had taken three years to complete, had been built, decorated and equipped almost without regard to cost. (When manufacturers of lavatory fixtures competed for the Shamrock order, the winner, we are told, was a firm that declared: 'We didn't even consider the cost.') The total sum was about $21 million. A staff of 1,200 was engaged, all at comparatively high wages. The manager was from New York's famous Waldorf-Astoria. The opening ceremony and the celebrations to follow it had been planned on the most lavish scale, at a cost to Mr. McCarthy and his associates of $300,000. An intensive publicity campaign had made everybody in Texas, and many people in other regions, familiar with all the exciting details of the occasion; the newspapers devoted columns to it; the newsreels offered the public many privileged glimpses both of the hotel itself and the personages involved in its opening; the more fashion-

275

able stores in Houston and Dallas specially featured furs, dresses, shoes, gloves, that might be worn with confidence on that evening. Thus, all the cultural resources of *Admass* were pressed into service to celebrate the occasion. Radio was to be represented by such admirable programmes as the Breakfast Club, the Original Amateur Hour, and the Sealtest, which, at a charge of $15,000, would present the dazzling Dorothy Lamour herself, to broadcast during the evening from the Emerald Room. Nor were commercial and advertising interests slow to appreciate the value of these celebrations. They responded with eager goodwill and immediate enterprise, both typical of our new society at its best. Among their contributions we may briefly note: the Harry Winston establishment's $10-million display of emeralds, diamonds, and rubies, to delight the guests; the erection and maintenance by the American Orchid Society of two twelve-foot orchid-hung trees in the Lobby; the provision of bottles bearing special Shamrock labels by the distillers of Old Forrester bourbon; and, by no means least, a capital friendly gesture from the Goodyear Company, whose airship soared high above the great white building and towed an immense sign that read *The Shamrock Has Airfoam By Goodyear*. Seeing this attractive and striking sign, breaking for once the blue monotony of their native skies, many people must have realised once again how fortunate they were to be members of our *Admass* society, sensibly oligarchic in its financial and industrial structure but genuinely democratic in its culture and social outlook, bringing together characteristically to celebrate this splendid occasion all its leadership, expert

276

advertising and salesmanship, zestful good-fellowship.

My authorities differ on the number of invitations issued by Mr. McCarthy for the opening party: some say it was 2,500, others 3,500. There is some difference again, ranging from 200 to 250, in the estimated number of special invitations, with all expenses paid, to persons of notable distinction; but all agree that these invitations were printed in gold on white doeskin. Other invitations offered free hospitality but were not on doeskin. The remainder of the guests, probably some two thousand citizens of Houston delighted to attend such festivities, paid $42 and $38 and even as little as $32 per head, according to the particular dining-room to which they were allotted, the Emerald Room, from which Miss Lamour would broadcast, being the most expensive. The gold-and-doeskin invitations had been sent to the gayer members of *Admass* aristocracy—film stars, radio comedians, and a few celebrities of the Press. (Probably due to some mistake, an architect, a Mr. Frank Lloyd Wright, was included among the guests, and did little to justify his choice. We are told that he went sniffing through the hotel, found the long green corridors depressing, said that the building was a tragic imitation of Rockefeller Centre out there on the prairie, and was ungrateful enough to declare 'There should be written in front of it, in great tall letters, in electric lights, W-H-Y-?') It was a daring move to bring so many representative figures of our time on one day to Houston, but there can be no doubt about its success; later, when the stars went in open cars, wisely imitating royalty elsewhere, to attend a film première in the city, a crowd of 250,000 packed itself along Main Street to cheer them. The crack train of the South-West, the renowned *Super Chief*, was borrowed at a cost of $40,000 to transport this astonishing bevy of celebrities. To mark the occasion, not without a charming touch of sentiment, the ladies from Hollywood had been presented with panties and brassières decorated with shamrocks. No expense was spared to relieve the tedium of the desert journey: it was described by one of the reporters on the train as 'Just a good clean drunk all the way'. Special airplanes brought guests of equal distinction from New York. By air too, 2,500 shamrocks were imported from Ireland. With them came copies of the *Irish Independent*, bringing greetings and congratulations, and its editor, who brought a shillelagh for Mr. McCarthy.

That the occasion more than justified the money and careful planning it called for, cannot be doubted. From the first it was stamped with the hallmark of Success. The subsequent failure of the hotel must not prejudice our judgment here. Whatever may have happened afterwards, this great opening must be considered one of the most remarkable, yet one of the most characteristic, events of our age, with *Admass*, we might say, fully flowering in a single gorgeous night. *Admass* called, and *Admassians* eagerly answered the call. They stood outside the wonder building in their hundreds of thousands. Some two or three thousand of the privileged found their way into it. Not, it is true, without difficulty. After all, this splendid occasion was something of a pioneering feat, with commercial and social enterprise on tiptoe to reach the highest mark of achievement. It was expressing the age, inspired by the *Zeitgeist*, but so ambitiously, in such a bold heightened fashion, that

some mishaps were inevitable. But we must remember
that these mishaps were due to the overwhelming
success of the event, to the eager desire of so many
people fully to participate in it, in fact to its very *Admass*
character. There was probably some justice in the com-
parison between the Lobby, early in the evening, and
the Fort Worth stockyards, where thousands of doomed
animals push and shove and bellow with rage. The
guest who gasped 'Rich people push worse than poor
people' at least discovered a valuable truth. It was
unfortunate that the Mayor of Houston and his entire
retinue were helplessly jammed in the entrance for two
hours; and less unfortunate perhaps that among others
who could neither get in nor get out was Mr. McCarthy's
older rival, Mr. Jesse Jones, the owner of a Houston
newspaper and several hotels down-town. It is said that
some members of Mr. McCarthy's own family soon
found themselves widely separated from him, lost in a
struggling mob of guests that the special squad of 150
hotel police could not begin to control. Men in evening
dress, gorgeously gowned women, fought their way in
and out of the Grecian, Normandy, Castillian and Ming
Rooms, no matter to which room their tickets assigned
them; but the pressure, scrimmage, and uproar were
greatest in the Emerald Room, where drunken admirers
struggled to reach the film stars for autographs, Miss
Lamour tried to sing above the bedlam, with angry
male guests asking the microphones where the hell
their seats were; with the result that the $15,000 broad-
cast was cut off the air and its star fled in tears. It must
be admitted that the Hollywood guests, who had
arrived so triumphantly, were not happy. The hotel's

room service had been hours behind time all that day. Breakfast came at lunch-time. When one film star finally struggled to her place at the evening banquet, she said 'At last we're having lunch'. Chaos itself came with the night stampede. One wit, fighting his way through the densely packed crowd, kept on repeating: 'If you're not doing anything, I'm giving a big party in about twelve minutes.' For waiters and diners it was an inferno: soup, drinks, coffee were knocked or swept off trays, to spill over the guests; at one important table, jammed with millionaires' wives, a whole tray of fruit cocktails, appropriately called *pineapple surprise* on the menu, was scattered over bare shoulders. One waiter, weary of being screamed at, replied to an order: 'Sorry, I don't work here. I work four blocks down the street. I just got caught in the mob.' Guests were still being served dinner after midnight. Speeches that should have been made at the beginning of the evening, by the Governor, Mr. McCarthy, the film stars, had to be kept until the end, by which time it must have looked as if a cyclone had swept through the building. (The two trees in the Lobby had been stripped of all their orchids much earlier.) The Haroun Al Raschid of this Arabian Night, Mr. McCarthy, was driven to confess: 'I'm kinda peeved about a few things.' But the final word must be left to the Southwestern Bell Telephone Company, which, after coldly considering its statistics, announced on the following day that the opening of the Shamrock, regarded as an emergency operation, ranked with the Texas City disaster and the Galveston Flood.

Yes, it all happened in Texas, which explains some of the more obvious absurdities and crudities, the slapdash bigness of the thing. Nevertheless, most of it, and most of what is essentially wrong with it, belongs to *Admass*, where we are all beginning to live now. Beat the big drum as hard, make sure of that initial build-up, bring in the same circus of film, TV and radio names, and there is hardly a city in America, the British Commonwealth, and Western Europe, which would not show you the same pandemonium. If stupidity and vulgarity are more obvious on this occasion than they might be elsewhere, that is because behind it were more energy and enthusiasm than most of us have to spare. The values expressed on that St. Patrick's Day are the values of our new society: the Irish-American tycoon and Texas merely added shamrock panties for film stars. If Houston's choice of the nation's representative figures amuses you, find out what is happening in fifty other cities and then laugh your head off. In Washington, for example, where President Eisenhower, we read, gives informal dinner parties for the men whose opinions are important. The guest lists, heavy with top brass, are very different from Mr. McCarthy's, but are no more concerned with speculative thought, social philosophy, and all the arts, than his was. We find there merely the power end of our mechanical civilisation. The shoddy standards are the same. And if sense and dignity could be so easily and completely banished from the Shamrock opening, it is largely because they are being defeated everywhere. Men who begin in poverty and then acquire millions before they are forty, chiefly by guessing right, are bold intuitives; and though Mr. McCarthy might at this time have still been a Texas rough-neck, he perceived intuitively what would impress not only

Houston but our whole society. If he failed, it was not because he guessed wrong for once and adopted the wrong standards, but because he was too impatient and his organisation was faulty. If his great evening had gone according to plan, none of these newspapers and magazines would have jeered at him, for they have long adopted the very same standards, and have made it their business to wave them continually in the faces of their readers. There was a time when stupid people had to make some effort to understand and enjoy what was in print. But now every foolish or dangerous prejudice, every moronic symptom, every gaping idiocy is carefully catered for, endlessly flattered.

If the multimillionaire and all the men whose services he could buy, if the gimcrack celebrities and the higher-income mob that pushed and jostled to see them, if the dumb mass that stared open-mouthed outside the hotel, all behaved as they did, it is because there is now no particular reason why anybody should behave any better. Who are we, anyhow? What is there outside the factory, to give us temporary security against the menace of the dark, except the lighted fun-fair? Having disinherited ourselves, we have to keep on inventing new ways of forgetting what we once had and who we were. So like our cousins in *Propmass*, who are only at the other end of the same boat, the end where the mate wields a lash, we try to find satisfaction in an existence that is two dimensions short, that has length, straight from here to the grave, but neither breadth nor height. What breadth, what height? The breadth once known as eternity, life experienced outside time; the height that represents the possibility of man becoming something other than he is now, the flowering of that seed which sometimes, especially when the game grows stale, seems to stir in the depths of our being. The old symbols, belonging to that breadth and height, are losing their last glimmer of magic. No new shapes seem to rise from the black water. If they do, then they are quickly driven from consciousness, in our terror of being alienated from sound normality, of being compelled to return awkward answers when we are questioned by the authorities, the sentries of the citadels of power. (As existence narrows, as experience loses colour and taste, some men, harder and fiercer than the rest, must have power at all cost. What else is there?) So we scamper back to the solidity and security of mass life, never dreaming, except when an occasional nightmare makes us sweat with inexplicable apprehension, that nothing more fragile and insecure was ever seen on earth. Once there, we try mostly to pass the time. But if time is itself the unending road on which we must travel, how can time be passed?

Feeling hungry now, and with time on my mind, I stared hard at my watch, which I could have sworn seemed to give me something like a wink. It was not too late, just about my dinner hour. As before, I remembered that I had only to pick up the telephone to recruit into my service one of those stainless steel pressure cookers (40 lbs. per square inch) up to 150-gallon size or mixers with three speeds and bowls up to 100-quart capacity, all roaring and churning away, far below. But I had been in that room—Doublette (Efficiency Apartment)—long enough. Making myself look a little less like a 200-lb. ash-tray, I decided to dine in the club at the end of the Lobby, for which I had a card as a temporary member. (I am very much a man with a temporary member's card, even on this planet, which I often feel is not mine at all.) It was not bad down there; the glittering bar was nearly always noisy with booming facetious men, like giant schoolboys, and their impatient, rather bored girls; but the dining-room beyond, fairly large and very dimly lit, with a soothing under-the-sea atmosphere, was usually deserted when I visited it. The waiters were young, darkly handsome, products of some frantic unknowable cross-breeding, and, while brisk enough, had that air of insolence which comes of believing that you are better-looking and more sophisticated than most of the people you serve. And that evening, I seem to remember, was the one when I gained a victory, not only over my own waiter but also over the headwaiter who was at least five years older, nearly thirty, in the essential matter of serving slices of brown bread and butter with smoked salmon; thereby deserving, though not receiving, the thanks of many a member of the club and patron of the Shamrock Hotel, to which, like the horrible voices in the travelogue films, I now say Farewell.

18

**J. H. and
J. B. P. meet
at Santa Fé**

The travel agency business in America has been largely taken over by women. I make a point of giving them my custom. They are not quite as good at reading time-tables as the men are, but any weakness here is more than compensated by their more sympathetic and imaginative interest in other people's journeys. They see you as a person not a parcel; they take more trouble. So I said to the pleasant middle-aged woman: 'I want to join my wife in Santa Fé. Please work out the quickest way.' All pleasant middle-aged women want men to join their wives; they are ready to toil at bringing them together as soon as possible; I was shown the quickest way. So after a very early breakfast I caught the big plane that was going from Houston to San Francisco. It would drop me at El Paso, and from there a smaller local plane would take me up to Albuquerque.

In the air I am the representative man of our time. A thousand sermons could be preached on me. To begin with, I am always flying though I don't really like flying. Often I have boarded ships and trains with a deep feeling of relief and thankfulness, but never once have I climbed into an airplane experiencing this feeling. It has to be done, so I do it. I have read about gay scenes at airports but though I have arrived at and departed from all manner of airports, from Heath Row to Honolulu, Stockholm to Tiflis, Tangier to Guadalajara, I have never been around when this gaiety is lighting up the scene. And indeed it is absurd to suggest that there are all manner of airports; there is only one airport, and wherever you fly you take it with you. Nor will it be long before you take more than the airport with you; the city near the airport will be just like the city you flew away from; and not long after that, at our present rate of progress, there will be no point in travelling at a thousand miles an hour even to join a person, because that person will be no different from all the people you have left behind. But though I am haunted by such thoughts, though I don't really like flying, I persist in flying, chiefly, I suppose, because I am hag-ridden by greed and impatience. I want to get on with something else, hoping it will bring me the satisfaction I missed in the last experience. Here I am the representative man of our time. My behaviour while I am up in the air is typical too. I don't do anything thoroughly. I half read, half think. I am neither really asleep nor properly awake. Even when I eat and drink—and I look forward to eating and drinking, grumbling to myself because my end of the plane always seems to be the one served last —I am not wholeheartedly giving myself to the food and wine, as a peasant would, but am eating and drinking half in a dream. And not a pleasant dream. What I am really feeling—the core of the whole experience—is a mixture of impatience and boredom, darkened at the edges by anxiety. On the ground, where I belong, I can do better, now and again; but when I am carried through the air at two hundred and seventy-five miles an hour I am a typical specimen of *Homo Sapiens circa mid-Twentieth Century*.

A ribbed desert came through the haze to meet us. We seemed to circle over miles of airfields. We landed in a great glare of noon. Tiny private planes, crimson, blue, emerald-green, seemed to hover like humming birds, scuttle like tropical beetles, above and below the massive hulls of the transcontinental aircraft. I had two hours to wait but decided against leaving the airport to find El Paso itself. I checked the time of my plane to Albuquerque, had a wash, looked at the usual display of cheap cigars, magazines, paper-backed books all with blondes who had had their clothes torn, and had a leisurely lunch. Just to show myself that I was still on the job, I scribbled some notes; and now, months afterwards, five thousand miles away, I am staring at them: *Children in restaurant. The women who receive you at doors of restaurants—their routine smiles—they keep invalid husbands. Barefoot boys. English in America.* How fatuous they look, these notes! What a horrible way to earn a living! Now I neither know nor care what I meant by *Barefoot boys* and *English in America.* Yet I can still remember myself sitting in that lunch-room at the El Paso airport: the place itself, dim and cool after the dusty glare outside; my seat just to the left of the entrance to the kitchen; the middle-aged waitress with a pancake make-up, nearly as thick as the old silent film make-up; the two small children and their mother sitting not far away, the children vaguely staring, sleep already in their eyes, the mother, behind her rouge and orange lipstick, looking warily defensive like an animal among traps; the gabbling sad voices coming through the loud-speakers, the engines spitting, rattling, roaring, on the dazzle of concrete beyond the window.

Over the desert again, this time with two engines instead of four, heading north for Albuquerque. So long, Texas! Not that I had really visited Texas. I had in fact taken care not to visit it, going out of my way to avoid what was characteristically Texan and concentrating entirely on the cities and urban living. I knew little more about that vast region, bigger than Western Europe, than when I first entered it. But cities are cities everywhere, and are probably less regional every year. It may well be that the major technical achievement of our time, the one that will do most to shape the world of the immediate future, has nothing to do with nuclear fission, antibiotics, aviation: it is air conditioning. Once his air is suitably conditioned, a man can exist and work almost anywhere. He can work but can he play? He can exist but can he really live? I tried to remember a single moment of happiness I had experienced while breathing conditioned air. I failed. Apparently it was always the messy old stuff, too hot, too cold, full of smells, thoroughly unhealthy, that brought me to life.

We came bumping down into the little Albuquerque airfield. Just as I set foot on it, an excitable young man came shouting my name, telling me to jump on the plane that was about to take off for Santa Fé. I caught it, so to speak, by the tail, and there in the tail I stayed, thinking this was one airplane too many, as we bounced over the jagged hills to the north. No distance, of course; it took about twenty minutes of solar time, about twenty hours of poor Jack Priestley's interior time. As soon as the little brute came to rest, I shot out of it terrified that it might take off again and bounce me for months among the savage peaks of New Mexico. The air up there was wonderful, mountain fresh, warm in the sun but with a hint of the cold night and all the snow to the north; I greeted my wife in my favourite weather. We shared the ramshackle car into Santa Fé with some crates of fruit. I would have shared it with parcels of alligators. We arrived at what was virtually a place of our own, which might almost have been a warm cave. There we talked and talked, had a drink or two and talked, prepared dinner and talked, ate the dinner and talked. Afterwards we went out to feel the icy breath of night on our cheeks, to see the huge glitter of stars, from the familiar blaze of constellations to the silver dust that was a vista of illimitable worlds. They regarded us, for once, without irony. I forbore, for once, to make my speech about higher levels of being. It was a night when a man could believe there was a good life up there, a good life down here, and perhaps some possible connection between them, without saying too much about it.